THE RIGHT IS WRONG

BY

T. J. O'HARA

TELEMACHUS PRESS

If you purchased this book without a cover you should be aware that this book is stolen property. It was reported as "unsold and destroyed" to the publisher and neither the author nor the publisher has received any payment for this "stripped book."

This book is a work of satire. As such it is meant as a humorous yet thought-provoking look at the Platform of the 2008 Republican Party. With the exception of the text of the Republican Party Platform, the opinions expressed within this book are solely those of the author.

THE RIGHT IS WRONG
Copyright © 2010 by T. J. O'Hara. All rights reserved, including the right to reproduce this book, or portions thereof, in any form. No part of this text may be reproduced, transmitted, downloaded, decompiled, reverse engineered, or stored in or introduced into any information storage and retrieval system, in any form or by any means, whether electronic or mechanical without the express written permission of the author. The scanning, uploading, and distribution of this book via the Internet or via any other means without the permission of the publisher is illegal and punishable by law. Please purchase only authorized electronic editions, and do not participate in or encourage electronic piracy of copyrighted materials.

This book incorporates the original text of the 2008 Republican National Platform (Copyright © 2008 by the Republican National Committee) under the doctrine of Fair Use (17 USC 107).

The publisher does not have any control over and does not assume any responsibility for author or third-party websites or their content.

Cover Art Design: Lorraine Hansen
Cover Art Photography: Kimberly O'Hara
Cover Art Illustrations:
    Copyright © istockphoto/Mark Stay (8180012)
    Copyright © istockphoto/Mark Stay (1089076)
    Copyright © istockphoto/Bob Ash (8115166)

Interior Art Illustration:
    Copyright © istockphoto/Mr_Vector (2366458)

Visit The Common Sense Czar's website at
http://www.TheCommonSenseCzar.net

Become a "Follower" of The Common Sense Czar's blog at
http://TheCommonSenseCzar.blogspot.com

ISBN: 978-1-935670-30-8 (eBook)
ISBN: 978-1-935670-29-2 (Paperback)

Published by: Telemachus Press, LLC
http://www.telemachuspress.com

Printed in the United States of America

10 9 8 7 6 5 4 3 2 1

THE RIGHT IS WRONG

T. J. O'HARA

Dedication

To my beautiful bride, Kimberly, who inspires and supports me in everything I do … and to the rest of *"the Pack,"* Nikki, London and Chanel, who lay by my side as I write and bring me their toys when they think I need a break.

FOREWORD

In the interest of full disclosure ... or should I say *"complete transparency?"* ... I am the product of a *mixed marriage:* my father was a Republican, and my mother was a Democrat. To add to the complexity: my father was of Irish heritage, and my mother was of Italian heritage; my father was Catholic, and my mother was Protestant; and, my father was a male, and my mother was a female (... I think you have to *specify* that these days).

My father grew up on an Irish-only street. By that I mean, as the son of an Irish immigrant, he was safe ... on *his* street. However, he could not walk through the street that stood only a block away, because *that* was a German street, and he would likely be attacked. In case you haven't seen the movie *The Streets of New York*, suffice it to say that the Irish held a unique status at the time that was somewhere between that of the early colonial slaves ... and pond scum.

My mother was the first-born child of Italian immigrants. Back in those days, Italians enjoyed a higher status that the Irish (... but then, who didn't?) until that nettlesome thing called World War II broke out. Italy, you see, was part of the *Axis of Power* along with Germany and Japan; bad news for Italian descendants living in the United States. Never mind that my grandparents were more proud of their United States citizenship than anyone you can imagine or that my mother never set foot in Italy; they were singled out during WWII, and their home was painted by the apparent progeny of today's *"taggers"* with a less-than-artistic swastika.

To add to the confusion, my father was a blue-collar worker, who worked for the newspaper as a journeyman and served as his union's Secretary/Treasurer. In that latter capacity, my sister and I earned part of our meager allowances by helping him balance the books and write the monthly union report. When technology displaced the need for his craft, my father's union lost its battle with a competing union for jurisdiction. As a result, he became an entrepreneur and started a modest but successful house painting business. He had bravely served as a commando in the Navy during WWII, often hitting the beaches in the South Pacific with the first wave of Marines. It was an experience in his life that he generally chose not to discuss. But I have no doubt, were he alive today and this country's freedom at stake, he would take up arms once again without a moment's hesitation ... for he loved this country that much.

Let me apologize ahead of time for the *"political incorrectness"* of the next statement, but it's the truth: my mother was a *"stay-at-home-mom."* There, I said it! Boy, it was sure hard to get it out, but I feel quite relieved.

My mother was always there for my sister and me when we came home from school; she cared for us when we were ill and was active in anything that she thought might contribute in a meaningful way to our lives (*e.g.*, PTA, Playground Mother's Club, etc.). She was passionate about art and music and made sure that we had an appreciation for both. And Mom was in the audience anytime we spoke, sang, acted or played. She also was a member of the local Civic Association, which was as close as she came to political activism. Yet, she was deeply steeped in the national pride that is so often associated with America's *Greatest Generation* and was further driven by one of her parents' favorite phrases: *"God bless America!"*

So now you know! I take my citizenship *very* seriously. While I was *born* into it and didn't have to traverse an ocean or learn a new language, as both sets of my grandparents did, I have a *profound* respect for what it means. Neither did I have to survive the economic hardships of *The Great Depression* nor defend my country on foreign soil as my parents did. However, perhaps it is through the intensity of my family members' experiences and their devotion to what this Nation stands for that has given birth to my undying *love* for ... and *commitment* to ... the United States of America.

And as far as *"political correctness"* goes ... if that concept is meaningful to you, you may wish to read no further because I have no time for such folly. I was raised to *"tell the truth, the whole truth, and nothing but the truth ... so help me God."* If unvarnished honesty offends you, read no further. If the fact that I choose to occasionally call upon the *"help"* of a higher power offends you, read no further. However, if you can muster the strength to weather those two concepts, I encourage you to read on.

I write *not* to *convince* you but rather to *entertain* you and to *stimulate your thoughts* so that your opinion, moving forward, is more *informed* and reflects *your* true feelings rather than what *someone else* would have you believe. Brace yourself and enjoy the journey!

THE RIGHT IS WRONG

INTRODUCTION

*** *If you've already read the Introduction in one of the other books you may skip this chapter* ***

By way of introduction, I am the self-appointed *Common Sense Czar*. With all due respect to Thomas Paine, author of *Common Sense*, I think I deserve the job. Besides, Thomas Paine has been dead for over 200 years ... even though he's still registered to vote in three States according to Acorn.

Being a Czar is really cool. Unlike politicians, you don't have to have to raise money to run; you generally don't have to be vetted in a rigorous way; and you have reasonably unbridled authority ... *plus*, you get to be called *"Czar!"*

As the *Common Sense Czar*, I apply *common sense* to the issues of the day; something that has been missing in our Nation's capital for quite some time. As my first official act, I applied *common sense* to the current glut of Czars and dismissed all of them except for the *Faith-Based Czar*. Personally, I can't imagine why the ACLU hasn't attacked that particular position with its normal zeal. The *issue* would seem to be *obvious*. Maybe it's *Devine intervention*. If that's the case, my *common sense* tells me not to *mess* with it.

As for the rest of the positions, the decisions were easy. The *Guantanamo Closure Czar* was going to lose his job anyway since his position was driven by an Executive Order issued by President Obama on January 22, 2009, to close Gitmo *"no later than one year from now"* to quote the President, and we all know how well that's been going.

The *TARP Czar* and *Stimulus Accountability Czar* were also expendable. On February 25, 2009, just eight days after signing the $787-billion dollar economic stimulus package, President Obama stated that he was putting Vice President Joe Biden in charge of the *"tough, unprecedented oversight effort"* of the fiscal stimulus plan *"because nobody messes with Joe."* I can't imagine why we would need these two Czars if Vice President Biden has everything under control.

The departure of the *Government Performance Czar* was another easy call given our Government's performance in recent years.

I dumped the *Afghanistan Czar* and the *Sudan Czar* because, the last time I looked, these are independent countries. If we have military or humanitarian initiatives in *any* country, it's Congress' responsibility to address the issues. We don't need Czars for specific countries. If we did, then we should at least start with Russia. They're used to it.

Then, we've got the *Mideast Peace Czar*. Talk about a dead-end job! These countries have been fighting for over 2,000 years. What are the odds that a political appointee in the United States will be able to resolve their differences? That's one more position we can eliminate. And while we're at it, let's eliminate the *Central Region Czar* who is responsible for our policies in, you guessed it, the same part of the world; needless duplication. Gone!

While we're on the subject, we presently have a *Terrorist Czar*. No, not Bill Ayres (although he might be a good choice under the assumption that *"it takes one to know one"*) … a fellow named John Brennan. This is the same John Brennan who allegedly nixed a plan to kill or capture Osama bin Laden back in 1998. Way to establish job security! Eliminating this position shouldn't exactly create a void.

Staying with the terrorist theme for a moment, I see we have a *Weapons Czar* and a *WMD Policy Czar*. Why differentiate? If the *Weapons Czar* only tackles issues of conventional weaponry (like sling-shots), we don't need him. If there really are *"no weapons of mass destruction,"* we don't need the *WMD Policy Czar* either. Assuming for the moment that weapons of mass destruction are *not* just a figment of former President Bush's imagination, I'll establish the policy. Weapons of mass destruction are bad things; particularly in the hands of unstable people. There you have it … a *common sense* policy and two more positions eliminated.

Along these same lines, we have an *Intelligence Czar*. Let's just agree that it's an obvious oxymoron and eliminate the position to stop the snickering!

We have a *Border Czar* to protect us from illegal immigration. If you call this Czar's office, press 1 for English, press 2 for Spanish, press 3 for Tagalog, press 4 for Farsi, press 5 for ... well, you get the picture. Applying *common sense*: we have immigration laws in place. Enforce them! One more position eliminated.

This same solution can be applied to two more positions: *Domestic Violence Czar* and *Drug Czar*. *Common sense* tells us that domestic violence and the illegal use of drugs are bad. We have laws in place against both negative behaviors. Enforce them! That gets rid of those two Czars.

Next, we have a few positions tied to specific locations within our country. We have a *Great Lakes Czar*. I've been to the Lakes. They're indeed *"Great."* That should cover it. Position eliminated!

We also have a *California Water Czar* ... as if there aren't any other problems in that State. Interestingly enough, this particular one is man-made. Last year, California and the surrounding States enjoyed record snowfalls, which created an abundance of water. However in 2007, a Federal judge ruled that endangered smelt might get caught in the pumps. So, the pumps were ordered to be shut down to preserve the habitat for the tiny, silver fish. As a result, taxpayers from San Diego to San Jose have been placed on water allocation and have suffered significant rate hikes; farmers have been threatened with foreclosures and bankruptcies because they can't irrigate their crops; but I'm happy to say that the smelt are enjoying living their lives and being eaten by natural predators. I apologize in advance to environmentalists, but there comes a time when *common sense* must intervene. So, I say open the pumps, restore the agrarian economy, fish fry at my house, and eliminate this position.

Since I've already offended my fellow environmentalists, let's take a look at three other unnecessary positions: *Climate Czar*, *Energy and Environment Czar*, and *Green Jobs Czar*. If we accept the premise of Global Warming (as established by world-renowned scientist and inventor of the Internet, Al Gore), our climate would seem to be a legitimate issue. Luckily, the Federal and State governments have authority to create laws that make us better *"citizens of the planet."* Unfortunately, we have no authority to legislate what China, India and the rest of the world do. So, the *Climate Czar* can step down.

Similarly, we don't have a need for an *Energy and Environment Czar*. The environmental element is repetitive and, as for energy, I can set the policy:

eliminate our dependence on foreign oil; cultivate our natural resources in a responsible way (which doesn't mean *"rape the earth"* any more than it means that accessing them will destroy the world as we know it); and develop new and better alternative fuels.

This brings us to the *Green Job Czar*, but I need not address this one. Apparently, the White House has already excused him when it was discovered that he took the whole Czar thing a little too literally and pledged allegiance to Stalin. Besides, the title evokes a theme of racial discrimination.

Speaking of jobs, I find it interesting that we don't have a *Jobs Czar*. No problem ... I can handle it. We do have an *Economic Czar*, so maybe there's some overlap. Paul Volcker headed the Federal Reserve during the latter stages of the Carter Administration and through the Reagan years. The good news is that he is credited with helping our Nation overcome *"stagflation."* The bad news is that he did it by raising the prime lending rate to 21.5% and driving the economy into a deep recession that created a level of unemployment not seen since the Great Depression. I'm eliminating his position because we're already there when it comes to creating a recession and experiencing an untenable level of unemployment.

Correspondingly, I'm going to eliminate the *Regulatory Czar*. I've soured on the self-righteousness of our regulatory agencies ever since the *"anointed one,"* Eliot Spitzer, prostituted his position as Governor of New York after ruling herd over the bastions of Wall Street. I'll only reconsider if Bernie Madoff gets an early parole and assumes the role of Frank Abagnale, Jr. (I hope that reference isn't too esoteric). Besides, the current *Regulatory Czar* apparently wants to *"regulate"* everything including *"free speech"* (of which I am obviously a fan); having called for taxing or censoring conspiracy theories ... such as the theory that Global Warming may be a deliberate fraud. He also wants to lobby for the right for animals to bring lawsuits. This would give even more power to the ACLU (America's Crazy Lunatic Unit) to bring "udderly" worthless lawsuits on behalf of sacred cows; barring them from grazing on government property as a violation of the separation of church and state. Gone!

We also have a *Pay Czar*. This is the individual who, like the *Regulatory Czar*, remains ever vigilant over those fat-cat CEOs in high-profile industries we all love to hate. However, I can't help noticing that he hasn't imposed any restrictions on the compensation of the executives at Fannie Mae and Freddie Mac, who have almost single-handedly destroyed the economy. I also don't recall seeing any *"smack downs"* of the union officials who can consistently deliver political votes in volume. *Common sense* tells me he has to go!

While we're talking about unions, I feel compelled to point out that we have two Czars for the automotive industry: a *Car Czar* and an *Auto Recovery Czar*. By now, you know how I feel about redundancy. I'm not sure what either does, but I'm *sure* we don't need two. Under the *Car Czar's* guidance, both General Motors and Chrysler have gone bankrupt. Since I'm reasonably confident they could have accomplished that without him, his position is being eliminated. As for the *Auto Recovery Czar*, I'm not sure if he's vested with the responsibility to help the automotive industry *"recover"* from the bankruptcies the *Car Czar* has overseen, or if his responsibility is to *"recover"* the taxpayer dollars that have been funneled into the industry without any noticeable results. Once again, this is a position we can safely eliminate.

Moving along into the vital science, technology and information sectors, I am happy to say we have a Czar for each one. Our *Science Czar* is a top-flight academic, which means that *common sense* isn't a part of his world. He once proffered the idea of forced abortions, *"compulsory sterilization,"* and the creation of a *"Planetary Regime"* to control human population and natural resources to save the Earth. *"Earth to Science Czar,"* I'll only consider keeping you if the *"compulsory sterilization"* idea begins with Members of our current Congress.

Our *Technology Czar* and *Information Czar* are good friends. Together, they will lead the evolution of Information Technology within our government. You guessed it ... I see this as redundant. Given that the *Information Czar* came first and brought the *Technology Czar* on board, I've got to give the nod to him. Unfortunately, he's been linked to hiring individuals with criminal records to protect our information. Since I'd hate to break up a team, they both have to go.

With healthcare reform on the forefront, we have two Czars that touch upon it: an *AIDS Czar* and a *Health Czar*. The *AIDS Czar* can go. AIDS is a disease. Other than its associated political capital, it does not rank in the top ten causes of death in the United States (which are: (1) Heart Disease; (2) Cancer; (3) Stroke; (4) Chronic Lower Respiratory Diseases; (5) Accidents (unintentional injuries); (6) Diabetes; (7) Alzheimer's disease; (8) Influenza and Pneumonia; (9) Nephritis, Nephrotic Syndrome, and Nephrosis; and (10) Septicemia). Sorry, but until the Top Ten have their own Czars, AIDS doesn't merit one. Because the *Health Czar* hasn't had the *common sense* to recognize this either, she's gone too!

I'm sad to report that we have a comparatively unaccomplished *Urban Affairs Czar*. Why settle? This is America. We have John Edwards, Bill Clinton, Mark Sanford and, most recently, Tiger Woods. Now, *these* men clearly know how to have urban affairs! If none of them will step up to embrace their civic duty, let's just eliminate this position.

So, with that task completed, let's get to work!

PREMISE

We may be disenchanted with our politicians, but it's not necessarily fair to blame the inmates for the way they run the asylum. After all, they do *warn* us … particularly in Presidential election years when they author National Platforms that define their positions. Yet, few of us ever take the time to *read* those documents to truly understand each Party's position … even though their positions and underlying beliefs will drive the decisions that dictate the direction in which our country will *be headed* … or should that be spelled *"beheaded?"* Shame on us!

Instead, we tend to take the easy way out and just listen to their speeches and debates (at least as much of them as we can stand); we watch their negative ads (positive ones went away a generation ago); and we let politically jaded wolves, who like to parade around in the sheep's clothing of *"reporting the news"* (once an honored profession), deliver thinly veiled versions of their personal opinions and beliefs. As the *Common Sense Czar*, I say we take a new approach: *let's read the words the Parties have committed to writing and for which we can hold them accountable.*

Now, I know this is a challenging suggestion because Party Platforms are always filled with political platitudes to their own greatness, grossly exaggerated vilifications of the *"Opposition,"* and a tediously repetitive casting of the same old drivel in hopes of gaining a vote. Well, as the *Common Sense Czar*, I've decided to make the endeavor far more entertaining, informative, and worthy of your time … and completely devoid of *"political correctness!"*

In hopes of getting you to actually *read* what the two major Parties have written, I've *"channeled"* them (in two separate books) … not only providing you with the *exact* transcript of their Platforms (misspellings and grammatical errors included) ... but my own satirical interpretation of what they were *actually thinking* at the time. <u>*The Left isn't Right*</u> has fun with the Democratic National Platform; <u>*The Right is Wrong*</u> has fun with the Republican National Platform; and the third book, <u>*The National Platform of Common Sense*</u>, provides a satirical look at how the Parties *could* have structured their Platforms if they had paid attention to the *Declaration of Independence*, the *Constitution*, and the *Bill of Rights* ... and applied some *"common sense."*

As far as trilogies go, this one is devoid of magical rings, wizards, and diminutive beings, but I strongly encourage you to read *all* three books. At the end of the day, regardless of your Party affiliation, you'll have a far better understanding of *both* of our major political Parties' philosophies ... and a *"common sense"* appreciation of our country and the Republic *"for which it stands."*

WHAT YOU NEED TO KNOW BEFORE YOU START

This book incorporates the original text of the 2008 Republican National Platform (Copyright © 2008 by the Republican National Committee) under the doctrine of Fair Use (17 USC 107) to maintain the accuracy of the Platform, and it distinguishes its satirical comments, criticisms, and research clearly to avoid any confusion. Its purpose is to stimulate political thought and promote a more informed electorate. The RNC does not endorse any of the views or opinions expressed by the book's author, and the author recommends that you visit www.gop.com/2008Platform/2008platform.pdf for a downloadable, full-color copy of the 2008 Republican National Platform.

> **The *Common Sense Czar's* satirical comments, criticisms, and research start with the *Common Sense Czar's* very own *"idea"* light bulb. They are further distinguished by their indentation and bolded text (with this section serving as an example).**
>
> **To fully appreciate the satirical nature of the comments, read them *as if* they are being expressed *by* the Party ... but in the end, remember that they are just meant to be entertaining comments that stimulate thought.**

When the indentation and bolded text end, so do the *Common Sense Czar's* embellishments and you are returned to the Republican National Platform's original text.

CHAIRMEN'S PREAMBLE

This is a platform of enduring principle, not passing convenience; the product of the most open and transparent process in American political history. We offer it to our fellow Americans in the assurance that our Republican ideals are those that unify our country: Courage in the face of foreign foes. An optimistic patriotism, driven by a passion for freedom. Devotion to the inherent dignity and rights of every person. Faith in the virtues of self-reliance, civic commitment, and concern for one another. Distrust of government's interference in people's lives. Dedication to a rule of law that both protects and preserves liberty.

 **You're going to quickly find out that we're not a very creative Party. We threw in the phrase** *"most open and transparent process in American political history"* **because it's a hot topic right now and we heard that the Democrat's were going to make the same claim.**
We feel that it's particularly important to *"distrust ... government's interference in people's lives."* **Over the years, we've interfered in people's lives all the time, so we know how dangerous it can be!**

We present this platform at an uncertain point in time. Our country remains at war and committed to victory, but reckless political forces would imperil that goal and endanger our nation. In the economy and in society at large, it is a time of transformation. But the American people will meet these challenges. Even with its uncertainties, they embrace the future, but they are also too wise to rush headlong into it. We are an adventurous, risk-taking people, but we are not gamblers. A sound democracy trusts new leadership but insists that it demonstrate the old virtues: the character and the command that, in times of conflict and crisis, have led the Republic through its trials.

This platform likewise rests on proven truths and tested wisdom as it looks ahead, both to deal with present challenges and to explore possibilities that may sometimes seem beyond our grasp. It shows what the American people can accomplish when government respects their rights, conserves their resources, and calls upon their love of country. It is not a tribute to bigger government.

If you're wondering about the *"maverick"* comment, our candidate, John McCain, was once at odds with our Party and became defined as a *"maverick."* Now, since we've somehow chosen to have him represent our Party, we've got to turn this into a positive. It's the same reason we use terms like *"old virtues,"* *"proven truths,"* and *"tested wisdom."* Let's face it, our candidate is pretty old, and he's as white as a sheet that's been hung out to dry in the sun too long. We're running him against an opponent who's much younger and has a better tan. We've just got to play the cards we're dealt.

Our platform is presented with enthusiasm and confidence in a vision for the future, but also with genuine humility – humility before God and before a nation of free and independent thinkers. As the party of ideas, rather than a mere coalition of interests, we consider vigorous debate a strength, not a weakness.

Of course, *"debate"* is not one of our strong suits. Just ask anyone who remembers Dick Nixon *"getting it on"* with Jack Kennedy. We all remember Jack Kennedy. He was an opponent of ours. And … well … John McCain is *"no Jack Kennedy"* when it comes to debating.

Indeed, we are a party – as we are a nation – of mavericks. Yet we stand united today because we are the one party that speaks to all Americans – conservatives, moderates, libertarians, independents, and even liberals. We welcome all to our deliberations in the firm belief that the principles embodied in this platform will prove to be as compelling and persuasive as they are vital and enduring. We do not fear disagreement, and we do not demand conformity, but we do fight for our principles with confidence that the best ideas will prevail in the end.

Notice how we slipped in *"maverick"* again? It's going to be an uphill battle. And while we speak *"to all Americans,"* we're not sure if very many of them are listening. Probably because for a great many years ... while we did not *"demand conformity"* ... we all pretty much looked alike.

Our party embodies a uniquely American spirit. It is the spirit of independent minds, the conviction that open and honest debate is essential to the freedom we enjoy as Americans. This platform is a testament to that freedom and stands as our promise to future generations that we will do whatever it takes to preserve it. It is grounded on our heartfelt belief that our principles, our policies, and our vision will lead our American family, not just through present dangers, but to a horizon of prosperity and liberty mankind has only begun to explore.

With gratitude for eight years of honorable service from President George W. Bush and Dick Cheney, the Republican Party now stands united behind new leadership, an American patriot, John McCain. In support of his candidacy and those of our fellow Republicans across the nation – and ever grateful to Almighty God for the political, religious, and civil liberties we enjoy – we, the representatives of the Republican Party in the states and territories of the United States, offer this platform to the American people.

Oh sure, we know that the press has vilified President Bush and suggested that Vice President Cheney is the love child of Satan. But like we said before, *"old virtues,"* *"proven truths,"* and *"tested

wisdom" are our mantras, so we have to follow tradition and *"beat the dead horse"* one more time. Giddy-up, cowboy!

DEFENDING OUR NATION

SUPPORTING OUR HEROES, SECURING THE PEACE

Three decades ago, in a world as dangerous as today's, Americans of all stripes came together to advance the cause of freedom. They had witnessed the wreckage of inexperienced good intentions at the highest levels of government, the folly of an amateur foreign policy. And so, in defiance of a worldwide Marxist advance, they announced a goal as enduring as the vision of Isaiah, to "proclaim liberty to the captives," and summed up America's strategy for achieving that end in a timeless slogan: Peace through strength – an enduring peace, based on freedom and the will to defend it.

We couldn't wait any longer to invoke Ronald Reagan and take a shot at the inexperience of Barrack Obama. After all, President Reagan is our *"pedestal"* President ... you know ... the type you put up on a pedestal and pretend they didn't have any faults. Kind of like the Democrats use to do with Kennedy and are now doing more with FDR ... since Roosevelt was more of a Socialist. Hey, we're only going back about 25 years to find a role model. The Democrats have to go back 65!

That goal still requires the unity of Americans beyond differences of party and conflicts of personality. The rancor of past years must now give way to a common goal of security for our country and safety for our people. For seven years, the horror of September 11, 2001 has not been repeated on our soil. For that, we are prayerfully grateful and salute all who have played a role in defending our homeland. We pledge to continue their vigilance and to assure they have the authority and resources they need to protect the nation.

You've got to give us this point. There hasn't been an attack on our soil prior to any change in leadership since September 11, 2001. The best the Democrats can do is to speculate that there wouldn't have been one if they were in office. Of course, we may have been a little *over-zealous* in trampling on some Constitutional rights, but who really cares?

Defending Our Nation

The Current Conflict Abroad

All Americans should affirm that our first obligation is the security of our country. To all those who defend it, we owe our full support and gratitude.

The waging of war – and the achieving of peace – should never be micromanaged in a party platform, or on the floor of the Senate and House of Representatives for that matter. In dealing with present conflicts and future crises, our next president must preserve all options. It would be presumptuous to specify them in advance and fool-hardy to rule out any action deemed necessary for our security.

"*The waging of war – and the achieving of peace – should never be micromanaged in a party platform, or on the floor of the Senate and House of Representatives.*" We know. We've been doing it that way for years when *we* were in control, and it just doesn't work!

Since the Democrats have pushed the *"peace"* button again and tried to make people believe that the War in Iraq was ill-conceived and without justification (just because we couldn't *find* the weapons of mass destruction we said were there), we need to strike back and say their diplomatic approach is *"fool-hardy"* so we can generate some *fear*, and in

return, garner some votes. It's another attempt to play off of Obama's inexperience.

The reality is that we know that *fear* generates *votes*. The Democrats use that tactic all the time. We're just not quite as good at as they are ... but we're trying!

<u>Homeland Security</u>

We acknowledge and appreciate the significant contributions of all of America's First Responders, who keep us safe and secure and who are ever ready to come to our aid. The security of our country is now everyone's responsibility, from the Department of Homeland Security to state and local first responders, private businesses, and individual families. The fact that eighty percent of our critical infrastructure is in private hands highlights the need for public-private partnerships to safeguard it, especially in the energy industry.

We don't have as many constituencies as the Democrats, so we have to *"suck up"* **to the business sector. It gets us in trouble with the** *"little guy"* **sometimes because the Democrats have been really good at convincing people who identify themselves as** *"lower"* **or** *"middle class"* **... and virtually** *all* **union members ... that business people are** *"bad to the bone."* **We're doing a good job of trying to shift that opinion, but it's so hard to turn away the campaign donations we receive from the** *fat cats* **... not to mention the** *great* **trips they take us on to ... uh ... discuss the economy. Yeah, that's right ... to discuss the economy! Of course, every now and then, our trip is ruined because we bump into Charlie Rangel, but you have to take the bitter with the sweet.**

Along with unrelenting vigilance to prevent bioterrorism and other WMD-related attacks, we must regularly exercise our ability to quickly respond if one were to occur. We must continue to remove barriers to cooperation and information sharing. Modernized 9-1-1 services must be made universally available and be adequately funded. We must be able to thwart cyber attacks that could cripple our economy, monitor terrorist activities while respecting Americans' civil liberties, and protect against military and industrial espionage and sabotage. All this requires experienced leadership.

Give us credit. It takes real chutzpah to bring up *"WMDs"* again after the fiasco in Iraq, but we've got balls! We slip in the jab about *"experienced leadership,"* but truth be told, we've done very little to improve the tools and funding of our first responders since 9/11. Their communication and triage systems are nearly archaic, yet we still haven't made it a priority to correct the problem.

Terrorism and Nuclear Proliferation

The attacks of September 11, 2001 were a pivot point in our national experience. They highlighted the failure of national policy to recognize and respond to the growth of a global terror network. They should have put an end to the Democrats' naive thinking that international terrorists could be dealt with within the normal criminal justice system, but that misconception persists.

The gravest threat we face – nuclear terrorism – demands a comprehensive strategy for reducing the world's nuclear stockpiles and preventing proliferation. The U.S. should lead that effort by reducing the size of our nuclear arsenal to the lowest number consistent with our security requirements and working with other nuclear powers to do the same.

Actually, we think our nuclear arsenal should be about 10 *times* the size of the rest of the world's *combined* nuclear arsenals. You just can't be too careful!

In cooperation with other nations, we should end the production of weapons-grade fissile material, improve our collective ability to interdict the spread of weapons of mass destruction and related materials, and ensure the highest possible security standards for existing nuclear materials wherever they may be located.

But that is not enough. We must develop and deploy both national and theater missile defenses to protect the American homeland, our people, our Armed Forces abroad, and our allies. Effective, layered missile defenses are critical to guard against the unpredictable actions of rogue regimes and outlaw states, reduce the possibility of strategic blackmail, and avoid the disastrous consequences of an accidental or unauthorized launch by a foreign power.

The defense industry's Political Action Committees are to the Republican Party what the unions are to the Democratic Party. We enjoy the *"benefits"* of its lobbying efforts. Of course, we have to work a little harder. While the unions deliver money and votes to the Democrats, the defense industry just lines our pockets with money. Then, we have to figure out how to use it to attract votes ... you know, by investing in negative ads, etc.

<u>Better Intelligence — the Key to Prevention</u>

Intelligence is America's first line of defense. We must increase the ranks and resources of our human intelligence capabilities, integrate technical and human sources, and get that information more quickly to the warfighter and the policy maker. The multi-jurisdictional arrangements that now prevail on Capitol Hill should be replaced by a single Joint Committee on Intelligence.

Don't be alarmed. We mean *"intelligence"* in the sense of gathering critical data ... not in the sense of actually *doing* something *"intelligent."* As Dirty Harry would say, *"A man's got to know his limitations."*

INTELLIGENCE IS KEY TO FIGHTING BIOTERRORISM AND CYBERTERRORISM

Bioterrorism and cyberterrorism, once the stuff of science fiction films, are immediate threats to our nation's health and safety. Our food and water distribution systems require special vigilance. By the same token, a well-placed cyber-attack could cripple our economy, shut down our energy and transportation systems, wreck our health care delivery systems, and put millions of lives at risk. Although our country has thwarted new terrorist attacks since 2001, those threats do persist. That is why our reform of the Foreign Intelligence Surveillance Act was so vital, and why the Democrats' opposition to it was so wrong.

 We're not really sure what it means, but we have to pay lip-service to *"cyberterrorism."* We're not even sure how to spell it. Heck, most of us think *"tweeting"* is something a bird does! But we know that the Internet is apparently catching on, so we need to acknowledge it ... as a *threat* to national security. Now, that's something we can relate to! We just wish that Al Gore hadn't invented the darn Internet. Then, we wouldn't have to deal with all this new-fangled technology stuff.

Immigration, National Security, and the Rule of Law

Immigration policy is a national security issue, for which we have one test: Does it serve the national interest? By that standard, Republicans know America can have a strong immigration system without sacrificing the rule of law.

ENFORCING THE RULE OF LAW AT THE BORDER AND THROUGHOUT THE NATION

Border security is essential to national security. In an age of terrorism, drug cartels, and criminal gangs, allowing millions of unidentified persons to enter and remain in this country poses grave risks to the sovereignty of the United States and the security of its people. We simply must be able to track who is entering and leaving our country.

 Since we need to *"strike fear in the hearts of Americans"* (a key tactical strategy) and we can't mimic the Democrats' patented *"oppressed minority"* strategy, we tend to conjure up groups for whom most people harbor some degree of trepidation. In that regard, *"terrorists," "drug cartels"* and *"criminal gangs"* work well for us.

Our determination to uphold the rule of law begins with more effective enforcement, giving our agents the tools and resources they need to protect our sovereignty, completing the border fence quickly and securing the borders, and employing complementary strategies to secure our ports of entry. Experience shows that enforcement of existing laws is effective in reducing and reversing illegal immigration.

 We've created and maintained a *"Law and Order"* image for our Party (one of our core strategies). Heck, we even tried to run one of the TV series' actors for President. Some of our greatest politicians have been actors since they can deliver our Party's lines in a convincing manner. We just wish that Clint Eastwood wasn't a Libertarian.

As far as the border fence goes, we got that from a movie as well. It is our fervid belief that *"if we build it, they won't come."*

Our commitment to the rule of law means smarter enforcement at the workplace, against illegal workers and lawbreaking employers alike, along with those who practice identity theft and traffic in fraudulent documents. As long as jobs are available in the United States, economic incentives to enter illegally will persist. But we must empower employers so they can know with confidence that those they hire are permitted to work. That means that the E-Verify system – which is an internet-based system that verifies the employment authorization and identity of employees – must be reauthorized. A phased-in requirement that employers use the E-Verify system must be enacted.

 **We're just going to keep pounding in the *"rule of law"* phrase, so get used to it. It's a play on our *"Law and Order"* strategy.**

Of course, we've had *years* to address these immigration issues, but we're serious this time! And notice how we acknowledged the Internet again. We even used the *"E"* term to show how hip we are. Quick, somebody give John McCain a cell phone and take the one with the rotary dial away from him.

The rule of law means guaranteeing to law enforcement the tools and coordination to deport criminal aliens without delay – and correcting court decisions that have made deportation so difficult. It means enforcing the law against those who overstay their visas, rather than letting millions flout the generosity that gave them temporary entry. It means imposing maximum penalties on those who smuggle illegal aliens into the U.S., both for their lawbreaking and for their cruel exploitation. It means requiring cooperation among federal, state and local law enforcement and real consequences, including the denial of federal funds, for self-described sanctuary cities, which stand in open defiance of the federal and state statutes that expressly prohibit such sanctuary policies, and which endanger the lives of U.S. citizens. It does not mean driver's licenses for illegal aliens, nor does it mean that states should be allowed to flout the federal law barring them from giving in-state tuition rates to illegal aliens, nor does it mean that illegal aliens should receive social security benefits, or other public benefits, except as provided by federal law.

 **We've got to reinforce this issue because if the Democrats win the White House, Obama may try to put a Hispanic woman on the Supreme Court who might rule from her personal *"experience"* as a Latino rather than based on the *law*. Sure, you think that won't happen, but it could. He might even try to put another woman**

on the Supreme Court who doesn't even have *any* judicial experience. And we've got to stem the tide on this immigration thing before the States start taking the law into their own hands.

We oppose amnesty. The rule of law suffers if government policies encourage or reward illegal activity. The American people's rejection of en masse legalizations is especially appropriate given the federal government's past failures to enforce the law.

Truth be told, we oppose amnesty because we know the Democrats will use it to expand the welfare state they use to curry favor with the masses. They've already got a big enough majority among voters (both living and dead), so we don't *dare* let them grow their base.

Embracing Immigrant Communities

Today's immigrants are walking in the steps of most other Americans' ancestors, seeking the American dream and contributing culturally and economically to our nation. We celebrate the industry and love of liberty of these fellow Americans.

Both government and the private sector must do more to foster legally present immigrants' integration into American life to advance respect for the rule of law and a common American identity. It is a national disgrace that the first experience most new Americans have is with a dysfunctional immigration bureaucracy defined by delay and confusion; we will no longer tolerate those failures.

In our multiethnic nation, everyone – immigrants and native-born alike – must embrace our core values of liberty, equality, meritocracy, and respect for human dignity and the rights of women.

We threw in the *"rights of women"* as opposed to leaving it at *"respect for human dignity"* because we want to take a firm stand that the Democrats don't

> have our *carte blanche* approval to carve out women as an "oppressed minority." We have women who support our "Old Boys' Club" as well ... and most of them are rather good looking!
>
> And just ignore the fact that we've done *nothing* to resolve the immigration issue that has been growing over the years. If we'd fixed it, we wouldn't have it to use any more to employ our *"strike fear in the hearts of Americans"* strategy.

One sign of our unity is our English language. For newcomers, it has always been the fastest route to prosperity in America. English empowers. We support English as the official language in our nation, while welcoming the ethnic diversity in the United States and the territories, including language. Immigrants should be encouraged to learn English. English is the accepted language of business, commerce, and legal proceedings, and it is essential as a unifying cultural force. It is also important, as part of cultural integration, that our schools provide better education in U.S. history and civics for all children, thereby fostering a commitment to our national motto, E Pluribus Unum.

English is our national language. We're adamant about it. That's why we emphasize the importance of *"fostering a commitment to our national motto, E Pluribus Unum,"* which, of course, we express in Latin.

We are grateful to the thousands of new immigrants, many of them not yet citizens, who are serving in the Armed Forces. Their patriotism is inspiring; it should remind the institutions of civil society of the need to embrace newcomers, assist their journey to full citizenship, and help their communities avoid patterns of isolation.

WELCOMING REFUGEES

Our country continues to accept refugees from troubled lands all over the world. In some cases, these are people who stood with America in dangerous times, and they have first call on our hospitality. We oppose, however, the granting of refugee status on the basis of lifestyle or other non-political factors.

 *"We oppose ... the granting of refugee status on the basis of lifestyle or other non-political factors."* Besides, we have a tacit agreement with the Democrats about this. They stay out of our *"Law and Order"* domain, and we stay out of their *"oppressed minority"* territories.

SUPPORTING OUR HEROES

Republican leadership, from the presidency to the Congress, has given America the best-manned, best-trained, best-equipped, and best-led military in the world. That is a radical change from the late 1990's, when national defense was neglected and under-funded by the Clinton Administration. Our Armed Forces today are modern, agile, and adaptable to the unpredictable range of challenges in the years ahead. We pledge to keep them that way.

 **Forgive us, but we hadn't slammed a Democratic President in a while, and we were due. And while the Clinton Administration had its good points, other parts of it obviously sucked.**

Providing for the Armed Forces

The men and women who wear our country's uniform – whether on active duty or in the Reserves or National Guard – are the most important assets in our military arsenal. They and their families must have the pay, health care, housing, education, and overall support they need. We must significantly increase the size of our Armed Forces; crucial to that goal will be retention of combat veterans.

Injured military personnel deserve the best medical care our country has to offer. The special circumstances of the conflict in Iraq have resulted in an unprecedented incidence of traumatic brain injury, which calls for a new commitment of resources and personnel for its care and treatment. We must make military medicine the gold standard for advances in prosthetics and the treatment of trauma and eye injuries.

We must always remember those who have given the ultimate sacrifice; their families must be assured meaningful financial assistance. It is the solemn duty we owe and honor we give to those who bravely don the uniform of freedom.

Because it integrates so well with our *"Law and Order"* strategy, we've always done well with the military. The Democrats like to stereotype us is as *neo-fascist, military supporters* ... and we're okay with that. Most people accept the fact that Democrats are *left-wing, socialist, nut jobs* ... because their most demonstrative members are! As a result, we virtually own the veterans' population, except for an occasional *left-wing, socialist, nut job* ... like John Kerry.

NATIONAL GUARD AND RESERVES

We pledge to maintain the strength of the National Guard and Reserves and to ensure they receive pay, benefits, and resources befitting their service. Their historic role as citizen-soldiers is a proud tradition linking every community with the cause of national security. We affirm service members' legal right to return to their civilian jobs, whether in government or in the private sector, when their active duty is completed, and we call for greater transition assistance from employers across the nation to smooth their return to the work force.

The National Guard and Reserves have grown, both in size and importance, over the last decade, so now they merit their own paragraph. If the Merchant Marine ever expands, we'll give them a paragraph too!

PERSONNEL POLICIES

The all-volunteer force has been a success. We oppose reinstituting the draft, whether directly or through compulsory national service. We support the advancement of women in the military and their exemption from ground combat units. Military priorities and mission must determine personnel policies. Esprit and cohesion are necessary for military effectiveness and success on the battlefield. To protect our servicemen and women and ensure that America's Armed Forces remain the best in the world, we affirm the timelessness of those values, the benefits of traditional military culture, and the incompatibility of homosexuality with military service.

We're not going to get their votes anyway, so we're willing to risk offending homosexuals … even though *our* Presidential and Vice Presidential lineage have more of a homosexual flair to them than the Democrats', whose elected officials are far better known for their *heterosexual* activities outside the bonds of marriage. Of course, we can always ask John Edwards to back us in this regard as he did when he *"complimented"* the Cheney's for still loving their gay daughter.

<u>Fulfilling our Commitment to our Veterans</u>

To military personnel who have served honorably and then retire or leave active duty, we owe a smooth transition to civilian life. Funding for the programs that assist them should be sufficient, timely, and predictable and never be subject to political gamesmanship.

While we state that the funding of veterans' programs should *"never be subject to political gamesmanship,"* our actions suggest that *every-thing* is *"subject to political gamesmanship"* … or this wouldn't still be an issue today.

ECONOMIC OPPORTUNITY FOR VETERANS

Returning veterans must have access to education benefits, job training, and a wide variety of employment options. We want to build on the bipartisan expansion of the GI Bill by encouraging private colleges to bridge the gap between GI Bill education benefits and tuition costs. We will strongly enforce the Uniformed Services Employment and Reemployment Rights Act so that returning veterans can promptly return to their former jobs. Our existing "veteran preference" regulations must lead to real action, not hollow promises. We encourage private businesses to expand their outreach to the veterans community, especially disabled veterans.

We think we truly have a shot at *"build(ing) on the bipartisan expansion of the GI Bill"* because it involves spending money … and the Democrats are *always* on board with that idea.

VETERANS' HEALTH CARE AND DISABILITY SYSTEM

We will hold the VA accountable for tangible results and steady improvement of its services. The VA must become more responsive and more efficient by eliminating its disability backlog and reducing waiting times for treatment. To ensure that the VA provides veterans with world class medical care, both at its own facilities and through partnerships with community providers, we must recruit the next generation of highly qualified medical professionals. Where distance or crowding is an obstacle to traditional VA facility-based care, our veterans should be provided access to qualified out-of-network providers. We call for greater attention by the VA to the special health care needs of women veterans, who will comprise an even larger percentage of VA patients in the future.

"We will hold the VA accountable for tangible results and steady improvement of its services." Thank goodness no one holds us *"accountable for tangible results and steady improvement of its services."* We'd almost *all* be *"one-termers."*

The VA's current disability compensation formulas need to be restructured and modernized. Those who have borne the burden of war must have access to training, rehabilitation, and education. Their families and caregivers deserve our concern and support.

We pledge special attention to combat stress injuries. There must be adequate counseling when veterans return home – for them and their families. They should have ongoing professional care, whether in a VA facility or closer to home, so that the natural and usually temporary responses to the horrors of war do not become permanent conditions. We recognize the need for more mental health professionals who can give the highest quality treatment to our veterans.

We applaud the non-profit organizations which assist veterans and their families materially and in other ways. They represent the best of the American spirit and merit our support.

Procurement Reform

The military's partners are the men and women who work in the defense industry and civilian sector, supplying the Armed Forces with weapons and equipment vital to the success of their mission. To ensure that our troops receive the best material at the best value, we must reform the defense budgeting and acquisition process to control costs and ensure vigorous and fair competition. We will not allow congressional pork to take the place of sound, sustained investment in the nation's security.

The days of the *"$800 hammer"* are gone ... unless it's a *really* good hammer! The electorate is beginning to wise-up ... or at least a *small* percentage of it is. So, we're going to have to be careful about how we *"process the pork."* We were more lackadaisical about it when we weren't putting our military personnel in *"harm's way,"* but now people are actually starting to pay attention to the Defense programs we're funding, and the press isn't particularly inclined to cut us any slack.

SECURING THE PEACE

The Republican vision of peace through strength requires a sustained international effort, which complements our military activities, to develop and maintain alliances and relationships that will lead to greater peace and stability.

 **Again, when in doubt, use Reagan's language. *"Peace through strength"* resonates with our constituency. As far as being able to *"develop and maintain alliances and relationships that will lead to greater peace and stability"* ... well, let's just say that wasn't exactly a *strong point* of the Bush Administration's or "W" would have received a Nobel Peace Prize.**

Promoting Human Rights and American Values

The international promotion of human rights reflects our heritage, our values, and our national interest. Societies that enjoy political and economic freedom and the rule of law are not given to aggression or fanaticism. They become our natural allies.

Republican leadership has made religious liberty a central element of U.S. foreign policy. Asserting religious freedom should be a priority in all America's international dealings. We salute the work of the U.S. Commission on International Religious Freedom and urge special training in religious liberty issues for all U.S. diplomatic personnel.

 **Of course, we haven't been particularly successful in securing religious freedom at *home*, much less *abroad*, during recent year. We've become so afraid of being *"politically incorrect"* that we've let special interest groups dictate the terms by which religion can be celebrated in the United States. Crosses have been torn down; Christmas trees have disappeared from our political landscape (not to mention that Christmas songs can't be sung during the Christmas season); and the Ten Commandments can no longer make an appearance on public property for fear that our**

citizens may stop killing each other, stealing each other's property, and committing adultery ... just to mention a few. But, no worries ... we're going to tell *China* how to manage the religious freedom of *its* people.

To be successful international leaders, we must uphold international law, including the laws of war, and update them when necessary. Our moral standing requires that we respect what are essentially American principles of justice. In any war of ideas, our values will triumph.

Being the Party of *"Law and Order,"* we're more comfortable relating to war analogies. Discussions of peace reminds us too much of leftist, liberal hippies; a constituency with which we have consciously disassociated ourselves.

STATE DEPARTMENT REFORM

Advancing America's values should be the core mission of every part of the federal government, including the Department of State. America's diplomatic establishment must energetically represent our country's agenda to the world. We propose a thorough reform of its structure to ensure that promotions and appointments are based on performance in supporting the nation's agenda. Our diplomats must be the best our country has to offer, and America's diplomatic abilities must be an integral part of America's national security system.

Until now, the over-riding qualifications to be considered for a diplomatic appointment were: (a) you had to be a *"political embarrassment"* that we needed to move *"off-shore;"* (b) you had to have performed *a lot* of political favors in the past (so you could call in your *"markers"* so to speak), and you had to have a *high tolerance* for *limited sleep* and *the excessive consumption of alcohol* to survive all of the Embassy parties; or (c) you had photographs of one of our senior political officials who *didn't*

have a *high tolerance* for *limited sleep* and *the excessive consumption of alcohol* at one of our political balls.

PUBLIC DIPLOMACY

Throughout the Cold War, our international broadcasting of free and impartial information promoted American values to combat tyranny. It still does, through Radio Free Europe/Radio Liberty and Radio/TV Marti, and it remains an important instrument in promoting a modernizing alternative to the culture of radical terror. Getting America's message out to the world is a critical element in the struggle against extremism, and our government must wage a much more effective battle in the war of ideas.

 **As a Party, we're big on the** *"international broadcasting of free and impartial information promot(ing) American values to combat tyranny."* **Radio shows like Rush Limbaugh's and Sean Hannity's come to mind; shows that promote the America *we* believe in. And who's the wise guy who submitted the name *Al Jazeera* anyway? We want *high-visibility* celebrities to host our radio broadcasts, and we don't even know who this "Al" guy is!**

HUMAN TRAFFICKING

Generations after the end of slavery in America, new forms of bondage have emerged to exploit men, women and children. We salute those across the political spectrum who have come together to end the commerce in our fellow human beings. We advocate the establishment of an Inter-Agency Task Force on Human Trafficking, reporting directly to the President, and call for increased diplomatic efforts with foreign governments that have been negligent toward this evil. The principle underlying our Megan's Law – publicizing the identities of known offenders – should be extended to international travel in order to protect innocent children everywhere.

 *"We advocate the establishment of an Inter-Agency Task Force on Human Trafficking."* We're pretty sure we can get the Democrats to support this because it will cost money and requires the formation of yet one more new agency.

We know what you're thinking ... we can't even establish an effective *"No Fly"* list, but we think we can create an international list of far more innocuous individuals who *"exploit men, women and children"* in a disgraceful way. *"Yes we can!"* Oops, we can't believe we just said that ... but it *is* kind of catchy.

The real challenge will be to define the disgraceful *"exploit(ation) of men, women and children"* in a way that doesn't *inherently* include politicians. Now, *that* might take some time!

<u>Sovereign American Leadership in International Organizations</u>

The United States participates in various international organizations which can, at times, serve the cause of peace and prosperity, but those organizations must never serve as a substitute for principled American leadership. Nor should our participation in them prevent our joining with other democracies to protect our vital national interests.

 We say that we believe that *"United States participates in various international organizations,"* but what we really believe is that the United States should be able to do whatever it wants. It doesn't *need* some international organization monitoring its choices. We're the *"big dog"* in this fight. We just don't want to offend anyone by stating this out loud. You see, we need to be *"politically correct!"*

At the United Nations, our country will pay a fair, but not disproportionate, share of dues, but we will never support a UN-imposed tax. The UN must reform its scandal-ridden and corrupt management and become more accountable and transparent in its operations and expenses. As a matter of U.S. sovereignty, American forces must remain under American command.

 Over the years, the UN has gone from being an organization of *hope* ... to one with *"scandal-ridden and corrupt management."* We firmly believe that *"scandal-ridden and corrupt management"* is *best* reserved to the United States Congress. Will someone please pass the pork? Thank you!

Discrimination against Israel at the UN is unacceptable. We welcome Israel's membership in the Western European and Others Group at the UN headquarters and demand its full acceptance and participation at all UN venues. We likewise oppose the ideological campaign against Vatican participation in UN conferences and other activities.

 *"Discrimination against Israel at the UN is unacceptable."* We *really* believe this! You can tell because, try though we may, we've never really been able to capture the Jewish vote; Catholic, yes ... but Jewish, no. There's no money in it for us, and we can count the votes we get on one hand, but we still continue to support Israel for some reason. What's wrong with us? It seems so un-democratic (no pun intended).

What we'd really like to emphasize is how much we *hate* the way the UN gives credence to the leadership of countries like Iran and Lebanon. It allows those cretins to have an international forum to spew forth their venomous ideas. But again, we don't come out and say this because it would be *"politically incorrect."*

Because the UN has no mandate to promote radical social engineering, any effort to address global social problems must respect the fundamental institutions of marriage and family. We assert the rights of families in all international programs and will not fund organizations involved in abortion. We strongly support the long-held policy of the Republican Party known as the "Mexico City policy," which prohibits federal monies from being given to non governmental organizations that provide abortions or actively promote abortion as a method of family planning in other countries. We reject any treaty or agreement that would violate those values. That includes the UN convention on women's rights, signed in the last months of the Carter Administration, and the UN convention on the rights of the child. For several reasons, particularly our concern for US sovereignty and America's long-term energy needs, we have deep reservations about the regulatory, legal, and tax regimes inherent in the Law of the Sea Treaty.

While many people understand our restriction against the federal funding of abortion, we begin to lose the masses when we try to *legislate* our religious *beliefs* as well. This is particularly true when we try to mandate our social *mores* on diverse cultures that are *markedly* dissimilar to ours. So, we'll continue to ignore this reality and steadfastly argue our point ... often to the *extreme*.

To shield the members of our Armed Forces and others in service to America from ideological prosecutions, the Republican Party does not accept the jurisdiction of the International Criminal Court over Americans. We sup port the American Servicemembers Protection Act, to shield U.S. personnel and officials as they act abroad to meet global security requirements.

If only we could get the Democrats to stop prosecuting our military personnel while giving Miranda rights to captured terrorists, it would be a perfect world. And remember, we're the Party of *"Law and Order,"* so our *"laws"* and our *"order"* should apply to *everyone* throughout the world.

Helping Others Abroad

Americans are the most generous people in the world. No nation spends more in combined public and private efforts to combat disease and poverty around the world, and no nation works harder to ensure the continued vitality of the global economy. Our reasons for doing so are both moral and practical, for a world where half of the human race lives on a few dollars a day is neither just nor stable.

We may not be able to effectively *"combat disease and poverty"* in our *own* country, but we sure think we can get the job done *elsewhere* in the world. As an aside: John McCain says if he had a brother in Kenya who was only earning $1 a month, he'd give him a couple of hundred dollars, feed him a Big Mac (Super-sized, of course), and buy him a new set of clothes. One thing we Republicans aren't is *cheap!*

Including the world's poor in an expanding circle of development is part and parcel of the Republican approach to world trade through open markets and fair competition. It must also be a top priority of our foreign policy. Decades of massive aid have failed to spur economic growth in the poorest countries, where it has often propped up failed policies and corrupt rulers. We will target foreign assistance to high-impact goals: fostering the rule of law through democratic government; emphasizing literacy and learning; and, concentrating on the foundations for economic development – clean water, agricultural improvement, and microcredit funding for small enterprises. Maternal and child health, especially safer childbirthing and nutrition, must be priorities, especially in countries affected by epidemics of HIV/AIDS, malaria, and tuberculosis.

Did you catch the phrase *"fostering the rule of law through democratic government?"* It allowed us to combine the terms *"rule of law"* and *"democratic government"* in a single phrase. Never mind that the Framers of our Constitution created a Republic rather than

a Democracy ... most people don't know the difference. Notice that we used the term *"democratic government"* but spelled *"democratic"* with a lower-case "d." If we would have used *"Democratic"* with a capital "D," it would have been an oxymoron.

Just imagine if we were able to *"target"* the same *"high-impact goals"* in our own country rather than wasting time and money on things like Congressional perks, reelection campaigns, political dinners, and jet-setting to *"strategic"* conferences. What a difference *that* would make.

Further, we call for the development of a strategy for foreign assistance that serves our national interest. Specifically we call for a review and improvement of the Foreign Assistance Act of 1961 oriented toward: alignment of foreign assistance policies, operations, budgets and statutory authorities; development of a consensus on what needs to be done to strengthen the non-military tools to further our national security goals; greater attention to core development programs – education, child survival, and agricultural development; and greater accountability by recipient countries so as to ensure against malfeasance, self-dealing, and corruption, and to ensure continued assistance is conditioned on performance.

"We call for a review and improvement of the Foreign Assistance Act of 1961 oriented toward" essentially eliminating waste and corruption in other countries. Now, if only we could figure out a way to eliminate waste and corruption within *our* government. Then again ... Washington, D.C. just wouldn't be the same.

<u>Strengthening Ties in the Americas</u>

Faith and family, culture and commerce, are enduring bonds among all the peoples of the Americas. Republicans envision a western hemi-sphere of sovereign nations with secure borders, working together to advance liberty and mutually-beneficial trade based on sound and proven free enterprise principles. Our relations with our immediate neighbors, Canada and Mexico, are grounded on our shared values and common purpose, as well as our steadily increasing trade. We pledge to continue this close association and to advance mutually beneficial trade agreements throughout Latin America, promoting economic development and social stability there while opening markets to our goods and services. Our strong ties with Canada and Mexico should not lead to a North American union or a unified currency.

We don't think for a minute that we have *"shared values and common purpose"* with Mexico ... or even Canada for that matter. As far as trade goes, Ross Perot was right when he warned us about NAFTA: *"There will be a giant sucking sound going south."*

It's a joke for us to suggest that we will *"continue this close association and to advance mutually beneficial trade agreements throughout Latin America, promoting economic development and social stability there while opening markets to our goods and services."* Our trade relationship with Mexico is far from *"mutually beneficial"* unless you consider exporting our jobs south of the border to be *"beneficial"* to our country in some way. And if you look at how we've done in evolving Mexico's *"social stability,"* we'll bet you just can't wait to see how well we do with the *rest* of Latin America.

Two factors distort this hemispheric progress. One is narco-terrorism, with its ability to destabilize societies and corrupt the political process. In an era of porous borders, the war on drugs and the war on terror have become a single enterprise. We salute our allies in the fight against this evil, especially the people of Mexico and Colombia, who have set an example for their neighbors. We support approval of the free trade agreement with Colombia, currently blocked by Capitol Hill Democrats and their union boss supporters, as an overdue gesture of solidarity for this courageous ally of the United States.

You have to acknowledge that the Mexican and Columbian governments have made an effort to reduce *"narco-terrorism,"* but they haven't *really*

made much of a dent in the trafficking. The real Republican opportunity in this whole *"narco-terrorism"* thing is in weapons deals. That's right ... selling weapons to the Mexican and Columbian governments. You see, they're tremendously outgunned by the drug cartels at this point in time. We're not sure where the cartels are getting their weapons, but we sure *hope* it's from the good old U S of A. We'll take any kind of contribution to the economy we can get today.

The other malignant element in hemispheric affairs is the anachronistic regime in Havana, a mummified relic from the age of totalitarianism, and its buffoonish imitators. We call on the nations of Latin America and the Caribbean to join us in laying the groundwork for a democratic Cuba. Looking to the inevitable day of liberation, we support restrictions on trade with, and travel to, Cuba as a measure of solidarity with the political prisoners and all the oppressed Cuban people. We call for a dedicated platform for transmission of Radio and Television Marti into Cuba and, to pre-pare for the day when Cuba is free, we support the work of the Commission for Assistance to a Free Cuba. We affirm the principles of the Cuban Adjustment Act of 1966, recognizing the rights of Cubans fleeing Communist tyranny, and support efforts to admit more of them through a safe, legal, orderly process.

We're taking a hard line on Cuba. We might be more flexible on this if Fidel Castro wasn't so *old* and infirmed. We figure the old coot can't *last* much longer ... and when he's gone, the new regime will welcome us with open arms to get some U.S. dollars flowing in its direction. We might welcome it as well because, frankly, it's been so long ... there aren't many of us who *remember* exactly why we imposed the embargo ... other than our dislike of Castro. We're *also* pretty excited about reconnecting with Cuba since the first thing we're going to do is lift the ban on its smooth smoking cigars. Right now, we have to smoke them in private. We can't *wait* to be able to smoke them in public again like the old days.

Advancing Hope and Prosperity in Africa

The great promise of Africa has been dimmed by disease, hunger, and violence. Republicans have faced up to each of those challenges because, in addition to humanitarian concerns, the U.S. has important security interests in the stability and progress of African nations. The devastating toll of HIV/AIDS threatens to destabilize entire societies through large numbers of orphaned youths. In response, the U.S. has become the unrivaled leader in fighting the diseases that are the scourge of much of the continent. Republican-sponsored legislation has brought jobs and investment to sub-Saharan Africa. To continue that progress, we advocate continued expansion of trade with African nations.

When "W" pushed the President's Emergency Plan for AIDS Relief (PEPFAR) through, it went a long way toward addressing the HIV/AIDS threat in Africa. We think we can ride on those coattails for awhile, even though we've never really figured out how to politically capitalize on one of the monumentally successful programs that "W" created. The Bush Administration is still viewed as an evil, incompetent part of our nation's history.

As for *"Republican-sponsored legislation (bringing) jobs and investment to sub-Saharan Africa"* … if we *really* knew how to create *"jobs and investment,"* we'd be doing it *here!*

Genocide must end. The horrendous suffering of the people in the Darfur region of Sudan, as well as less publicized human tragedies elsewhere, calls for a far more energetic and determined response from Africa's elected leaders. The United States stands ready to assist them with materiel, transportation, and humanitarian supplies. We will continue America's diplomatic efforts to secure a comprehensive and humane settlement for the people of the southern and western Sudan.

We're against *"genocide."* There, we said it! This is our opportunity to position ourselves as a Party that *cares*. Our party has

gotten a bad rap about being uncaring. We think we're every bit as caring as the Democrats! Of course, that's not really saying much.

The promise of democracy and freedom in Africa is diminished by the government of Zimbabwe, which has seized lands without compensation, debased the currency, murdered and tortured its people, and so intimidated voters that free and fair elections are impossible. We support sanctions against this government, free elections, and the restoration of civil government in Zimbabwe.

 *"Zimbabwe ... has seized lands without compensation, debased the currency, murdered and tortured its people, and so intimidated voters that free and fair elections are impossible."* **Hmmm ... while the *"torture"* part is okay with us, we consider the murdering of citizens to be a bad thing. We're also against *"seiz(ing) lands without compensation, debas(ing) the currency,... and so intimidate(ing) voters that free and fair elections are impossible"* because it sounds too much like the Democratic Platform.**

<u>Partnerships across the Asia-Pacific Region</u>

The U.S. is a Pacific nation, and our historic ties to Asia will grow stronger in the years ahead. Australia has stood shoulder to shoulder with us in every major conflict. The ties between our peoples, our economies, and our governments are extraordinary. We cherish our bonds with our Freely Associated States in the Pacific Islands. Our long-standing alliance with Japan has been the foundation for peace and prosperity in Asia, and we look for Japan to forge a leadership role in regional and global affairs. Another valued ally, the Republic of Korea remains vigilant with us against the tyranny and international ambitions of the maniacal state on its border. The U.S. will not waver in its demand for the complete, verifiable, and irreversible dismantlement of North Korea's nuclear weapons programs, with a full accounting of its proliferation activities. We look toward the restoration of human rights to the suffering people of North Korea and the fulfillment of the wish of the Korean people to be one in peace and freedom.

We're basically *"blowing smoke"* here because we've *never* really done anything meaningful to reign in North Korea. Oh sure, every now and then we puff up our diplomatic chests and threatened *"significant trade restrictions,"* but we're always hard pressed to get any of the other nations to join in to make our threats more meaningful. As a result, we're just waiting for Kim Jong-*il* to get a little more *"ill"* and pass on to his reward; kind of like our *"Castro Strategy"* for Cuba.

India

We welcome America's new relationship with India, including the U.S.-India Civil Nuclear Accord. Our common security concerns and shared commitment to political freedom and representative government can be the foundation for an enduring partnership.

We've got to maintain strong relationships with India. Otherwise, we'll *never* be able to get phone support for our computers and printers.

Pakistan

We must expand our ties with the government and the people of Pakistan. We support their efforts to improve democratic governance and strengthen civil society, and we appreciate the difficult but essential role Pakistan plays in the fight against terror.

Pakistan's role in *"the fight against terror"* is *"difficult."* It's *tough* to play *both* sides like the Pakistani government has been doing for years. It's even more of a balancing act for us to support Pakistan and India since these two countries get along about

as well as the two Koreas ... or Israel and the Arab nation of your choice.

Taiwan

Our policy toward Taiwan, a sound democracy and economic model for mainland China, must continue to be based upon the provisions of the Taiwan Relations Act. We oppose any unilateral steps by either side to alter the status quo in the Taiwan straits on the principle that all issues regarding the island's future must be resolved peacefully, through dialogue, and be agreeable to the people of Taiwan. If China were to violate these principles, the U.S., in accord with the Taiwan Relations Act, will help Taiwan defend itself. As a loyal friend of America, the democracy of Taiwan has merited our strong sup-port, including the timely sale of defensive arms and full participation in the World Health Organization and other multilateral institutions.

The U.S./China conflict over Taiwan: this is a stalemate of epic proportions. China is benefiting *way* too much from its new found infatuation with capitalism to throw it all away for a tiny little island of 23 million people. That's about the population of a block in downtown Beijing.

China needs to continue to build its economy ... so it can continue to loan money to *us*. We, in turn, need to work with China to expand our business and supply presence on the mainland ... so we can *service* the debt we're creating for ourselves with China. And neither of us is going to let Taiwan get in the way of big business.

China

We will welcome the emergence of a peaceful and prosperous China, and we will welcome even more the development of a democratic China. Its rulers have already discovered that economic freedom leads to national wealth; the next lesson is that political and religious freedom leads to national greatness. That is not likely to be learned while the government in Beijing pursues advanced military capabilities without any apparent need, imposes a "onechild" policy on its people, suppresses basic human rights in Tibet and elsewhere, and erodes democracy in Hong Kong. China must honor its obligations regarding free speech and a free press as announced prior to the Olympics.

This is all for show. It's not like we really believe that China is going to focus on delivering *"political and religious freedom"* any time soon. As for the *"one child"* policy, we'd normally be in *favor* of it since they already have about 1.4 billion people. But then we realized it would limit our business potential in China at some point ... so now we're *against* it.

Our bilateral trade with China has created export opportunities for American farmers and workers, while both the requirements of the World Trade Organization and the realities of the market-place have increased openness and the rule of law in China. We must yet ensure that China fulfills its WTO obligations, especially those related to protecting intellectual property rights, elimination of subsidies, and repeal of import restrictions. China's full integration into the global economy requires that it adopt a flexible monetary exchange rate and allow free movement of capital. China's economic growth brings with it the responsibility for environmental improvement, both for its own people and for the world community.

Again, if we were a political party within China, we might be able to actually influence these issues ... but we're not. Then again, if we were a political party within China, we might disappear from the face of the Earth for even *suggesting* they consider changing their position on these issues.

Vietnam

Our relations with Vietnam have improved, but two grave matters remain. The first is the need for unceasing efforts to obtain an accounting for, and repatriation of the remains of, Americans who gave their lives in the cause of freedom.

"Our relations with Vietnam have improved" ... ever since we stopped killing them and they stopped killing us. It's funny how that works. The same thing happened between our country and Germany and Japan.

The second is continued repression of human rights and religious freedom, and the retribution by the government of Vietnam against its ethnic minorities and others who assisted U.S. forces there. We owe them a debt of honor and will do all we can to relieve their suffering.

"We owe ... a debt of honor" to the *"ethnic minorities and others who assisted U.S. forces"* in Vietnam. Of course, the war has been over since 1975, so we should probably start planning what we're going to do for them before the entire generation to whom we owe *"a debt of honor"* passes away.

Burma

We urge all the nations of East Asia to join the world-wide effort to restore the suffering people of Burma to the democratic family of nations. The military dictatorship in Burma is among the worst on the planet. Its savagery demands a strong response from the world community, including economic and financial sanctions and isolation of the illegitimate regime.

"We urge all the nations of East Asia to join the world-wide effort to restore the suffering people of Burma to the democratic family of nations." This is our *number one* priority. Just kidding! Most of us don't even know where Burma is, and our older Party leaders think it's the headquarters for some sort of shaving cream company.

Seriously though, we want a *"response from the world community, including economic and financial sanctions and isolation of the illegitimate regime."* You know ... the type we've used in the past to bring Iran and North Korea to their knees!

<u>Strengthening Our Relations with Europe</u>

Our country's ties to the peoples of Europe are based on shared culture and values, common interests and goals. We particularly appreciate our close friendship with the United Kingdom, a relationship that has led the forces of freedom for generations. The enduring truth – that America's security is inseparable from Europe's – was reaffirmed by our European allies after September 11, 2001. NATO, the most successful military alliance in history, has been greatly strengthened by the addition of new members in Central and Eastern Europe. We believe the door to NATO membership should remain open to all democratic nations who share our values and meet the requirements for NATO membership. We strongly support NATO-endorsed efforts to deploy missile defenses to protect our European allies from the threat of Iranian missiles, and we appreciate the willingness of the governments of Poland and the Czech Republic to host these needed defensive systems. We condemn the Russian Federation's attempts to intimidate states, formerly under Soviet domination, in order to prevent their deploying missile defenses. The decision on this question is for each sovereign nation to decide.

As we stated earlier, a good war or two seems to solidify our relationship with other countries. You can add England to the list with Germany and Japan. If we're right about this, North Korea will come around some time soon, and Iraq is just going to love us.

As for NATO, we think *"membership should remain open to all democratic nations who share our values and meet the requirements."* Of course, if the Democrats dismantle the missile defense system we've built over the years, there may not be much of a reason for any country to join.

We support the ongoing reconciliation efforts in Cyprus and Northern Ireland, including the appointment of a U.S. Special Envoy for Northern Ireland. We condemn the escalation of anti-Semitic violence, arson, and desecration in Europe and other areas of the world.

"Reconciliation" ... good; "anti-Semitic violence, arson, and desecration" ... bad! **We love to say it this way because it reminds us of "41's" rhetoric ... the *good* Bush.**

When this part of our Platform arose, we had to explain to some of the old codgers that we didn't mean *"reconciliation"* between Cyprus and Northern Ireland; we meant *"reconciliation"* within Cyprus and Northern Ireland. They thought they had missed a war!

Russia

Americans and the Russian people have common imperatives: ending terrorism, combating nuclear proliferation, promoting bilateral trade, and more. But matters of serious concern remain, particularly the Russian government's treatment of the press, opposition parties, and institutions of civil society. It continues its aggressive confrontations with its neighbors, from economic intimidation to outright warfare, and has aligned with dangerous anti-democratic forces in the Middle East. As a condition for its continued acceptance in world organizations, Russia must respect the independence and territorial integrity of all the nations of the former Soviet Union, beginning with the republic of Georgia, and move toward a free and democratic society.

This is yet another example of what we've discussed previously. We're still at odds with the Russians. Part of it is probably just out of habit; the other part is because a *"cold war"* just isn't a replacement for a real war! We'd probably be BFFs (like the kids say these days) if we'd actually fought each other rather than just choosing sides and selling weapons to other

countries that were at odds. Of course, that assumes that we wouldn't have *annihilated* each other in the process.

And, once again, for our more senile ... uh, we mean ... *senior* Party members, it's not the Georgia *you're* thinking of. It's not where your peaches come from and the pea-NUT farmer lives.

The Middle East

The momentum of change in the Middle East has been in the right direction. From Morocco to the Gulf States, the overall trend has been toward cooperation and social and economic development, especially with regard to the rights of women. We acknowledge the substantial assistance the U.S. has received from most governments in the region in the war on terror. Those countries that have made peace with Israel, whether officially or in fact, deserve our appreciation and assistance.

We obviously are using the term *"most"* loosely when we're describing the Middle East governments that *"have made peace with Israel"* and helped us wage our *"war on terror."* Truth be told, *"most"* of these countries either fund or harbor anti-American and anti-Israeli terrorist training programs. They've just become less *overt* about it.

We urge the continued isolation of groups like Hamas and Hezbollah because they do not meet the standards of the international community. We call for the restoration of Lebanon's independence and sovereignty and the full implementation of all UN resolutions concerning that country.

It's pretty easy to dislike Hamas and Hezbollah. They both start with "H" ... you know, like *"Holocaust"* ... that little event that they deny ever happened but would apparently be happy to repeat.

It galls us to support the UN in any way since it's become such a pathetically emasculated organization, but we're even less fond of Lebanon ... ever since the bombing of our Marines' barracks in Beirut in 1983. So, on this rare occasion, we *support* the UN and its resolutions against Lebanon.

The struggle in which we are engaged is ideological, not ethnic or religious. The extremists we face are abusers of faith, not its champions. We appreciate the loyalty of all Americans whose family roots lie in the Middle East, and we gratefully acknowledge the contributions of American Arabs and Muslims, especially those in the Armed Forces and the intelligence community.

"We gratefully acknowledge the contributions of American Arabs and Muslims, especially those in the Armed Forces" **... except maybe for Major Nidal Malik Hasan at Ft. Hood.**

Israel

Israel is a vigorous democracy, unique in the Middle East. We reaffirm America's commitment to Israel's security and will ensure that Israel maintains a qualitative edge in military technology over any potential adversaries. Israel must have secure, defensible borders and we support its right to exist as a Jewish state able to defend itself against homicide bombings, rocket and mortar fire, and other attacks against its people. We support the vision of two democratic states living in peace and security: Israel, with Jerusalem as its capital, and Palestine. For that to become a reality, the Palestinian people must support leaders who reject terror, embrace the institutions and ethos of democracy, and respect the rule of law. We call on Arab governments throughout the region to help advance that goal. We support Jerusalem as the undivided capital of Israel and moving the American embassy to that undivided capital of Israel.

 **Do you wonder *why* we always side with Israel? When was the last time you saw a protest in Israel where they were burning or stomping on an American flag? When was the last time you saw an angry crowd in Israel hang our President in effigy? When was the last time an Israeli terrorist cell attacked our country? When was the last time Israel threatened the United States in any way? This isn't even a *"close call"* for the Republican Party.**

The U.S. seeks a comprehensive and lasting peace in the Middle East, negotiated between the parties themselves, without the imposition of an artificial timetable, and without the demand that Israel deal with entities which continue to pledge her destruction. At the heart of any peace process must be a mutual commitment to resolve all issues through negotiation. Part of that process must be a just, fair, and realistic framework for dealing with the Palestinian refugee issue. Like all other elements in a meaningful agreement, this matter can be settled only on the basis of mutually agreed changes that reflect today's realities as well as tomorrow's hopes.

 **We generally don't like *"artificial timetables"* because ... well, they're *artificial!* This thing has been going on for 2000 years. It's not likely that we can pick a definitive time frame and get the job done just because we set a date. We're talking about *"a comprehensive and lasting peace in the Middle East"*. The phrase is almost an oxymoron!**

Now, there is a downside to our unwillingness to set an *"artificial timetable;"* it could result in a *laissez faire* attitude toward ever resolving the issue. We have a *history* of doing that ... never completing a task because we believe that things will take care of themselves. So far, that hasn't worked particularly well either ... but we'll probably keep trying because we're more comfortable with that approach.

Iraq

A stable, unified, and democratic Iraqi nation is within reach. Our success in Iraq will deny al Qaeda a safe haven, limit Iranian influence in the Middle East, strengthen moderate forces there, and give us a strategic ally in the struggle against extremism. To those who have sacrificed so much, we owe the commitment that American forces will leave that country in victory and with honor. That outcome is too critical to our own national security to be jeopardized by artificial or politically inspired timetables that neither reflect conditions on the ground nor respect the essential advice of our military commanders. As the people of Iraq assume their rightful place in the ranks of free and open societies, we offer them a continuing partnership.

 **There's that *"artificial timetable"* thing again. We keep bringing it up because the Democrats are always willing to *"bail"* from anything that doesn't come across as a *"kumbaya"* peace rally. They want to withdraw from Iraq without a plan for *"completion."* We want to stay in Iraq ... well, because we don't have a plan for *"completion"* either.**

Afghanistan

In the seven years since U.S. troops helped topple the Taliban, there has been great progress – but much remains to be done. We must prevail in Afghanistan to prevent the reemergence of the Taliban or an al Qaeda sanctuary in that country. A nationwide counterinsurgency strategy led by a unified commander is an essential prerequisite to success. Additional forces are also necessary, both from NATO countries and through a doubling in size of the Afghan army. The international community must work with the Afghan government to better address the problems of illegal drugs, governance, and corruption. We flatly reject the Democratic Party's idea that America can succeed in Afghanistan only by failure in Iraq.

 *"A nationwide counterinsurgency strategy led by a unified commander is an essential prerequisite to success."* It's a good thing we have a unified commander in place with General McChrystal! He's a rolling stone that won't gather any moss. What? *You're kidding!* He's been fired. How did that happen on our watch? Oh ... so it's not *our* watch anymore!

Iran

We express our respect for the people of Iran who seek peace and aspire to freedom. Their current regime, aggressive and repressive, is unworthy of them. The Iranian people, many of whom risk persecution to speak out for democracy, have a right to choose their own government. As a rogue state, Iran's leadership supports terror, threatens its neighbors, and provides weapons that are killing our troops in Iraq. We affirm, in the plainest words we can use, that the U.S. government, in solidarity with the international community, will not allow the current regime in Tehran to develop nuclear weapons.

 **We should have known we were going to have a few problems with Iran. Iran used to be known as Persia. Its name was changed in 1935. The name *"Iran"* is a modern cognate of *"Aryan"* meaning *"the Land of Aryans."* It is said to have been made upon recommendation of Persia's Ambassador to Germany, who had become enamored with the influence of the Nazi movement. That seems to have been a bad launching point for future relationships between our countries.**

At least Iran's current political leader has a full, if somewhat scruffy beard. We'll just consider that to be an upgrade from the hideous partial mustache his Führer used to sport. There is one other importance between the two men: Hitler was *proud* of the Holocaust ... while Mahmoud Ahmadinejad won't admit that it ever happened.

We call for a significant increase in political, economic, and diplomatic pressure to persuade Iran's rulers to halt their drive for a nuclear weapons capability, and we support tighter sanctions against Iran and the companies with business operations in or with Iran. We oppose entering into a presidential-level, unconditional dialogue with the regime in Iran until it takes steps to improve its behavior, particularly with respect to support of terrorism and suspension of its efforts to enrich uranium. At the same time, the U.S. must retain all options in dealing with a situation that gravely threatens our security, our interests, and the safety of our friends.

 **Even though few, if any, of our prior efforts involving** *"political, economic, and diplomatic pressure"* **have every yielded any measure of success, we'll keep calling for them. Truth be told, we rather invade the bloody country and depose its leadership like we did in Iraq. Who knows ... our countries might become very friendly down the road if we went to war with them today. In any event, we don't think we'll get the chance ... Israel's probably not going to wait for us to make a decision** *after* **Iran establishes a nuclear capability.**

REFORMING GOVERNMENT TO SERVE THE PEOPLE

The American people believe Washington is broken – and for good reason. Short-term politics overshadow the long-term interests of the nation. Our national legislature uses a budget process devised long before the Internet and seems unable to deal in realistic ways with the most pressing problems of families, businesses, and communities. Members of Congress have been indicted for violating the public trust. Public disgust with Washington is entirely warranted.

 It took us years to get to this point, but it may be the one area in which the Democrats worked together with us – *ruining* a perfectly good political system. Over the years, we have become *"elitist"* in our behavior … as have the Democrats. We think we're *"entitled"* … and the rest of the citizens are not. While this has radically improved our lifestyles, it's gotten to the point where the American public is starting to take note and respond with anger. There's going to come a time when we're going to have to *admit* that we're just civil servants who didn't have to pass a test … and then get back to serving the people. We just hope we're out of office and living on our special pensions before that happens!

Republicans will uphold and defend our party's core principles: Constrain the federal government to its legitimate constitutional functions. Let it empower people, while limiting its reach into their lives. Spend only what is necessary, and tax only to raise revenue for essential government functions. Unleash the power of enterprise, innovation, civic energy, and the American spirit – and never pretend that government is a substitute for family or community.

 **Okay, so we *didn't* do this the last time we were in power. We spent like we were Democrats; we seized as much power as we could; and we ignored our core principles of supporting the entrepreneurial spirit that has made our country excel over the years. But *now*, we're *really* serious about doing things right ... particularly since we've become politically *"neutered"* in the backlash of the public's outrage. It might be time to go back to that old document that used to guide us ... what's it called? Oh yeah ... the *Constitution!***

The other party wants more government control over people's lives and earnings; Republicans do not. The other party wants to continue pork barrel politics; we are disgusted by it, no matter who practices it. The other party wants to ignore fiscal problems while squandering billions on ineffective programs; we are determined to end that waste. The entrenched culture of official Washington – an intrusive tax-and-spend liberalism – remains a formidable foe, but we will confront and ultimately defeat it.

WASHINGTON'S FAILURE: THE SCOPE OF THE PROBLEM

The federal government collects $2.7 trillion a year from American families and businesses. That's $7.4 billion a day. Even worse, it spends over $3 trillion a year: $8.2 billion a day. Why? Largely because those who created this bloated government will not admit a single mistake or abolish a single program. Here are some staggering examples of the overall problem:

 **Notice how we're acting as if we didn't have anything to do with creating the deficit. We're hoping that the Democrats are so *"over-the-top"* when it**

comes to spending money on worthless causes and social *"reform"* programs, that you'll just ignore the fact that we voted for a lot of the *"out-of-control"* spending that began our economy on its downward spiral. Oh sure, the Democrats can make *our* excesses look *trivial* in comparison. But then again, that's what we're counting on!

- Recent audits show that 22% of all federal programs are ineffective or incapable of demonstrating results.
- 69 separate programs, administered by 10 different agencies, provide education or care to children under the age of 5.
- Nine separate agencies administer 44 different programs for job training.
- 23 separate programs, each with its own overhead, provide housing assistance to the elderly.

With so many redundant, inefficient, and ineffective federal programs, it is no wonder that the American people have so little confidence in Washington to act effectively when federal action is really needed.

 **Again, please ignore the fact that many of these agencies were formed, and programs were passed on *our* watch. We just weren't sure what to do. If only we had established a few more agencies and programs to address the issue.**

The Budget Process — A Fraud that Guarantees Runaway Spending

For more than three decades – since enactment of the Budget Act of 1974 by a Democrat-controlled Congress – the federal government has operated within a rigged system notable for its lack of transparency. The earlier approach – annual passage of the appropriation bills, amended and voted up or down, with the numbers there for all to see – had its flaws and generated much red ink. But its replacement, the current budget process, only worsened the money flow and came to rely on monstrous omnibus spending bills. The results are adverse to all seeking to limit government's growth. For example:

 In the 18 Congressional terms that have been served since *"enactment of the Budget Act of 1974,"* *four* have been split (between who controls the House and the Senate), *nine* have been controlled by the Democrats, and we have been in controlled on *five* occasions (*all* of which occurred within the last eight Congressional terms). Yet, when we had the chance, we did *nothing* to fix the problem. And when the Democrats are in total control (including the House, the Senate, and the Presidency), brace yourselves; it will be like a political Spring Break (*i.e.,* one big spending spree with *no thought ... no morals ... and no responsibility*).

- The budget process assumes every spending project will be on the books forever, even if the law says the spending will expire – but it assumes tax relief will be temporary.

 Based upon past history, the assumption that *"every spending project will be on the books forever, even if the law says the spending will expire – (and all) tax relief will be temporary"* appears to be valid.

- It treats well-deserved tax cuts as a kind of spending, so that letting Americans keep more of their earnings is considered the same as more spending on pork projects.
- It fails to recognize the positive impact that lowering tax rates has on economic growth.

 This is another area where history rears its ugly head, and it also demonstrates one of our worst weaknesses: our inability to communicate *anything* effectively to the America people. History conclusively demonstrates that tax cuts stimulate economy growth, but we can't seem to present the facts in a way that people accept it. In a sense, this is yet one more thing we have

in common with the Democrats; we collectively validate the insight of George Santayana, who famously shared: *"Those who do not learn from history are doomed to repeat it."* The Democrats try to solve everything by raising taxes, and we just keep trying to make our point in the same, ineffective way we always have.

- In its deceptive and irresponsible accounting, an increase in a program's funding is actually a decrease if it is less than the rate of inflation.

 **The latest trick we're learning from our far more experienced brethren is to claim victories in areas that can't be disproven. For example: the Democrats are now giving themselves credit for *"jobs saved."* We need to jump on this bandwagon and find some similar issues that are near and dear to our hearts but that *can't* be proven or refuted. We should be running on a basis of some fictitious numbers like *"lives saved"* because of our stance on the abortion issue or *"jobs created"* due to tax relief. Since no one is apparently paying any attention to the facts, we need to learn to exploit this *"new math"* to get people to vote for *us!***

- Once a budget is produced under that system, the budget law itself limits the time Congress can consider it before voting.

 **Truth be told, the compressed time frame we have is more than sufficient to review legislation that's only a few thousand pages long. That's because most of us aren't competent to *understand* what we're reading anyway. That's why we vote along Party lines so often ... because we don't really know what's in the legislation or what its impact might be.**

Seriously, do you remember the adage *"Those who can ... do; those who can't ... teach?"* Well, most of us on both sides of

the aisle can't even *teach*. So, we have no alternative other than to run for office.

Moreover, the budget's review process is a sham. Of the $3 trillion spent annually, only one-third is reviewed each year during the budget and appropriations process. The remaining $2 trillion automatically goes to interest on the national debt or entitlements. And because the budget process assumes an automatic increase in spending, the debate on the remaining one-third is only over how much more spending to approve.

 **Again, we didn't do anything about this during the ten recent years in which we controlled both the House and the Senate (and even the Presidency for four of those years). But then again, we were in control, so it wouldn't have benefited us at the time to *fix* the problem.**

Finally, while government requires corporations to budget for future pension and health care costs, our government ignores those requirements. No family or private sector business could keep its books the way Washington keeps ours.

 **We're not saying we should change anything. We kind of like the current system. We deserve the best that money can buy ... particularly when the money isn't ours.**

<u>A Plan to Control Spending</u>

Republicans will attack wasteful Washington spending immediately. Current procedures should be replaced with simplicity and transparency. For example:

 **Okay, we know what you're thinking: nothing gets done in Washington, D.C. *"with simplicity and transparency"* ... and you're *right*! But this is an**

election year, so we're going to appear to be *really* sincere about this when we say it.

- We favor adoption of the Balanced Budget Amendment to require a balanced federal budget except in time of war.

Keep in mind that if we gain a majority, we'll reintroduce the concept of an *"unending"* War on Terrorism, so we'll always have an *"out"* if we need it.

- Earmarking must stop. To eliminate wasteful projects and pay-offs to special interests, we will impose an immediate moratorium on the earmarking system and reform the appropriations process through full transparency. Tax dollars must be distributed on the basis of clear national priorities, not a politician's seniority or party position.

Just to be clear ... we said we'd impose an *"immediate moratorium on the earmark system."* A *"moratorium"* is generally defined as a *temporary* suspension. In the unlikely event that we regain a *dominant* majority in the House and Senate any time soon, we want to have the ability to cancel the *"moratorium"* to get back to business as usual.

- Government waste must be taken off auto-pilot. We call for a one-year pause in non-defense, non-veterans discretionary spending to force a critical, cost-benefit review of all current programs.

Look, we don't serve a lot of *"oppressed minorities,"* so we're stuck playing the few cards we've been dealt: Defense, veterans, and big business. Just like the Democrats pander to *their* constituencies, *we* pander to *ours*.

- We call for a constitutionally sound presidential line-item veto.

 The *"line-item veto"* goes back to "41's" presidency. It's the only thing *"George the First"* was really passionate about ... other than his lip-reading promise of *"No new taxes."* While it makes great sense, neither Party wants it because it could *really* mess up the graft and bribery we have in place. It's one of those things we can throw out to score some points with the American public without *any* fear that it might actually come to fruition.

- If billions are worth spending, they should be spent in the light of day. We will insist that, before either the House or Senate considers a spending bill, every item in it should be presented in advance to the taxpayers on the Internet.

 This is another one that sounds good. We're in lock-step with Obama on this one. Yes, sir! We'll give everyone 72 hours to read through every 1,000+ page bill we can crank out. The Democrats might actually have some explaining to do among their voters (at least among those who can read), but we don't expect this to have much impact on our constituents since they have jobs and can't take 72 hours off to read some unfathomably complex bill on a subject in which they have little to no expertise.

- Because the problem is too much spending, not too few taxes, we support a supermajority requirement in both the House and Senate to guard against tax hikes.

 Being in a filibuster-proof Senate sucks! A supermajority requirement would insulate us from essentially being a non-entity when it comes to a vote.

- New authorizations should be offset by reducing another program, and no appropriation should be permitted without a current authorization.

 **You can put this idea in the** *"Do as we say, not as we do"* **file.**

- Congressional ethics rules governing special interests should apply across the board, without the special exemptions now granted to favored institutions.

 **Okay, you can stop laughing now. We know that** *"Congressional ethics"* **is an obvious oxymoron, but we still needed to raise the issue because it sounds good during an election year.**

- We support the Government Shutdown Protection Act to ensure the continuance of essential federal functions when advocates of pork threaten to shut down the government unless their wasteful spending is accepted.

 **If we actually cared, it would be better to** *expose* **the worst** *"pork"* **offenders and either throw them out of Congress or get the voters to do it during the next election.** *Unfortunately***, we also have a hard time not succumbing to the temptation of** *"pork"* **when it's elegantly** *"prepared"* **in a bill, so it would be a little like committing suicide within our own Party.**

- We will insist that the budget reasonably plan for the long-term costs of pension and health care programs and urge the conversion of such programs to defined contribution programs.

 **You've probably noticed that we like to use words like "insist." It's almost as if we still have some *real power* on the Hill.**

EMPOWERING THE STATES, IMPROVING PUBLIC SERVICES

The long term solution for many of Washington's problems is structural. Congress must respect the limits imposed upon it by the Tenth Amendment: "The powers not delegated to the United States by the Constitution, nor prohibited by it to the States, are reserved to the States respectively, or to the people."

 **While you would think this would be dispositive of the issue, the Tenth Amendment has been circumvented for years by the broadening of the interpretation of the Constitutional powers granted to the Federal government. We've been grabbing power for so long that it will be difficult to share it with the States.**

We look to the model of Republican welfare reform, which, since its enactment in 1996, has accomplished a major transfer of resources and responsibility from the federal government back to the states – with an accompanying improvement in the program itself. Applying that approach to other programs will steer Congress back into line with Constitution, reversing both its intrusion into state matters and its neglect of its central duties.

 ***"Transfer(ing) of resources and responsibility from the federal government back to the states"* isn't so much of a Tenth Amendment issue as it is a shifting of the *cost* and the *blame* to the States ... which is a *far* superior political strategy than to take responsibility for the programs at a Federal level. Instead, *welfare* can drive California and the other States into bankruptcy instead of *us*. We prefer to legislate our *own* way into *national* bankruptcy.**

To aid in the fulfillment of those duties, we propose a National Sunset Commission to review all federal programs and recommend which of them should be terminated due to redundancy, waste, or intrusion into the American family. The Congress would then be required by law to schedule one yea or nay vote on the entire sunset list with no amendments.

Again, *"propos(ing) a National Sunset Commission to review all federal programs and recommend which of them should be terminated due to redundancy, waste, or intrusion into the American family"* sounds good but doesn't really accomplish anything. We know that one more commission is just another waste of time and money. If we were *really* serious, we'd proposed a zero-based budget that would require each program, agency, commission, etc. to justify its own existence.

And did you notice that we included a single *"yea or nay vote on the entire sunset list?"* Since we also want the President to have a *"line item veto,"* wouldn't the President then be allowed to veto any or all of the programs on the list on a line item basis? Oh, let's not worry about it since we really don't think we can get any of this passed any way.

Additionally, as important as returning power to the states is returning power to the people. As the Declaration of Independence states, our rights are endowed to us by our Creator and are unalienable: rights to life, liberty, and property. Government does not confer these rights but is instituted by men to protect the rights that man already possesses. The Republican Party strongly affirms these rights and demands that government respect them.

What we really like to do is have the ACLU and any of its supporters *deported* to some third-world country where they could spend the rest of their natural lives in exile.

Congress Must Improve Oversight of Government Programs

Congress has a fundamental duty to conduct meaningful oversight on the effectiveness of government programs, not use every hearing as an opportunity for political grandstanding. To that end:

- We urge every congressional committee to reserve at least one week every month to conduct oversight of the nearly 1,700 separate grant and loan programs of the federal government.

 **Sure, we know that's about 1,600 more grant and loan programs than we need, but like we said, we're really not *serious* about reducing the size of government.**

To prevent conflicts of interest, a Truth in Testimony mandate should require all committee witnesses to detail the amount of federal funding they and their employer currently receive and, in the case of associations, how much federal money their members would receive from the proposed legislation.

 **We know this is a pipe dream. We can't even mandate that Presidential candidates disclose their birth certificates or college transcripts. So, what right do we have to expect witnesses to be more forthcoming about their federal funding? Why that would be like asking *us* to disclose how much money *we've* taken from Congressional Committee witnesses before we would be allowed to participate in *their* questioning. It's downright un-American.**

Because official Washington does not even know how much land it owns, we call for a national audit of all federally-owned properties as a first step toward returning unnecessary properties to the American people or to state and local government for public use.

 This is the *"first step toward returning unnecessary properties to the American people or to state and local government for public use."* Notice that we don't even speculate how many actual steps there will be, but trust us, it will be *several* unborn generations before *any* of this land changes hands. Otherwise, why not just give it back to whatever Native American tribe we stole it from ... rather than giving it *"to state and local government for public use?"*

IMPROVING THE WORK OF GOVERNMENT

Modern management of the federal government is long overdue. The expected retirement over the next ten years of more than 40 percent of the federal workforce, and 60 percent of its managers, presents a rare opportunity: a chance to gradually shrink the size of government while using technology to increase its effectiveness and reshape the way agencies do business.

 Here's our dilemma, if we *shrink* the size of government, there will less people with meaningless jobs that nonetheless pay wages, which in turn generate taxes. We need the tax base to forestall the government bankruptcy our ridiculously expensive programs will inevitably cause ... at least until we retire to our generous pensions and can pass the blame onto our successors in office.

Each agency must be able to pass a financial audit and set annual targets for improving efficiency with fewer resources. Civil service managers should be given incentives for more effective leadership, including protection against the current guilty-until-proven-innocent grievance procedures which disgruntled employees use against them to thwart reform. Due process cannot excuse bad behavior.

 **This may be expecting too much.** It would mean treating *"big government"* as if it was *"big business."* The Democrats won't support this unless there's a way to *unionize* all the employees. Besides, we're not sure anyone in the government really has the experience or knowledge to compete in a *real world* environment.

We will provide Internet transparency in all federal contracting as a necessary step in combating cost overruns. We will draw on the expertise of today's successful managers and entrepreneurs in the private sector, like the "dollar-a-year" businesspeople who answered their country's call during the Second World War, to build real-world competence and accountability into government procurement and operations.

 **A special *"shout out"* to Al Gore for inventing the Internet: *"Thanks, Al!"* We predict that the *"'dollar-a-year' businesspeople who answered their country's call during the Second World War"* concept is going to make a comeback. After running preliminary numbers on the Democrat's latest tax proposal, a *"dollar-a-year"* is essentially going to be the take-home pay of anyone earning $250,000 or more.**

DOMESTIC DISASTER RESPONSE

Americans hit by disaster must never again feel abandoned by their government. The Katrina disaster taught a painful lesson: The federal government's system for responding to a natural calamity needs a radical overhaul. We recognize the need for a natural disaster insurance policy.

 **We actually see the *"natural disaster insurance policy"* to be a new area of profit for our constituents in the insurance industry. The reality is that it would be *far* more helpful to actually**

create a standardize response protocol that could be *efficiently executed* in the case of a natural disaster than to create an insurance policy to pay for our *ineffective response*. That way, we wouldn't still be processing claims and working on a strategy to rebuild an American city five years *after* a hurricane hits ... or trying to cap an oil well in the Gulf and affect a cleanup process before too many species are extinct or our food supply is tainted for decades.

State and local cooperation is crucial, as are private relief efforts, but Washington must take the lead in forging a partnership with America's best run businesses to ensure that FEMA's Emergency Operations Centers run as well as any Fortune 500 Company. We must make it easier for both businesses and non-profits to act as force-multipliers in relief situations. We believe it is critical to support those impacted by natural disasters and to complete the rebuilding of devastated areas, including the Gulf Coast.

Trying *"to ensure that FEMA's Emergency Operations Centers run as well as any Fortune 500 Company"* ... without its management being incarcerated ... is a laudable goal. Today, it's operating more like it should be known as the Federal Emergency Equipment, Buildings, and Logistics Enterprise (FEEBLE for short). Another possible consideration would be to impose a ban on Internet porn to help the Mineral Management Services become more efficient (not to mention the Securities and Exchange Commission).

RESTORING OUR INFRASTRUCTURE

The American people can have safer roads and bridges, better airports and more efficient harbors, as long as we straighten out the government's spending priorities. The politics of pork distorts the allocation of resources for modernizing the nation's infrastructure. That can leave entire communities vulnerable to natural disasters and deprive others of the improvements necessary for economic growth and job creation. We pledge a business-like, cost-effective approach for infrastructure spending, always mindful of the special needs of both rural and urban communities.

 *"Safer roads and bridges, better airports and more efficient harbors"* **... who can argue with these goals? Of course, we could have started this initiative 40 *years* ago. Then, maybe we wouldn't be so buried in debt. But hey, better late than never!**

We support a level of investment in the nation's transportation system that will promote a healthy economy, sustain jobs, and keep America globally competitive. We need to improve the system's performance and capacity to deal with congestion, move a massive amount of freight, reduce traffic fatalities, and ensure mobility across both rural and urban areas. We urgently need to preserve the highway, transit, and air facilities built over the last century so they can serve generations to come. At the same time, we are committed to minimizing transportation's impact on climate change, our local environments, and the nation's energy use. Careful reforms of environmental reviews and the permitting process should speed projects to completion.

 **Now, you're starting to see a small semblance of another core strategy. We work well with business, so our strategy is to frame everything we can around business opportunities.**

We don't promise the *"oppressed minorities"* any type of entitlements. The Democrats have that approach all but locked up. Instead, we promise *lifestyle* improvements that appeal to *everyone*: better roads, housing, jobs, etc.; a safer environment within which to live; and a better quality of life based on the opportunity to actually *keep* some of the money you earn. That's what we offer ... along with our *"Defense Strategy"* based upon protecting you from terrorist attacks, unfriendly nuclear-armed nations, etc. We'll call this one our *"Quality of Life"* strategy. It's as close as we come to blurring the distinction between our Party and the Democrats'.

Safeguarding our transportation infrastructure is critical to our homeland security. An integrated, flexible system – developed and sustained in partnership between state and local governments and the federal government – must also share responsibilities with the private sector. We call for more prudent stewardship of the nation's Highway Trust Fund to restore the program's purchasing power and ensure that it will meet the changing needs of a mobile nation.

Did you notice how we merged our *"Defense Strategy"* into the infrastructure discussion by incorporating *"homeland security?"* We also slipped in our *"Business Strategy"* by mentioning the *"private sector."* That's pretty smooth for us. We tend to be more *"in your face"* from a strategic standpoint because our core strategies aren't *"warm and fuzzy"* like the Democrats'.

ENTITLEMENT REFORM

The job of modernizing Social Security, Medicare, and Medicaid calls for bipartisanship, not political posturing. Through the last four presidential terms, we have sought that cooperation, but it has not been forthcoming. The public demands constructive action, and we will provide it.

Our view of *"bipartisanship"* is getting the Democrats to agree to what *we* want ... and voting *"no"* on everything else. The Democrats do the exact same thing ... but they're better at getting away with it because they've become much better at positioning themselves as the *"protectors of the huddled masses"* while we've been stereotyped as the *"protectors of the rich and famous."*

Social Security

We are committed to putting Social Security on a sound fiscal basis. Our society faces a profound demographic shift over the next twenty-five years, from today's ratio of 3.3 workers for every retiree to only 2.1 workers by 2034. Under the current system, younger workers will not be able to depend on Social Security as part of their retirement plan. We believe the solution should give workers control over, and a fair return on, their contributions. No changes in the system should adversely affect any current or near-retiree. Comprehensive reform should include the opportunity to freely choose to create your own personal investment accounts which are distinct from and supplemental to the overall Social Security system.

 **Social security has been in place since 1935. We've know about the demographic shift between the Baby Boomer generation versus Generation X since the mid 1970s. So, we think we should follow the time-honored tradition of** *"closing the barn door after the horse has bolted."*

Medicare and Medicaid

As discussed in the health care section of this document, we commit to revive Medicare by rewarding quality care, promoting competition, eliminating waste, fraud, and abuse, and giving patients and providers control over treatment options. We envision a new Medicaid partnership with the states, improving public health through flexibility and innovation.

 **We still don't know why we lost the trust of seniors. Our marketing strategy has been** *woefully* **deficient. The Democrats have successfully campaigned against us over the past two decades by suggesting that our Party will eliminate** *"prescription drugs for seniors,"* **etc., and we haven't been effective at refuting those charges. You'd think the fact that we've** *never* **done** *any* **of those things when we've been in control would be enough ... but** *no* **... until recently, seniors thought we were against them and that the AARP represented their best interests. We've just been too stubborn to change our communication**

strategy, and the results have been fairly disastrous for us among seniors. We're just not very good at politics!

APPOINTING CONSTITUTIONALIST JUDGES FOR THE NATION'S COURTS

Judicial activism is a grave threat to the rule of law because unaccountable federal judges are usurping democracy, ignoring the Constitution and its separation of powers, and imposing their personal opinions upon the public. This must stop.

Personal opinions have no place in our judicial systems. If we don't end this trend, some leftist, Pinko, Commie, Socialist will even try to get people appointed to the Supreme Court that either have *no* judicial experience or who pledge to bring their *personal* experiences into play when deciding a case. If you think we're kidding and that this is just another extreme exaggeration on our part, you're wrong! We really believe that this could happen years down the road. Seriously!

We condemn the Supreme Court's disregard of homeowners' property rights in its Kelo decision and deplore the Court's arbitrary extension of Americans' habeas corpus rights to enemy combatants held abroad. We object to the Court's unwarranted interference in the administration of the death penalty in this country for the benefit of savage criminals whose guilt is not at issue. We lament that judges have denied the people their right to set abortion policies in the states and are undermining traditional marriage laws from coast to coast. We are astounded that four justices of the Supreme Court believe that individual Americans have no individual right to bear arms to protect themselves and their families.

As you can tell, we generally don't like the direction the Supreme Court is heading ... and it's a *"life sentence."* It used to be that they at least *acknowledged* the *Constitution*. Now, they just

seem to *ignore* it. Of course, several of the recalcitrants are Justices that *we* appointed to the Court. Our bad!

Republicans will insist on the appointment of constitutionalist judges, men and women who will not distort our founding documents to deny the people's right to self-government, sanction federal powers that violate our liberties, or inject foreign law into American jurisprudence.

 **We could have done this before ... but who knew?**

We oppose stealth nominations to the federal bench, and especially to the Supreme Court, whose lack of a clear and distinguished record leaves doubt about their respect for the Constitution or their intellectual fortitude. Nominees must have a record of fidelity to the U.S. Constitution and the rule of law.

 **We support *"stealth nominations"* to *Congress*, but *not* to the Supreme Court. With respect to Congressional seats, it's our way of giving back to people to whom we owe political favors. We don't necessarily back the *best* candidate, but we *always* back the one who has done the *most* to support us. We're loyal that way!**

We reject the Democrats' view that judicial nominees should guarantee particular results even before the case is filed. Judges should not be politicians. Jurists nominated by a Republican president will be thoughtful and open-minded, always prepared to view past error in light of stare decisis, including judicial fiats that disenfranchised the American people.

 **Okay, you're probably wondering what we meant when we said, *"We reject the Democrats' view that judicial nominees should guarantee particular results even before the case is filed ... Judges should not be politicians."* Well, we're just acknowledging that, as**

politicians, we're occasionally beholden to take a particular position on an issue, whether the facts support our position or not. A lot of the times, it just depends on how large the related campaign contribution was. Supreme Court Justices should *not* be so encumbered.

No qualified person should be denied the opportunity to serve on the federal bench due to race, ethnicity, religion or sex. In affirming Article VI of the Constitution – that no religious test shall ever be required for any office – we insist that the Senate should never inquire into a nominee's religious convictions and we condemn the opposition, by some members of the Democratic Party, to recent judicial nominees because of their ethnicity or religion.

If there's any group that we dislike *more* than the Supreme Court (and Ninth Circuit), it's the Democrats. We *"condemn"* pretty much *everything* they stand for. Why do they care what a nominee's religion is? For the most part, they don't even want to acknowledge the existence of God. Besides, none of *their* recent nominees have had any *"religious convictions."* Heck, they haven't even had any *"religious arrests!"* Correspondingly, in Congress, it's the *"moral convictions"* that can get you in trouble ... and we should apply the same standards to our Federal Justices.

PROTECTING THE RIGHT TO VOTE IN FAIR ELECTIONS

Many members of the Armed Services will find it difficult to participate in this year's elections because of the government's reliance on out-dated and inadequate voting, notification, and ballot delivery systems. The mishandling and delaying of registration forms and absentee ballots disenfranchises thousands of our servicemen and servicewomen. The Commander-in-Chief, the Department of Defense, and state and local election officials must do more to protect the voting rights of those on the front lines of freedom. That means using expedited mail delivery to bring ballots to and from our troops abroad, including those serving in areas of conflict, while completing work on an electronic ballot delivery system that will enable our military personnel to receive and cast their ballots in a secure and convenient manner.

"Enabl(ing) our military personnel to receive and cast their ballots in a secure and convenient manner" ... **we should have worked on this issue when *we* were in power. This is yet another example of our just how politically inept we are. Military personnel vote overwhelmingly in favor of the Republican Party, yet we allowed an archaic system to remain in place that could be exploited by the Democrats. How stupid is that?**

You can rest assured the Democrats would have found a way to expedite the votes of our military personnel if the shoe was on the other foot. Those guys have even figured out how to assist *dead* people in registering and casting absentee ballots!

We oppose attempts to distort the electoral process by wholesale restoration of the franchise to convicted felons, by makeshift or hurried naturalization procedures, or by discretionary ballot-reading by election boards. Preventing voting fraud is a civil rights issue. We support the right of states to require an official government-issued photo identification for voting and call upon the Department of Justice to deploy its resources to prevent ballot tampering in the November elections. We support efforts by state and local election officials to ensure integrity in the voting process and to prevent voter fraud and abuse, particularly as it relates to voter registration and absentee ballots.

"We oppose attempts to distort the electoral process by wholesale restoration of the franchise to convicted felons, by makeshift or hurried naturalization procedures, or by discretionary ballot-reading by election boards;" **basically, because we haven't been able to figure out how to get these things to work in *our* favor. It's *so* frustrating that we continually get out-flanked by the**

Democrats on opportunities like these. But once we figure it out, we'll be on it like Confederate colors on a Southern flag pole.

The rights of citizenship do not stop at the ballot box. They include the free-speech right to devote one's resources to whatever cause or candidate one supports. We oppose any restrictions or conditions upon those activities that would discourage Americans from exercising their constitutional right to enter the political fray or limit their commitment to their ideals.

We can't seem to stop liberal rallies ... the success of which the press seems to blow out of proportion; so, we're just trying to even the playing field. It would be *nice* for a change to see conservative rallies on TV. Of course, when they *are* shown, they're portrayed to be smaller than they really are, and the people are cast as a near-violent mob of vigilantes who have been *paid* by us to attend. It's almost as if the mainstream press is *biased!*

GUARANTEEING A CONSTITUTIONAL CENSUS IN 2010

The integrity of the 2010 census, proportioning congressional representation among the states, must be preserved. The census should count every person legally abiding in the United States in an actual enumeration. We urge all who are legally eligible to participate in the census count to do so; at the same time, we urge Congress to specify – and to constitutionally justify – which census questions require a response.

We were glad that Acorn was *"decommissioned"* as an agent of the 2010 census-taking campaign. We suspect that they may *not* have been fair and balanced in their approach to collecting the data.

The census is a big deal because, outside of gerrymandering, we have little control over Congressional representation. This is another area in which the Democrats have routinely *crushed* us. Since they capture the votes of

"oppressed minorities" (including the dead), we *can't* win the numbers game. Our only salvation is trying to attract constituents who actually care enough about the country to come to the polls without being offered a free pack of cigarettes.

WORKING WITH AMERICANS IN THE TERRITORIES

We appreciate the extraordinary sacrifices the men and women of the territories are making to protect our freedom through their service in the U.S. Armed Forces. We welcome greater participation in all aspects of the political process by Americans residing in Guam, the Virgin Islands, American Samoa, the Northern Marianas, and Puerto Rico. We affirm their right to seek the full extension of the Constitution, with all the political rights and responsibilities it entails.

Notice that we said, *"We welcome greater participation in all aspects of the political process by AMERICANS residing in Guam, the Virgin Islands, American Samoa, the Northern Marianas, and Puerto Rico."* If they're already American citizens, of course they should have the *"right to seek the full extension of the Constitution, with all the political rights and responsibilities it entails."*

What we *don't* support is statehood for these territories. Not only would it contribute to the welfare state that we *already* can't afford to support, it would just about *guarantee* that we could *never* again gain a majority in the House or Senate since there are a whole lot of *"oppressed minorities"* living in these territories ... and we *all* know how they'd end up voting.

We recognize the valuable contributions made by the people of the United States Virgin Islands to the common welfare of the nation, including national defense, and their contributions to the federal treasury in the form of federal excise taxes paid on products produced in the territory.

 **We support any territory that produces products and pays its taxes. It sounds like a Republican stronghold to us.**

We support the Native American Samoans' efforts to protect their right to self-government and to preserve their culture and land-tenure system, which fosters self-reliance and strong extended-family values. We support increased local self-government for the United States citizens of the Virgin Islands, and closer cooperation between the local and federal governments to promote private sector-led development and self-sufficiency. We recognize that Guam is a strategically vital U.S. territory, an American fortress in the western Pacific. We affirm our support for the patriotic U.S. citizens of Guam and the Commonwealth of the Northern Mariana Islands to achieve greater self-government, an improved federal territorial relationship, new economic development strategies, a strong health care system that meets their needs, and continued political self-determination. We support a review to determine the appropriate eligibility of territories as well as states for Supplemental Security Income and other federal programs.

 **Again, we're in support of *any* country that's trying to prevent the loss of self-government in return for the opportunity to add *their* star to *our* flag. We just don't think the additional business for the flag industry would be worth it.**

We also recognize that American Samoa, Guam and the Northern Mariana Islands are *critical* to our economy. After all, if it weren't for the remote little islands in their areas, where would we film *Survivor*?

We support the right of the United States citizens of Puerto Rico to be admitted to the Union as a fully sovereign state after they freely so determine. We recognize that Congress has the final authority to define the constitutionally valid options for Puerto Rico to achieve a permanent non-territorial status with government by consent and full enfranchisement. As long as Puerto Rico is not a state, however, the will of its people regarding their political status should be ascertained by means of a general right of referendum or specific referenda sponsored by the U.S. government.

 *"We support the right of the United States citizens of Puerto Rico to be admitted to the Union as a fully sovereign state after they freely so determine."* Of course, if we thought for a moment that native Puerto Ricans would sacrifice their own national pride for the privilege of becoming part of the United States, we might have to reconsider. Based upon their established voting patterns in New York City and Miami, as a Party, we can't *afford* to have that Puerto Rico become a State.

PRESERVING THE DISTRICT OF COLUMBIA

The nation's capital is a special responsibility of the federal government. Yet some of the worst performing schools in the country are mere blocks from the Department of Education, and some of the most crime-ridden neighborhoods in the country are blocks from the Department of Justice. Washington should be made a model city. Two major Republican initiatives – a first-time D.C. homebuyers credit and a landmark school choice initiative – have pointed the way toward a civic resurgence, and a third piece of GOP legislation now guarantees young D.C. residents significant assistance in affording higher education. Because Washington's buildings and monuments may be top targets of terrorist groups, the federal government must work closely with local officials to improve security without burdening local residents. We call on the District of Columbia city council to pass laws consistent with the Supreme Court's decision in the Heller case. We honor the contributions of the residents of the District of Columbia, especially those who are serving honorably, or have served, in our Armed Forces.

 **Once you set foot outside of the Beltway, you're taking your life in your hands in D.C. Historically, there have been more murders in Washington, D.C. each year than there've been military casualties in Iraq. It's a city where a Mayor can be convicted on drug charges**

and get *re-elected* after serving his term (see, Kwame, there *is* hope for you in Detroit).

We have no idea how a District that surrounds our Federal government could be *so* attracted to corruption. Where could the negative influence come from? The Democrats want to make Washington, D.C. a State. We think that Afghanistan should be given first consideration.

Also, we haven't gotten in a plug for the military in awhile, so forgive us for singling out *"the contributions of the residents of the District of Columbia, especially those who are serving honorably, or have served, in our Armed Forces."* It's just our lame attempt to reinforce our *"Defense Strategy."*

EXPANDING OPPORTUNITY TO PROMOTE PROSPERITY

America's free economy has given our country the world's highest standard of living and allows us to share our prosperity with the rest of humanity. It is an engine of charity, empowering everything from Sabbath collection plate to great endowments. It creates opportunity, rewards self-reliance and hard work, and unleashes productive energies that other societies can only imagine. Today, our economy faces challenges due to high energy costs. Our task is to strengthen our economy and build a greater degree of security – in availability of jobs, in accessibility of health care, in portability of pensions, and in affordability of energy. That is an urgent task because economic freedom – and the prosperity it makes possible – are not ends in themselves. They are means by which families and individuals can maintain their independence from government, raise their children by their own values, and build communities of self-reliant neighbors.

Truth be told, *"America's free economy"* is anything but *"free."* Sure, we blame the Democrats for their *"tax and spend"* philosophy, but we've passed *our* fair share of regulatory legislation to gain more power than the Framers ever intended for us to have. And it's tough to maintain our lifestyles as Senators and Congressmen without a lot of money rolling in. Worthless junkets abroad so we can travel on your dime, great Washington parties, special privileges, free travel ... these things all cost money ... *serious*

money! If we didn't fund them with your tax dollars, *we'd* be no better off than *you*.

Economic freedom expands the prosperity pie; government can only divide it up. That is why Republicans advocate lower taxes, reasonable regulation, and smaller, smarter government. That agenda translates to more opportunity for more people. It represents the economics of inclusion, the path by which hopes become achievements. It is the way we will reach our goal of enabling everyone to have a chance to own, invest, and build.

We may *"advocate lower taxes, reasonable regulation, and smaller, smarter government,"* but during "W's" second term, you'd have been hard pressed to find an example of how we actually *did* that. It was like we were trying to *"out-Democrat"* the Democrats. Of course, with their return to power, they'll show us that we're not even in the same *ballpark* when it comes to spending.

REPUBLICAN TAX POLICY: PROTECTING HARDWORKING AMERICANS

The most important distinction between Republicans and the leadership of today's Democratic Party concerning taxes is not just that we believe you should keep more of what you earn. That's true, but there is a more fundamental distinction. It concerns the purpose of taxation. We believe government should tax only to raise money for its essential functions.

Of course, for being professed Conservatives, we sure have a liberal interpretation of what *"essential"* means. From the perspective of a *"common man,"* a lot of what we deemed to be *"essential"* may seem to be *"extravagant."* Luckily, we do not consider ourselves to be *"common."*

Today's Democratic Party views the tax code as a tool for social engineering. They use it to control our behavior, steer our choices, and change the way we live our lives. The Republican Party will put a stop to both social engineering and corporate handouts by simplifying tax policy, eliminating special deals, and putting those saved dollars back into the taxpayers' pockets.

 **Actually, we act like *"today's Democratic Party"* is different from *yesterday's*, but we know it really isn't. The only *real* difference is that *we've* drifted closer to *their* approach over the past several years because *they* tend to be more politically adept at getting their way than *we* do … and we want to emulate their success. Besides, we've never really had a problem with orchestrating *"special deals."***

<u>The Republican Agenda: Using Tax Relief to Grow the Economy</u>

Sound tax policy alone may not ensure economic success, but terrible tax policy does guarantee economic failure. Along with making the 2001 and 2003 tax cuts permanent so American families will not face a large tax hike, Republicans will advance tax policies to support American families, promote savings and innovation, and put us on a path to fundamental tax reform.

 **Let's be honest: whenever we use the word *"permanent,"* take it with a grain of salt. To us, *"permanent"* means *"until we decide it doesn't serve our purpose to remain permanent any more."***
 As an aside: we occasionally throw in the term *"American families"* to affect a *personal* connection. While we know we can't exploit the *"oppressed minorities"* sectors of the electorate, we think the term *"American families"* has a distinctly conservative ring to it. The term *"families"* sounds so *Republican*. And we practically own the term *"American"* … since the Democrats are always *apologizing* for it.

Lower Taxes on Families and Individuals

American families with children are the hardest hit during any economic downturn. Republicans will lower their tax burden by doubling the exemption for dependents.

 **"Lower(ing) (the) tax burden by doubling the exemption for dependents"** isn't really a big deal. Sure, it will score emotional points with the individuals who benefit from it, but keep in mind that about 57% percent of all taxes are paid by 5% of the taxpayer population; about 87% of all taxes are paid by 25% of the taxpayers; and over 97% of all taxes are paid by 50% of the taxpayers. That means that 50% of the population is already getting a *"free ride."* So, to those families with children who are actually *paying* taxes, doubling the dependents' exemption helps, but its *real* impact is marginal at best.

New technology should not occasion more taxation. We will permanently ban internet access taxes and stop all new cell phone taxes.

 **We've already warned you about our use of the word *"permanent"* so when we say, "We will permanently ban internet access taxes and stop all new cell phone taxes,"** take it with a grain of salt. Besides, if we *really* meant that *"new technology should not occasion more taxation,"* we would be proposing that *no* new technology should be taxed ... and that simply isn't the case.

For the sake of family farms and small businesses, we will continue our fight against the federal death tax.

 *"Death to the Death Tax!"* **Kind of catchy ... but just between us ... who cares? If you're dead, it doesn't really matter. And besides, your heirs probably didn't help you earn the money with which you built your estate.**

The Alternative Minimum Tax, a stealth levy on the middle-class that unduly targets large families, must be repealed.

 **Why does there need to be an** *"alternative"* *"minimum tax?"* **Doesn't that suggest that the original** *"minimum tax,"* **calculated by applying the standard tax code, really is just a fiction if the IRS can find a way to set a** *higher* *"minimum?"* **Does the term** *"oxymoron"* **come to mind?**

Republicans support tax credits for health care and medical expenses.

 **We normally don't like to provide this much specificity with respect to what we support. People can get too caught up in the details. However in this case, since it pertained to health care and medical expenses ... which are** *inherently* **complex issues that touch the lives of** *every* **single American (and a whole bunch of** *"undocumented workers"***) ... we felt** *compelled* **to be specific. Try not to get lost in the detail that we have provided.**

Keeping Good Jobs in America

America's producers can compete successfully in the international arena – as long as they have a level playing field. Today's tax code is tilted against them, with one of the highest corporate tax rates of all developed countries. That not only hurts American investors, managers, and the U.S. balance of trade; it also sends American jobs overseas. We support a major reduction in the corporate tax rate so that American companies stay competitive with their foreign counterparts and American jobs can remain in this country.

Even without the tax code, we've proven that we can *regulate* business *out* of the United States. We constantly pass legislation that imposes regulations that make us *"non-competitive."* Admittedly, most of the legislation is proposed by the Democrats to pander to one of their *"oppressed minorities,"* but we're certainly *"enablers"* based upon our ineptness when it come to stopping ridiculous bills from being passed and regulatory agencies from being created.

Promoting Savings through the Tax Code

We support a tax code that encourages personal savings. High tax rates discourage thrift by penalizing the return on savings and should be replaced with incentives to save. We support a plan to encourage employers to offer automatic enrollment in tax-deferred savings programs. The current limits on tax-free savings accounts should be removed.

Saying that we *"support a tax code that encourages personal savings"* shows our *"concern."* We hope to make an emotional connection at the individual level by making this statement. The reality is that *"high tax rates"* don't just *"discourage thrift by penalizing the return on savings"* ... they *eliminate* the ability to have any money left at the end of the day to set aside as *"savings."*

Fundamental Tax Reform

Over the long run, the mammoth IRS tax code must be replaced with a system that is simple, transparent, and fair while maximizing economic growth and job creation. As a transition, we support giving all taxpayers the option of filing under current rules or under a two-rate flat tax with generous deductions for families. This gradual approach is the taxpayers' best hope of overcoming the lobbyist legions that have thwarted past simplification efforts.

As a matter of principle, we oppose retroactive taxation, and we condemn attempts by judges, at any level of government, to seize the power of the purse by ordering higher taxes.

We apologize! We've come dangerously close to making a recommendation that could *actually* have a positive impact. Of course, we recognized this at the last second and were sure *not* to include any *specific* recommendations. It's always *much* better to promise *nebulous ideas* for which we cannot be held accountable than it is to offer *details*.

Because of the vital role of religious organizations, charities and fraternal benevolent societies in fostering charity and patriotism, they should not be subject to taxation.

To be fair, we also probably shouldn't allow a *"charitable deduction"* since it, in effect, potentially defeats the purpose behind true *"donative intent."* It wasn't too long ago in our Nation's history that people willingly made donations to charities because it was the *right* thing to do rather than because they could write off the deduction. Of course, that was back in the old days, when people believed in God ... and integrity and honor were still held in high esteem.

In any fundamental restructuring of federal taxation, to guard against the possibility of hypertaxation of the American people, any value added tax or national sales tax must be tied to simultaneous repeal of the Sixteenth Amendment, which established the federal income tax.

We're taking a firm stand on this one. If we enact any new law that is in direct contravention of a Constitutional Amendment (in this case, the

Sixteenth Amendment), then we need to repeal the Amendment simultaneously. Otherwise, it could cause a great deal of consternation among the Justices of the Supreme Court when the inevitable litigation ends up on their docket. Given the fact that we are now considering the appointment of Justices who have little to no judicial experience, we don't need to make issues any more complex than they inherently need to be.

<u>The Democrats Plan to Raise Your Taxes</u>

The last thing Americans need right now is tax hikes. On the federal level, Republicans lowered taxes in 2001 and 2003 in order to encourage economic growth, put more money in the pockets of every taxpayer, and make the system fairer. It worked. If Congress had then controlled its spending, we could have done even more.

Please ignore the fact that *we* controlled Congress with majorities in both the House and the Senate from 2003 until 2007 ... not to mention that the President was also a Republican during that time. But, as we have admitted before, we are politically inept.

Ever since those tax cuts were enacted, the Democratic Party has been clear about its goals: It wants to raise taxes by eliminating those Republican tax reductions. The impact on American families would be disastrous:

- Marginal tax rates would rise. This is in addition to their proposal to target millions of taxpayers with even higher rates.
- The "marriage penalty would return for two-earner couples.
- The child tax credit would fall to half its current value.
- Small businesses would lose their tax relief.
- The federal death tax would be enormously increased.
- Investment income – the seed money for new jobs – would be eaten away by higher rates for dividend and capital gain income.

 **Unless you've been vacationing on Mars, none of this should come as** *"breaking news!"* **The Democrat's time-tested strategy is to** *"tax and spend"* **in a way that entices** *"oppressed minorities"* **to** *"pledge their allegiance"* **to the Democratic Party. No matter how much we rant and rave about it, we don't seem to know how to get people to** *"do the math"* **to recognize that this is a** *"wolf in sheep's clothing"* **strategy that perpetuates the status of the** *"oppressed minorities."* **We can't tell you how frustrating it is to be** *this* **incompetent as a Party.**

All that and more would amount to an annual tax hike upwards of $250 billion – almost $700 per taxpayer every year, for a total of $1.1 trillion in additional taxes over the next decade. That is what today's Democratic Party calls "tax fairness." We call it an unconscionable assault on the paychecks and pocketbooks of every hard-working American household. Their promises to aim their tax hikes at families with high incomes is a smokescreen; history shows that when Democrats want more money, they raise taxes on everyone.

 *"Tax fairness"* **is an oxymoron within the context of a progressive tax structure. Until every single American is paying what is truly their** *"fair share,"* **the term** *"tax fairness"* **should be banned. Why we can't articulate this in a way that people fundamentally** *"get it"* **remains an enigma. Like we said before, we apparently are just woefully inept!**

SMALL BUSINESS: THE ENGINE OF JOB GROWTH

We proudly call ourselves the party of small business because small businesses are where national prosperity begins. Small businesses such as Main Street retailers, entrepreneurs, independent contractors, and direct sellers create most of the country's new jobs and have been the primary means of economic advancement by women and minorities.

 We proudly call ourselves *"the party of small business,"* but we really pander (as charged) to *"big business"* instead. That's because it's easier to solicit significant campaign contributions from the smaller pool of big businesses than it is to *"go door-to-door"* among the much larger number of geographically dispersed small businesses. And because we've demonstrated a pronounced tendency to allow Political Action Committees (PACs) to unduly influence our votes, this is unlikely to change anytime soon.

You do have to admire that we dared to include the term *"Main Street"* in our diatribe. We think it demonstrates a new level of sophistication relative to taking a term that the Democrats use so derisively against us and turning it into a positive by attaching it to small businesses rather than big businesses. Then, we blended in *"women and minorities"* to show that the Democrats aren't the only ones who can feign to care about *"oppressed minorities."* This is our attempt to begin to emerge from our past state of political awkwardness to a new level of political sophistication ... at least comparatively.

Eight years ago, when Democrats controlled the Executive Branch, small business faced a hostile regulatory agenda, from OSHA's ergonomics standards and attempts to intrude into the homes of telecommuting employees to IRS discrimination against independent contractors. Republicans turned back those threats, along with much of the onerous taxation that limited the growth of small businesses. We reduced their marginal tax rates, quadrupled the limit on their expensing of investments, and phased out the death tax on family owned small businesses and family farms. We enacted Health Savings Accounts to help small business owners secure health insurance for themselves and their employees. All those gains are jeopardized if Democrats gain unfettered power once again.

 **We actually did have a positive impact in this regard. We're not sure *how* it happened as we were otherwise expanding spending and regulatory control during this same timeframe, but we accidently *did* have a positive impact.**

Republicans will advance a multi-pronged plan to support small business and grow good-paying jobs:

- Through the energy agenda laid out else-where in this platform, we will attack the rise in energy costs that is making it so difficult for entrepreneurs to compete.
- Our tax reduction and tax simplification agenda will allow businesses to focus on producing and selling their products and services – not on paying taxes.
- Our plan to return control of health care to patients and providers will benefit small business employers and employees alike.
- Our determination to vigorously open foreign markets to American products is an opportunity for many small businesses to grow larger in the global economy.
- Our approach to regulation – basing it on sound science to achieve goals that are technically feasible – will protect against job-killing intrusions into small businesses.
- Our commitment to legal reform means protecting small businesses from the effects of frivolous lawsuits.

 **Basically, this is our attempt to differentiate our Party's agenda from the Democratic Party's agenda ... without the risk of giving any details for which we could be held accountable. Besides, we haven't *really* thought through any of the *details!***

Using history as our guide, we look to innovative entrepreneurs for the ingenuity and daring that can give us the next generation of technological progress. The advances our country needs, in every-thing from health care to energy to environmental protection, are most likely to come from the men and women of small business.

 **We're hoping that there are others out there who are a whole lot smarter than us. Most of us have little to no *real world* experience. Oh sure, we can pontificate about what we believe and what we're going to do, but we have no real idea of *how* to do it. That's why we're counting on *"innovative entrepreneurs"* to bail us out at some point.**

TECHNOLOGY AND INNOVATION

American innovation has twin engines: technology and small business, employing over half the private-sector work force. The synergy of our technology and small business drove a world-wide economic transformation of the last quarter-century. To maintain our global leadership, we need to encourage innovators by reforming and making permanent the Research and Development Tax Credit as part of the overall agenda outlined in this platform.

 **Notice how we're distancing ourselves from *"big business?"* Big businesses contribute in a big way to the *"technology"* component of our argument, but we *never* mention them. We've been put in a box by the Democrats: *"big business"* is bad ... and the Republicans are comprised of fat-cat, senior executives from *"big business."* It's just not true. Even if they *all* voted for us, there aren't *enough* senior executives out there to win an election. If there were, we'd stop talking about small business owners and just concentrate on where the real money is!**

Innovation is our future – in our approach to energy, to education, to health care, and especially to government. As a symbol of that commitment, we share the vision of returning Americans to the moon as a step toward a mission to Mars. In advancing our country's space and aeronautics program,

NASA will remain one of the world's most important pioneers in technology, and from its explorations can come tremendous benefits for mankind.

 **This is just a cheap shot at Obama's pledge to shut down the Space Program. Our polls show that most Americans are proud of the Space Program, so we're trying to capitalize on that. It's not like we think we can legislate *"innovation."* Even we aren't *that* naïve! The operative phrase is that we support the Space Program *"as a symbol of (our) commitment"* to technology. And that's all it really is ... a *"symbol."***

DEVELOPING A FLEXIBLE AND INNOVATIVE WORKFORCE

To master the global economy, our work force must be creative, independent, and able to adapt to rapid change. That challenge calls for better education and training and new approaches to employer-employee relations. It means investing in people, not institutions.

 **The *"Catch-22"* here is that a more *educated* electorate is a *dangerous* electorate. Educated individuals might give real pause to considering those who currently serve in political office, on *either* side of the aisle, before ever casting a vote for us. Thank goodness we've got a great retirement program in place that's absolutely air-tight!**

The Failed Model of Employer-Employee Relations

The Democrats' approach to employment policy is a retreat to failed models of the past: new regulatory burdens on employers that make it more difficult for businesses, big and small, to hire and keep employees. That failed model empowers union bosses at the expense of their members, trial lawyers at the expense of small businesses, and government bureaucrats at the expense of employer-employee partnerships. Its goal is not to create jobs but to control the workplace and the work force.

 If we weren't afraid to tell the truth, we'd just spell out how the Democrats have sold out to the Labor Unions in return for their votes. Sure, we dance around it, but we don't just come out and say that the Democrats are in bed with Union leadership because Union leadership is willing to pledge big bucks to Democratic campaigns from the pension programs they control as well as to unduly influence their membership (by maintaining a *"We vs. They"* mentality against management and *"those dreaded Republicans")* in return for *huge* contracts and political *favors*. In today's day and age, it's *"politically incorrect"* to channel the spirit of Howard Cosell and *"tell it like it is!"*

<u>The Republican Model: Investing in People</u>

Republicans believe that the employer-employee relationship of the future will be built upon employee empowerment and workplace flexibility.

- The Industrial Revolution treated people like machines; today's economy must treat them as individuals. We recognize that work schedules should be more flexible when employers and employees are not negatively affected such as removing outdated distinctions between full time and part time, clock-punching and overtime. The federal government should set an example in that regard.
- The workplace must catch up with the way Americans live now. For increasing numbers of workers, especially those with children, the choice of working from home will be good for families, profitable for business, and energy efficient.
- All workers should have portability in their pension plans and their health insurance, giving them greater job mobility, financial independence, and security.
- Global competitiveness will increasingly require an entrepreneurial culture of cooperation and team work. Making the best talent part of our team is the rationale for the H-1B visa program, which needs updating to reflect our need for more leaders in science and

technology while we take the necessary steps to create more of them in our own school systems. By complementing the U.S. work force with needed specialists from abroad, we can make sure American companies and their jobs remain here at home.

Okay. We hope we didn't confuse you. You're probably going to need a scorecard to distinguish us from the Democrats in *this* section of our Platform. But here's the logic: we recognize that we've been reasonably unskilled from a political perspective; we recognize that the Democrats have been handing us our proverbial posteriors when it comes to *"connecting with the people."* So, we've chosen to *"shadow"* them in this regard; matching *our* rhetoric to *theirs*.

Our hope is that this will confuse the general public *so* much that some moderate Democrats will see us as a viable option and switch their allegiance to *us*. We don't know if this will work, but it's worth a try. From this day forward, never let it be said that the definition of being a Republican is *"doing the same thing over and over again and expecting a different result!"*

Businesses and employees, working together, are best suited to addressing the challenges ahead. Empowering official Washington and the trial bar, as Democrats prefer, will only lead to more antagonistic relations.

We side with Shakespeare on this one as he penned in *King Henry VI*: *"The first thing we do, let's kill all the lawyers."* The only chance we take is that the American people recognize just how many *lawyers* there are in Washington, D.C. ... and start with *us*.

<u>*Individual-Based Unemployment Insurance and Training*</u>

Government can play an important role in addressing economic dislocations by modernizing its re-training and unemployment assistance programs. We must make these programs actually anticipate dislocations so that affected workers can get new skills quickly and return to the workforce. We advocate a seamless approach to helping employees stay on the job and advance through education. Workers should be able to direct a portion of their unemployment insurance into a tax-free Lost Earnings Buffer Account that could be used for retraining or relocation. With financial incentives to return to work as soon as possible, this approach will also require strengthening community colleges and making them more accessible through Flexible Training Accounts.

We really wanted to say that if the Democrat's get their way when it comes to imposing new taxes, there will be little incentive to the unemployed to *ever* return to the workforce. If unemployed individuals *really* do the math, it probably makes more sense to transition to welfare ... rather than to return to work only to have your wages garnished by disproportionate taxes. You just have to accept the social stigma associated with being on welfare. But heck, how hard can *that* be? Tens of millions of people have *already* comfortably overcome that issue.

PROTECTING UNION WORKERS

We affirm both the right of individuals to voluntarily participate in labor organizations and bargain collectively and the right of states to enact Right-to-Work laws. But the nation's labor laws, to a large extent formed out of conflicts several generations ago, should be modernized to make it easier for employers and employees to plan, execute, and profit together. To protect workers from misuse of their funds, we will conscientiously enforce federal law requiring financial reporting and transparency by labor unions. We advocate paycheck protection laws to guard the integrity of the political process and the security of workers' earnings.

All together now, "♫ Look for... the union label! ♫" This is what we call a *"ventriloquist provision."* We entitle it *"Protect Union Workers"* ... then subtly *slam* unions. We'll bet you didn't even see our lips

move. We've been doing this for years and have become pretty good at it!

Stopping the Assault on the Secret Ballot

The recent attempt by congressional Democrats to deny workers a secret ballot in union referenda is an assault, not only against a fundamental principle of labor law, but even more against the dignity and honor of the American work force. We oppose "card check" legislation, which deprives workers of their privacy and their right to vote, because it exposes workers to intimidation by union organizers.

 **We're glad we caught this travesty. In recent years, we've been so busy trampling on individual *rights*, it would have been easy to *miss* this one. Luckily, it was a Democratic initiative, so it caught our eye. Otherwise, we might have been too busy listening to a wiretap of your private conversation to have noticed it.**

REBUILDING HOMEOWNERSHIP

Homeownership remains key to creating an opportunity society. We support timely and carefully targeted aid to those hurt by the housing crisis so that affected individuals can have a chance to trade a burdensome mortgage for a manageable loan that reflects their home's market value. At the same time, government action must not implicitly encourage anyone to borrow more than they can afford to repay. We support energetic federal investigation and, where appropriate, prosecution of criminal wrong-doing in the mortgage industry and investment sec-tor. We do not support government bailouts of private institutions. Government interference in the markets exacerbates problems in the marketplace and causes the free market to take longer to correct itself. We believe in the free market as the best tool to sustained prosperity and opportunity for all. We encourage potential buyers to work in concert with the lending community to educate themselves about the responsibilities of purchasing a home, condo, or land.

 **We really wanted to mention that our current economic crisis was precipitated by the collapse of the mortgage industry that was caused by ridiculous legislation involving Fannie Mae and Freddie Mac and the** *"community organizing"* **tactics of Acorn and its peers to** *pressure* **banks into making ill-fated loans that, in turn, created a class of tainted assets that were exploited by** *worthless profiteers* **on Wall Street. We decided** *not* **to be this direct because it would be** *"politically incorrect"* **... and it might** *offend* **the** *worthless profiteers* **on Wall Street who so** *generously* **contribute to our political campaigns.**

Republican policy aims to make owning a home more accessible through enforcement of open housing laws, voucher programs, urban homesteading and – what is most important – a strong economy with low interest rates. Because affordable housing is in the national interest, any simplified tax system should continue to encourage homeownership, recognizing the tremendous social value that the home mortgage interest deduction has had for decades. In addition, sound housing policy should recognize the needs of renters so that apartments and multi-family homes remain important components of the housing stock.

 **One more thing we should add: Hey, people! If the loan** *sounds* **too good to be true ... it probably** *is!* **If you can't believe that you could ever afford the home you're looking at on your current income ... it's because you probably** *can't!* **And if you mess up again ... we're not going to bail you out!**

REFORMING THE CIVIL JUSTICE SYSTEM TO IMPROVE COMPETITIVENESS

The rule of law demands that injured parties have access to the forums to vindicate their rights, but the rule of law does not mean the rule of lawyers – especially trial lawyers who manipulate the system to enrich themselves rather than protecting consumers, workers, or taxpayers. While no one should be denied access to the courts, the rule of lawyers threatens our global competitiveness, denies Americans access to the quality of justice they deserve, and puts every small business one lawsuit away from bankruptcy.

This is one thing we can all agree on: everybody seems to *hate* lawyers. Heck ... *lawyers* even *hate* lawyers! As we previously quoted Shakespeare, *"The first thing we do, let's kill all the lawyers."* Did we mention that Barney Frank, Chris Dodd and Harry Reid are *all* lawyers? And, we bet we could come up with an *honorary* law degree for Nancy Pelosi as well!

The Republican approach to eliminate frivolous lawsuits has advanced in Congress through efforts like the Class Action Fairness Act and in many states through the adoption of medical liability reforms, which we will continue to pursue on the federal and state level. But because their Democratic donees currently control Congress, the trial lawyers are on the offensive. They are trying to undermine federal health and safety regulations by allowing trial lawyers at the state level to preempt the reasoned judgments of independent experts. They seek to weaken lower-cost dispute resolution alternatives such as mediation and arbitration in order to put more cases into court. In bill after bill, their congressional allies insert new private causes of action – trial lawyer ear-marks – designed to drag more Americans into court.

All kidding aside, have you noticed how we specifically reference *"trial"* attorneys? That's just in case you take our Shakespearian reference to heart. Most of us are attorneys as well ... but we're not *"trial"* attorneys. *"Trial"* attorneys follow a different curriculum in law school. If you declare yourself to be a *"trial"* attorney, you apparently aren't allowed to take an Ethics class. Truth be told, law schools should probably offer a *similar* track for those of us who declare an interest in politics.

To resolve this issue, we think there should be an agency to regulate *"trial attorneys"* and that its leader should be a member of the Cabinet. In the spirit of bipartisanship, we'd like

to offer up John Edwards as a potential candidate. His background as a distinguished *"trial attorney"* as well as a Democratic Presidential candidate would allow him to bring his considerable experience to bear on the issue. Besides, we would just *love* to have the opportunity to question him *at length* ... and *in depth* ... *on national television* during his confirmation hearing.

Our repeated warnings about the corruption at the heart of the trial bar have been vindicated by high-profile criminal convictions and prison terms for some of the nation's leading class action and personal injury trial lawyers. All plaintiffs, especially those who must hire personal injury lawyers on a contingency basis, should be protected against abuse by their attorneys, and the attorney-client privilege should be defended as a bulwark in the defense of liberty.

 **We were right about these bums, and we've gotten to know them quite well. Several of them share cells with some of our *former* Congressional colleagues.**

FREE AND FAIR TRADE

Greater international trade, aggressively advanced on a truly level playing field, will mean more American jobs, higher wages, and a better standard of living. It is also a matter of national security and an instrument to promote democracy and civil society in developing nations.

With 95 percent of the world's customers out-side our borders, we need to be at the table when trade rules are written to make sure that free trade is indeed a two-way street. We encourage multilateral, regional, and bilateral agreements to reduce trade barriers that limit market access for U.S. products, commodities and services. To achieve that goal, Congress should reinstate the trade promotion authority every president should have in dealing with foreign governments. Trade agreements that have already been signed and are pending before Congress should be debated and voted on immediately.

 **If only we could eliminate the minimum wage, or at least roll it back to the level of pay given to *"undocumented workers,"* we'd become more competitive. It would also help if we could pollute a bit more indiscriminately and relax some of the laws that otherwise restrict our competitiveness; you know, like child labor laws, regulations that demand safe working environments, and overtime requirements. Oh, how we long for the days of the Company Town when the industrial revolution was in full swing.**

An aggressive trade strategy is especially important with regard to agriculture. Our farm economy produces for the world; its prosperity depends, more than ever before, on open markets. U.S. agricultural exports will top $100 billion this year. We will contest any restrictions upon our farm products within the World Trade Organization and will work to make the WTO's decision-making process more receptive to the arguments of American producers.

 **Farmers are one of our Party's few equivalents to an *"oppressed minority"* ... only they're too *proud* to be called an *"oppressed minority."* Still, they tend to vote for us religiously ... *literally!* In return, we continually renew farm subsidies that pay them *not* to farm their land. If they were left to their own devices and grew as much food as they could, food prices might eventually come down (as they would in a true, free market economy), and there would be a glut of food with which we could potentially eliminate hunger in the United States and abroad.**

We pledge stronger action to protect intellectual property rights against pirating and will aggressively oppose the direct and indirect subsidies by which some governments tilt the world playing field against American producers. To protect American consumers, we call for greater vigilance and more resources to guard against the importation of tainted food, poisonous products, and dangerous toys. Additionally, we recognize the need to support our growth in trade through appropriate development and support of our ports in order to ensure safe, efficient and timely handling of all goods.

 Does it strike anyone as just a bit ironic that we think we can identify and stop *"tainted"* products from crossing our borders when we seem to be so inept at stopping *"undocumented workers"* from penetrating our borders? Besides, we believe in American ingenuity. We believe *we* have the ability to produce all the *"tainted food, poisonous products, and dangerous toys"* we could ever need *without* having to import them.

SUPPORTING OUR AGRICULTURAL COMMUNITIES

Farming communities have been hard hit this year by flood and violent weather, as well as the escalation of fuel costs. Especially under those circumstances, federal agricultural aid should go to those who need it most as part of a sensible economic safety-net for farmers. We advocate the creation of Farm Savings Accounts to help growers manage risks brought on by turbulence in global markets and nature itself. Mindful that 98 percent of the 2 million farms in this country are owned by individuals or family farming partnerships, we affirm our fight against the death tax.

 Mindful also of the fact that about *"98 percent of the 2 million farms in this country"* vote Republican, we've even given them this additional section within our Platform. Notice that we only gave one or two sentences to issues concerning any of the Asian-Pacific countries. But then, no one in those countries votes for us.

Those who live on and work the land are our finest environmental stewards. They understand, better than most, the need for safe water, clean air, and conservation of open space. We oppose attempts to hamper agricultural production with heavy-handed mandates, including any expansion of the Clean Water Act to regulate ditches, culverts, converted cropland, and farm and stock ponds. We reaffirm traditional state supremacy over water allocations and will continue to make available renewable rangeland under sound environmental conditions. We support greater investment in conservation incentive pro-grams to help rural communities improve and sustain environmental quality. Agricultural policy should be formulated by giving careful consideration to the expert opinions of those most knowledgeable on the topic – the farmers and ranchers.

 **Of course, *"reaffirm(ing) traditional state supremacy over water allocations"* doesn't help much when you've got wing-nut judges sitting on the Federal bench that can force water allocation to protect a random species. It happens in California all the time.**

As for *"giving careful consideration to the expert opinions of those most knowledgeable on the topic,"* have you ever wondered why we don't apply this *same* rationale to other matters like health care reform, litigation reform, etc.? It's because it's too much *fun* wielding power over the *"innocent masses."* Otherwise, you might eventually figure out that most of us do not exactly fit the *"intellectual giant"* image we like to portray at political rallies.

To meet surging global demand for food and biofuel, farmers must have the technology to grow higher yields using fewer inputs. The USDA must remain the international leader in agricultural research to ensure that America and the world will never have to choose between food and fuel. The U.S. government should end mandates for ethanol and let the free market work.

 **We must also continue to invest in the development and application of pesticides, non-organic fertilizers, and genetic engineering of livestock that will continue to contribute in a significant way to our ever-increasing efficiency with respect to agricultural productivity. Just a mental note: we may *also* want to set aside some money to fund *medical research* on cancer and other major diseases that *inexplicably* seem to be on the rise.**

ENERGY INDEPENDENCE AND SECURITY

All Americans are acutely aware of the energy crisis our nation faces. Energy costs are spiraling upward, food prices continue to rise, and as a result, our entire economy suffers. This winter, families will spend for heat what they could have saved for college, and small businesses will spend for fuel what could have covered employee health insurance.

 **Just in case you didn't get the connection: rising** *"food prices"* **are tied to the** *"energy crisis"* **because, as the cost of fuel rises, the cost of transporting food rises and the increase is passed along to the consumer. It's either that ... or someone thought that since food provides energy to our bodies, it should be mentioned in this section.**

Our current dependence on foreign fossil fuels threatens both our national security and our economy and could also force drastic changes in the way we live. The ongoing transfer of Americans' wealth to OPEC – roughly $700 billion a year – helps underwrite terrorists' operations and creates little incentive for repressive regimes to accept democracy, whether in the Middle East or Latin America.

 **Please don't confuse OPEC (the Organization of the Petroleum Exporting Countries with *OPEC* (the Organization for the Political Exploitation of Consumers); although both exact a *"transfer of Americans' wealth,"* and an argument could be made that both *"help underwrite terrorists' operations and create little incentive for repressive regimes to accept democracy."* We're talking about the *first* OPEC; the second one is heretofore an undisclosed, quasi-organization through which we surreptitiously work in close cooperation with the Democrats ... and we take a lot more than *"$700 billion a year"* from the taxpayers to fund our boondoggles.**

It didn't have to be this way, and it must not stay this way. Our nation must have a robust energy supply because energy drives prosperity and increases opportunity for every American. We reject the idea that America cannot overcome its energy challenges – or that high gasoline prices are okay, as long as they are phased in gradually. We reject half-measures and believe "No, we can't" is not a viable energy policy.

 **We don't really say much in this paragraph, but we've been dying to mock the *"Yes We Can"* slogan of the Democrats. And *you* thought we weren't clever!**

Together we can build a future around domestic energy sources that are diverse, reliable, and cleaner. We can strengthen our national security, create a pathway to growing prosperity, and preserve our environment. The American people will rise to this challenge.

 **We're trying to *"rally the troops"* here, and we don't have a succinct phrase like *"Yes We Can."* After a great deal of caucusing, we came up with *"It is in the affirmative for which we positively assert that we, in fact, can accomplish all of the goals and aspirations of the**

achievements we so diligently strive to realize in our lives and the lives of those around us." While we thought it was quite "catchy," we couldn't get it to fit on any of our campaign posters, so we dropped the concept.

GROWING OUR ENERGY SUPPLY

We must aggressively increase our nation's energy supply, in an environmentally responsible way, and do so through a comprehensive strategy that meets both short and long term needs. No amount of wishing or hoping can suspend the laws of supply and demand. Leading economists agree that any actions that will increase future energy supplies will lead to lower energy prices today. Increasing our production of American made energy and reducing our excessive reliance on foreign oil will:
- Bring down the high cost of gasoline and diesel fuel.
- Create more jobs for American workers.
- Enhance our national security.

In the long run, American production should move to zero-emission sources, and our nation's fossil fuel resources are the bridge to that emissions-free future.

Manned-flight began with the Wright brothers in 1903. Less than 60 years later, President Kennedy proclaimed that we would put a man on the moon by the end of the decade. Eight years later, we accomplished that goal.

Conversely, oil has been used as a source of fuel for *hundreds* of years. The use of coal for heat dates back *tens* of *thousands* of years. Who knows? If we really commit to the process as politicians, we think we can achieve an *"emissions-free future"* ... in another few *millennia*.

Growing American Energy Production

If we are to have the resources we need to achieve energy independence, we simply must draw more American oil from American soil. We support accelerated exploration, drilling and development in America, from new oilfields off the nation's coasts to onshore fields such as those in Montana, North Dakota, and Alaska. The Green River Basin in Colorado, Utah, and Wyoming offers recoverable shale oil that is ready for development, and most of it is on federal lands.

Okay, we may back away from off-shore drilling for awhile until we learn how to cap those things when they blow. Otherwise, the cost of fish sticks could get out of hand. But we should be drilling on land and mining for coal as well. The reality is that we'll *all* be out of office for several generations before we run out of our traditional fuels.

To deliver that energy to American consumers, we will expand our refining capacity. Because of environmental extremism and regulatory blockades in Washington, not a single new refinery has been built in this country in 30 years. We will encourage refinery construction and modernization and, with sensitivity to environmental concerns, an expedited permitting process.

Any legislation to increase domestic exploration, drilling and production must minimize any protracted legal challenges that could unreasonably delay or even preclude actual production. We oppose any efforts that would permanently block access to the coastal plain of the Arctic National Wildlife Refuge.

It's true that we've been *"frozen"* for over 30 years when it comes to building refineries. But, don't worry about it. We also established the Department of Energy in 1977 under the Carter Administration. Its charter was to help our country evolve from its dependence upon foreign oil. During his military service, President Carter attended nuclear power school while on

assignment to the Navel Reactor branch, so you *know* the direction in which he was leaning.

Oh, and the last order for a nuclear power plant was ... you guessed it ... in the 1970's. The *same* environmentalists who complain about our dependence upon fossil fuels have done a great job of *shutting down* a transfer of our Nation's energy production to the *far* more efficient nuclear solution. The good news is that, in the interim, the Department of Energy has grown to about 16,000 Federal employees with a budget of about $26.5 billion ... and just *look* at how far we've evolved from our dependence upon oil under its guidance. Now, that's what we call *"bang for the buck!"*

Nuclear Power: the Earth's Clean Future

Nuclear energy is the most reliable zero-carbon-emissions source of energy that we have. Unwarranted fear mongering with no relationship to current technologies and safeguards has prevented us from starting construction of a single nuclear power plant in 31 years. Meanwhile, the U.S. Navy has for decades relied upon nuclear-powered vessels, and other nations have harnessed nuclear power to provide a major portion of their energy consumption. There is no reason why the United States cannot catch up and do the same. Confident in the promise offered by science and technology, Republicans will pursue dramatic increases in the use of all forms of safe, affordable, reliable – and clean – nuclear power.

 If we aren't successful in this regard, we'll just sit back and wait for Iran and North Korea to refine the technology they're so diligently working on to address their countries' need for power. These well-known, *environmentally sensitive* nations will undoubtedly share their *peaceful* discoveries with the rest of the world because they're all about the *"betterment of mankind."* Besides, Iran is particularly motivated since its environmentalists are undoubtedly concerned about running out of oil in the region.

As new plants are constructed using the highest safety and operation standards, the nation's industrial and manufacturing base will be rejuvenated. The labor force will expand, with nearly 15,000 high quality jobs created for every new nuclear plant built – and those workers will lead the nation away from its dependence on foreign oil.

 **This would be an even *better* argument if unemployment was a major concern in our great Nation. But what State could use 15,000 jobs spread over a decade or two anyway?**

Solar Wind, Geothermal, Hydropower

Alternate power sources must enter the main-stream. The technology behind solar energy has improved significantly in recent years, and the commercial development of wind power promises major benefits both in costs and in environmental protection. Republicans support these and other alternative energy sources, including geothermal and hydropower, and anticipate technological developments that will increase their economic viability. We therefore advocate a long-term energy tax credit equally applicable to all renewable power sources.

 **Truthfully, we really don't know much about these new-fangled energy sources. Big oil writes the checks for our campaigns. When the day comes that these *other* fuel sources start supporting the Republican Party, *we'll* start supporting them.**

That being said ... if hot air could be effectively harnessed, Congress alone could power our country for generations to come. We pledge to look into it.

Republicans support measures to modernize the nation's electricity grid to provide American consumers and businesses with more affordable, reliable power. We will work to unleash innovation so entrepreneurs can develop technologies for a more advanced and robust United States transmission system that meets our growing energy demands.

 *"We will work to unleash innovation"* to support the *"entrepreneurs"* we love so much. Yes, sir! We're going to *legislate* innovation. That will get the ball rolling!

Clean Coal

Although alternate fuels will shape our energy future, coal – America's most affordable and abundant energy resource and the source of most of our electricity – remains a strategic national resource that must play a major role in energy independence. We look to innovative technology to transform America's coal supplies into clean fuels capable of powering motor vehicles and aircraft. We support coal-to-liquid and gasification initiatives, just as we support investment in the development and deployment of carbon capture and storage technologies, which can reduce emissions. We firmly oppose efforts by Democrats to block the construction of new coal-fired power plants. No strategy for reducing energy costs will be viable without a commitment to continued coal production and utilization.

 While they have to hedge their bets, we get about 68% of the coal industry's political contributions, which run into the millions of dollars. Not only is coal a viable energy source in today's world, it's also an *excellent* source of political contributions.

Natural Gas

Natural gas is plentiful in North America, but we can extract more and do a better job of distributing it nationwide to cook our food, heat our homes, and serve as a growing option as a transportation fuel. Both independently and in cooperation with alternative fuels, natural gas will be an essential part of any long-term energy solution. We must ensure it gets to consumers safely and quickly.

The environmentalists want to take the fun out of *everything*. Now, they're against natural gas exploration because of the potential impact on water supplies. They fear the *"fracking"* technique by which millions of gallons of water (and now other chemicals) are pumped down a well and into shale at high pressure to create fractures that allow the gas to flow from the shale into the well. Correspondingly, a fairly high percentage of the tainted water is recovered, and no one is sure what to do with it. *We* say, just mix it back into our water supply. We already put a large number of chemicals into our water supply to treat it. What's a few more?

Mental note: weren't we supposed to *remind* ourselves to reserve some money for *medical research* on cancer and other major diseases that *inexplicably* seem to be on the rise? We might want to bump the amount up … just a bit.

<u>Energy Cooperation</u>

We embrace the open energy cooperation and trading relationship with our neighbors Canada and Mexico, including proven oil reserves and vast, untapped Canadian hydroelectric generation.

Canada seems to be a viable option, but Mexico probably won't be able to help us. They've been suffering from an incredible loss of their lower-end labor pool, which apparently has been migrating to other countries. We should look into this. Maybe *we* can help Mexico with their problem and, in return, *they'll* help us with *ours*.

REDUCING DEMAND FOR FOSSIL FUELS

While we grow our supplies, we must also reduce our demand – not by changing our lifestyles but by putting the free market to work and taking advantage of technological breakthroughs.

We're not really sure that this has much substance considering the fact that the free market hasn't exactly been restricted in the past. In any event, as the Baby Boom Generation ages, it will appear that we've cut demand as well since Gen-X is only about 60% of the size of the Baby Boomer Generation. We'll look like *geniuses!*

Increase Conservation through Greater Efficiency

Conservation does not mean deprivation; it means efficiency and achieving more with less. Most Americans today endeavor to conserve fossil fuels, whether in their cars or in their home heating, but we can do better. We can construct better and smarter buildings, use smarter thermo-stats and transmission grids, increase recycling, and make energy-efficient consumer purchases. Wireless communications, for example, can increase telecommuting options and cut back on business travel. The Republican goal is to ensure that Americans have more conservation options that will enable them to make the best choices for their families.

Conservation is a *good* thing. Besides it sounds a lot like *"Conservative,"* so we like it even *more*. However, these issues can only be addressed through bipartisan cooperation. In that regard, we'll call for a joint conference to be held between Democrats and Republicans ... perhaps over in Europe. We can all gather our staffs and families and fly to the site; taking limos to and from wherever else we may need to go when we get there. The first item on the agenda should be *"exploring a more intelligent use of electronic communication technologies."*

New Technologies for Cars and Other Vehicles

We must continue to develop alternative fuels, such as biofuels, especially cellulosic ethanol, and hasten their technological advances to next-generation production. As America develops energy technology for the 21st century, policy makers must consider the burden that rising food prices and energy costs create for the poor and developing nations around the world. Because alternative fuels are useless if vehicles cannot use them, we must move quickly to flexible fuel vehicles; we cannot expect necessary investments in alternative fuels if this flexibility does not become standard. We must also produce more vehicles that operate on electricity and natural gas, both to reduce demand for oil and to cut CO2 emissions.

If you run into us in public, please, dear God, don't ask us what *"cellulosic ethanol"* is. We have no real idea, but it makes our Platform sound more intelligent!
And remember, *"alternative fuels are useless if vehicles cannot use them."* That's why we've abandoned the idea of using wind turbines to generate power for electric cars ... en route. They kept snapping off when we tried to drive through tunnels.

Given that fully 97 percent of our current transportation vehicles rely on oil, we will aggressively support technological advances to reduce our petroleum dependence. For example, light-weight composites could halve the weight and double the gas mileage of cars and trucks, and together with flex-fuel and electric vehicles, could usher in a renaissance in the American auto industry.

This is particularly important since it now truly is the *"American auto industry,"* since the Democrats essentially nationalized it.

ENVIRONMENTAL PROTECTION

By increasing our American energy supply and decreasing the long term demand for oil, we will be well positioned to address the challenge of climate change and continue our longstanding responsibility for stewardship over the environment.

 Let's face it: we need to come across as environmentally sensitive. The *mainstream* press already *hates* us, so we can't come out and *say* we don't care about the environment. It just wouldn't be the *"politically correct"* thing to do. This relatively short section is our concession to that reality.

ADDRESSING CLIMATE CHANGE RESPONSIBLY

The same human economic activity that has brought freedom and opportunity to billions has also increased the amount of car-bon in the atmosphere. While the scope and long-term consequences of this are the subject of ongoing scientific research, common sense dictates that the United States should take measured and reasonable steps today to reduce any impact on the environment. Those steps, if consistent with our global competitiveness will also be good for our national security, our energy independence, and our economy. Any policies should be global in nature, based on sound science and technology, and should not harm the economy.

 **Working *"national security"* into this section makes us a little more comfortable. After all, one of our core strategies is *"Defense."* Other than that, we think Al Gore's rhetoric is the real source of global warming. If he'd stop flying around in his private jet and conserve some of his hot air, we'd all be better off ... and we mean that on a *global* basis. Then again, thank God that this particular science course was the only one that apparently ever inspired him. Can you imagine where we'd be if he'd taken an interest in economics?**

The Solution: Technology and the Market

As part of a global climate change strategy, Republicans support technology-driven, market-based solutions that will decrease emissions, reduce excess greenhouse gasses in the atmosphere, increase energy efficiency, mitigate the impact of climate change where it occurs, and maximize any ancillary benefits climate change might offer for the economy.

 **Republicans *also* support *"technology-driven, market-based solutions that will INcrease emissions, PROduce excess greenhouse gasses in the atmosphere, DEcrease energy efficiency, IGNORE the impact of climate change where it occurs"* as long as they *"maximize(s) any ancillary benefits climate change might offer for the economy."***

To reduce emissions in the short run, we will rely upon the power of new technologies, as discussed above, especially zero-emission energy sources such as nuclear and other alternate power sources. But innovation must not be hamstrung by Washington bickering, regulatory briar patches, or obstructionist law-suits. Empowering Washington will only lead to unintended consequences and unimagined economic and environmental pain; instead, we must unleash the power of scientific know-how and competitive markets.

 **We like to advance the cause of nuclear energy because you can also make a few good weapons along the way (just ask North Korea and Iran), and we're all about** *"Defense."*

We also don't think there's really a place for the government to get involved beyond that. Look how far private industry has taken us to date without government intervention. That's why we have a *high-speed rail system* that's the envy of every other nation and our cars are so much more *efficient* than those that were designed in *other* countries.

International Cooperation

Because the issue of climate change is global, it must become a truly global concern as well. All developed and developing economies, particularly India and China, can make significant contributions in dealing with the matter. It would be unrealistic and counterproductive to expect the U.S. to carry burdens which are more appropriately shared by all.

 **We think we should wait until India and China are on board with all this** *"climate change"* **stuff. China has already committed to address the issue as soon as they've become a beacon of leadership in the field of human rights. We think it's reasonable to wait for them to approach this in that order of prioritization.**

Using Cash Rewards to Encourage Innovation

Because Republicans believe that solutions to the risk of global climate change will be found in the ingenuity of the American people, we propose a Climate Prize for scientists who solve the challenges of climate change. Honoraria of many millions of dollars would be a small price for technological developments that eliminate our need for gas-powered cars or abate atmospheric carbon.

 **Initially, we thought the *"Climate Prize"* was a great idea. Now, we have some misgivings. When we took a straw poll, it turned out that the award would likely be given to Barack Obama ... based on the *"promise"* he offered. He apparently gave a speech on *"climate change"* at some point.**

Doing *No Harm*

Republicans caution against the doomsday climate change scenarios peddled by the aficionados of centralized command-and-control government. We can – and should – address the risk of climate change based on sound science without succumbing to the no-growth radicalism that treats climate questions as dogma rather than as situations to be man-aged responsibly.

 **If we're wrong, we're all going to be dead in five years anyway because Al Gore says the world will be under water by then. But we think Al *"massaged"* his numbers, if you know what we mean.**

A robust economy will be essential to dealing with the risk of climate change, and we will insist on reasonable policies that do not force Americans to sacrifice their way of life or trim their hopes and dreams for their children. This perspective serves not only the people of the United States but also the world's poorest peoples, who would suffer terribly if climate change is severe – just as they would if the world economy itself were to be crippled. We must not allow either outcome.

 **Okay ... off the record ... if *"a robust economy will be essential to dealing with the risk of climate change,"* we're in deep trouble. Start *"trim(ing) the hopes and dreams for (your) children"* ... the end is near!**

Continuing Our Stewardship over the Environment

The Republican perspective on the environment is in keeping with our long-standing appreciation for nature and gratitude for the bounty the Almighty has bestowed upon the American people. It was Republican President Theodore Roosevelt who said, "The conservation of natural resources is the fundamental problem. Unless we solve that problem, it will avail us little to solve all others." We agree. Whether through family vacations, hunting or fishing trips, backpacking excursions, or weekend hikes, Americans of all backgrounds share a commitment to protecting the environment and the opportunities it offers. In addition, the public should have access to public lands for recreational activities such as hunting, hiking, and fishing.

Now *this* ... is Americana! *"Hunting, hiking, fishing"* ... well, at least hunting and fishing ... are in *total* alignment with our Republican ideals. We're even willing to quote Teddy Roosevelt because he's viewed as a true outdoorsman. He was also a radical Progressive who we'd rather forget from a Party-affiliation standpoint, but we'll forgive him *this* time.

In caring for the land and water, private ownership has been the best guarantee of conscientious stewardship, while the world's worst instances of environmental degradation have occurred under governmental control. By the same token, it is no accident that the most economically advanced countries also have the strongest environmental protections.

We believe that the *strongest* environmental asset we have is our *bureaucracy*. If an environmental issue knocks on the door of the United States, we'll answer it in an expeditious manner by unleashing the full force of the bureaucracy that we have so diligently, and in a bipartisan manner, worked to establish over the years. Let the record show that we stand fast in our commitment to resolve *any* such challenge ... within a generation or two.

Our national progress toward cleaner air and water has been a major accomplishment of the American people. By balancing environmental goals with economic growth and job creation, our diverse economy has made possible the investment needed to safeguard natural resources, protect endangered species, and create healthier living conditions. State and local initiatives to clean up contaminated sites – brownfields – have exceeded efforts directed by Washington. That progress can continue if grounded in sound science, long-term planning, and a multi-use approach to resources.

"Brownfields" **create jobs, so we're all for them. They help stimulate the economy. If only we could have industry create more contamination without the** *press* **getting wind of it; then, we might have been able to orchestrate a faster economic recovery.**

Government at all levels should protect private property rights by cooperating with landowners' efforts and providing incentives to protect fragile environments, endangered species, and maintain the natural beauty of America. Republican leadership has led to the rejuvenation and renewal of our National Park system. Future expansion of that sys-tem, as well as designation of National Wilderness areas or Historic Districts, should be undertaken only with the active participation and consent of relevant state and local governments and private property owners.

We believe that *"Government ... should protect ... endangered species,"* **and we're working** *hard* **to have the Republican Party** *classified* **as such. If we're protected for a while and allowed to repopulate our territories, we can become relevant again. Trust us on this one!**

HEALTH CARE REFORM: PUTTING PATIENTS FIRST

Americans have the best doctors, the best hospitals, the most innovative medical technology, and the best scientists in the world. Our challenge and opportunity is to build around them the best health care system. Republicans believe the key to real reform is to give control of the health care system to patients and their health care providers, not bureaucrats in government or business.

It's tough to have *"the best doctors, the best hospitals, the most innovative medical technology, and the best scientists in the world"* **and still have a health care system that is too expensive and doesn't provide the quality of care that it should. Of course, we really think that part of it has to do with the fact that we are supporting about 46 million people who don't have any health care insurance. Most of them don't pursue care until their situations are elevated to an** *emergency* **level; the point where the related costs** *skyrocket***. But we can't really emphasize this point because it would be** *"politically incorrect"* **and our Party would be painted as** *"uncaring."* **So, we soft-peddle what we would do to reform health care as you'll see in the rest of this section of our Platform.**

There are reasons why American families and businesses are dissatisfied with the current state of health care:

The Right is Wrong

- Most Americans work longer and harder to pay for health care.
- Dedicated health care providers are changing careers to avoid litigation.
- The need to hold onto health insurance is driving family decisions about where to live and work.
- Many new parents worry about the loss of coverage if they choose to stay at home with their children.
- The need – and the bills – for long-term care are challenging families and government alike.
- American businesses are becoming less competitive in the global marketplace because of insurance costs.
- Some federal programs with no benefit to patients have grown exponentially, adding layers of bureaucracy between patients and their care.

 **Yes, we know. We could address the last point about *"federal programs"* in a heartbeat, but that would be too easy. Besides, there were a lot of favors handed out in return for the votes that were necessary to pass the related legislation, so we don't want to jeopardize politics as usual by having to *unwind* any of those deals.**

It is not enough to offer only increased access to a system that costs too much and does not work for millions of Americans. The Republican goal is more ambitious: Better health care for lower cost.

 **For politicians, trying to provide anything at a *"lower cost"* is a fairly radical idea. Does that make this a radical Republican idea? Can those two words even be *used* together?**

First Principle: Do No Harm

How do we ensure that all Americans have the peace of mind that comes from owning high-quality, comprehensive health cover-age? The first rule of public policy is the same as with medicine: Do no harm.

"Do no harm." **Hey, when you've got a tag line that works, don't tamper with it. Our Party is known for its hard-hitting strategies. This is just *another* one. When we say, *"Do no harm"* … people just *know* that we've really thought things through!**

The American people rejected Democrats' attempted government take-over of health care in 1993, and they remain skeptical of politicians who would send us down that road. Republicans support the private practice of medicine and oppose socialized medicine in the form of a government-run universal health care system. Republicans pledge that as we reform our health care system:

- We will protect citizens against any and all risky restructuring efforts that would complicate or ration health care.
- We will encourage health promotion and disease prevention.
- We will facilitate cooperation, not confrontation, among patients, providers, payers, and all stakeholders in the health care system.
- We will not put government between patients and their health care providers.
- We will not put the system on a path that empowers Washington bureaucrats at the expense of patients.
- We will not raise taxes instead of reducing health care costs.
- We will not replace the current system with the staggering ineffi-ciency, maddening irrationality, and uncontrollable costs of a gov-ernment monopoly.

We think most people would agree: these are *all* good positions to take. Unfortunately, it would have been a whole lot easier to accomplish even

one of them when we had a *majority* in the House and Senate. Now, that we're in the minority ... and by a *substantive* margin ... they're nice talking points, but we haven't got a snowball's chance of achieving *any* of them. However, we're Republicans, so we'll use strong, definitive phrases like *"we will"* and *"we will not"* to emphasize how *powerful* we are ... at least in our own minds.

Radical restructuring of health care would be unwise. We want all Americans to be able to choose the best health care provider, hospital, and health coverage for their needs. We believe that real reform is about improving your access to a health care provider, your control over care, and your ability to afford that care.

 **Of course, we don't mean this literally. If everyone were to choose *"the best health care provider, hospital, and health coverage for their need"* there'd only be one of each: *"the best."* What we *really* meant to say was that you should have a choice; like with an HMO versus a PPO. We just constantly struggle with our rhetoric.**

For example, we come on strong using the term *"radical restructuring of health care"* to imply that the Democrats are *"radical,"* which we deem to be synonymous with *"bad."* That would support the classic *"fear"* tactic of both Parties. But then, we *soften* the tone too quickly. Rather than finishing the sentence with a flourish (*i.e.,* radical restructuring of health care *"would create a cataclysmic disaster of epic proportions"* ... which is what we think), we instead wimp out and say it *"would be unwise."* "Unwise? "UNWISE?" It's like we're too *afraid* that we might offend someone if we dared to make a bold ... and honest ... statement. Then again, we're Republicans ... also known as the *"Party of Restraint."*

We will continue to advocate for simplification of the system and the empowerment of patients. This is in stark contrast to the other party's insistence on putting Washington in charge of patient care, which has blocked any progress on meeting these goals. We offer a detailed program that will improve the quality, cost, and coverage of health care through-out the nation, and we will turn that plan into reality.

 **We'll apologize in advance. Since we really aren't very polished at developing an effective political strategy, we've been relegated to playing the role of the *"Opposition Party."* Over the past several years, we've *forgotten* how to be relevant. However, in an attempt to scratch our way back to the top, we'll occasionally blend in the use of some of the Democrats' rhetoric. It may be confusing at times, but we'll try to explain it as we go.**

PATIENT CONTROL AND PORTABILITY

Republicans believe all Americans should be able to obtain an affordable health care plan, including a health savings account, which meets their needs and the needs of their families.

 **We *"believe all Americans should be able to obtain an affordable health care plan,"* but once again, we did *nothing* about it during the time that we could have made this a reality.**

Families and health care providers are the key to real reform, not lawyers and bureaucrats. To empower families, we must make insurance more affordable and more secure, and give employees the option of owning coverage that is not tied to their job. Patients should not have to worry about losing their insurance. Insurance companies should have to worry about losing patients' business.

 **If there's anything the American public hates more that Republicans, it's *lawyers* and *bureaucrats* … even though many members of *our* political leadership fall into both categories. As long as we**

use these inflammatory terms, we think we can curry some favor. Then, we throw in a pinch of *"empower(ing) families"* while simultaneously castigating insurance companies, and you'd almost think that we were Democrats.

The current tax system discriminates against individuals who do not receive health care from their employers, gives more generous health tax benefits to upper income employees, and fails to provide every American with the ability to purchase an affordable health care plan. Republicans propose to correct inequities in the current tax code that drive up the number of uninsured and to level the playing field so that individuals who choose a health insurance plan in the individual market face no tax penalty. All Americans should receive the same tax benefit as those who are insured through work, whether through a tax credit or other means.

Individuals with pre-existing conditions must be protected; we will help these individuals by building on the experiences of innovative states rather than by creating a new unmanageable federal entitlement. We strongly urge that managed care organizations use the practice patterns and medical treatment guidelines from the state in which the patient lives when making medical coverage decisions.

 **Uniform tax credits and the elimination of pre-existing condition restrictions should have been the case all the time. So,** *please* **don't ask us why we haven't done anything about it even though we had a majority in the House for 12 out of the last 15 years and in the Senate for 8 out of the last 15 years. But, now that we** *can't* **do anything about, we want to** *pretend* **that we can. Maybe we can attract a few of the more moderate members of the** *"oppressed minorities"* **who don't feel all that** *"oppressed"* **and will look past our record of non-performance in favor of our** *promise* **to address these issues going forward. It's worth a shot. After all, they've been conditioned to vote for** *"promise."*

Because the family is our basic unit of society, we fully support parental rights to consent to medical treatment for their children including mental health treatment, drug treatment, alcohol treatment, and treatment involving pregnancy, contraceptives and abortion.

 **Since we're supposed to be the right-wing, conservative party, we had to work something in to indicate our opposition to abortion ... without *really* saying it (so as not to offend our more moderate constituents). We also buffered it by throwing in *"mental health treatment, drug treatment (and) alcohol treatment."***

IMPROVING QUALITY OF CARE AND LOWERING COSTS

While delivering control of health coverage to families and individuals, Republicans will also advance a variety of targeted reforms to improve the quality of care, lower costs, and help Americans – men, women, and children – live longer and healthier lives.

 **Who can argue with this? It's just one more a small step toward mimicking the Democratic strategy. Notice how we promised a lot of *nebulous* things to everyone ... *"men, women, and children"* ... without giving *any* details. *Very* Democratic! Besides, we're tired of seeing how many people fall for this stuff and end up voting for the Democrats. Two can play at this game!**

Prevent Disease and End the "Sick Care" System

Chronic diseases – in many cases, preventable conditions – are driving health care costs, consuming three of every four health care dollars. We can reduce demand for medical care by fostering personal responsibility within a culture of wellness, while increasing access to preventive services, including improved nutrition and breakthrough medications that keep people healthy and out of the hospital. To reduce the incidence of diabetes, cancer, heart disease, and stroke, we call for a national grassroots campaign against obesity, especially among children. We call for continuation of efforts to decrease use of tobacco, especially among the young.

 **Wow! There may be a Nobel Prize in Medicine in this part of our Platform. Create** *"a national grassroots campaign against obesity, especially among children"* **... visionary!** *"Call for continuation of efforts to decrease use of tobacco, especially among the young"* **... astounding! No wonder people view us as the progressive, forward thinking force on America's political landscape.**

A culture of wellness needs to include the treatment of mental health conditions. We believe all Americans should have access to affordable, quality health care, including individuals struggling with mental illness. For this reason, we believe it is important that mental health care be treated equally with physical health care.

 **We have a selfish motive here. We want** *"access to affordable, quality health care (for) individuals struggling with mental illness"* **because we're pretty sure that** *doing so* **would cut into the Democrats' base. Of course, there** *is* **a risk that we would lose some of our Congressional Members to the program, but the Democrats would face the same challenge. You** *have to be* **mentally ill to** *run for public office* **these days!**

<u>Empower Individuals to Make the Best Health Care Choices</u>

Clear information about health care empowers patients. It lets consumers make better decisions about where to spend their health care dollars, thereby fostering competition and lowering costs. Patients must have information to make sound decisions about their health care providers, hospitals, and insurance companies.

 **Providing** *"clear information about health care ... (to help) consumers make better decisions"* **just makes common sense. We thought about extending this same premise to legislative bills, but**

that would open up a *real* can of worms. We're better off continuing the age-old practice of writing legislation that even *we* can't understand. At least it gives us the defense of *"plausible deniability"* when one of our bills *blows up* on us.

Use Health Information Technology to Save Lives

Advances in medical technology are revolutionizing medicine. Information technology is key to early detection and treatment of chronic disease as well as fetal care and health care in rural areas – especially where our growing wireless communications network is available. The simple step of modernizing recordkeeping will mean faster, more accurate treatment, fewer medical errors, and lower costs. Closing the health care information gap can reduce both under-utilization (the diabetic who forgets to refill an insulin prescription) and over-utilization (the patient who endures repetitive tests because providers have not shared test results).

"Information technology is key to early detection and treatment of chronic disease as well as fetal care and health care." Of course, it really only makes sense if the data is centralized, and we'll argue against that as a violation of privacy. But it *sounds* good and makes us seem a bit more *"high-tech."* And we really need to change our image in that regard ever since John McCain stated that he doesn't use e-mail and is just learning how to go online.

Protect Good Health Care Providers from Frivolous Lawsuits

Every patient must have access to legal remedies for malpractice, but meritless lawsuits drive up insurance rates to outrageous levels and ultimately drive up the number of uninsured. Frivolous lawsuits also drive up the cost of health care as health care providers are forced to practice defensive medicine, such as ordering unnecessary tests. Many leave their practices rather than deal with the current system. This emergency demands medical liability reform.

 **We want to pass legislation that would ban "frivolous lawsuits (that) also drive up the cost of health care."** We're thinking of calling it the *John Edwards Act* (not to be confused with the other act that John Edwards is famous for). This is one of our core strengths: kicking someone when they're down ... and in this case, no one will disagree with us!

Reward Good Health Care Providers for Delivering Real Results

Patients deserve access to health care providers they trust who will personalize and coordinate their care to ensure they receive the right treatment with the right health care provider at the right time. Providers should be paid for keeping people well, not for the number of tests they run or procedures they perform. The current cookie-cutter system of reimbursement needs restructuring from the view of the patient, not the accountant or Washington bureaucrat.

 **"Providers should be paid for keeping people well."** That sure sounds good! Of course, it could also potentially encourage Providers to discriminate against those who truly *need* care. We're hoping they'll be very altruistic ... but if *we* were physicians, we'd only treat the healthy so we could *maximize* our profits.

Drive Costs Down With Interstate Competition

A state-regulated national market for health insurance means more competition, more choice, and lower costs. Families – as well as fraternal societies, churches and community groups, and small employers – should be able to purchase policies across state lines. The best practices and lowest prices should be available in every state. We call upon state legislators to carefully consider the cost of medical mandates, and we salute those Republican governors who are leading the way in demonstrating ways to provide affordable health care options.

 **Again, this makes sense, and we could have pushed for it when we had control of Congress. It was just easier to continue to *"party hardy"* and enjoy the perks of our majorities in the House and the Senate rather than *do* anything constructive during those years.**

Modernize Long-Term Care Options for All

The financial burdens and emotional challenges of ensuring adequate care for elderly family members affect every American, especially with today's aging population. We must develop new ways to support individuals, not just institutions, so that older Americans can have a real choice whether to stay in their homes. This is true not only with regard to Medicaid, where we spend $100 billion annually on long-term care, but also for those who do not qualify for that assistance.

 **It wasn't until recently that we started to pay attention to the elderly. Someone mentioned that the country was about to experience a significant demographic shift because of the aging of the Baby Boomers. We've never done particularly well among the elderly because those darn Democrats got them to believe that they were an *"oppressed minority"* ... and AARP predominantly supported the Liberal agenda.**

We'd like to give special thanks to Barrack Obama, Nancy Pelosi, Harry Reid, *et al.*, who have done what *we* couldn't do on our own: *scare* the aging population enough to make them actually pay attention. While it's led to a bit of a splinter group (the Tea Party), at least they're finally starting to understand what we've been trying to tell them. We'll try to capitalize on this as much as possible going forward.

Encourage Primary Care as a Specialty

We believe in the importance of primary care specialties and supporting the physician's role in the evaluation and management of disease. We also encourage practice in rural and underserved areas of America.

 **We also think everyone should have drinking water. Oops! Sorry about that. We just got on a roll in stating the obvious. What were we *going* to say? It's not like we can say** *"We don't believe in the importance of primary care specialties, and we think auto mechanics can do the evaluation and management of disease ... and we think people who choose to live in rural and underserved areas of America should just be on their own."* **We needed to state the obvious; particularly since rural populations tend to vote overwhelmingly Republican.**

FUNDING MEDICAL RESEARCH

We support federal investment in basic and applied biomedical research. This commitment will maintain America's global competitiveness, advance innovative science that can lead to medical breakthroughs, and turn the tide against diseases affecting millions of Americans – diseases that account for the majority of our health care costs. The United States leads in this research, as evidenced by our growing biotechnology industry, but foreign competition is increasing. One way government can help preserve the promise of American innovation is to ensure that our intellectual property laws remain robust.

Federal research dollars should be spent as though lives are at stake – because, in fact, they are. Research protocols must consider the special needs of formerly neglected groups if we are to make significant progress against breast and prostate cancer, diabetes, and other killers.

Taxpayer-funded medical research must be based on sound science, with a focus on both prevention and treatment, and in accordance with the humane ethics of the Hippocratic Oath. In that regard, we call for a major expansion of support for the stem-cell research that now shows amazing promise and offers the greatest hope for scores of diseases – with adult stem cells, umbilical cord blood, and cells reprogrammed into pluripotent stem cells – without the destruction of embryonic human life. We call for a ban on human cloning and a ban on the creation of or experimentation on human embryos for research purposes.

We've been portrayed as being *against* medical research. We're not. However, to protect our right-wing, conservative base, we occasionally have to take an overzealous stand *against* things like stem-cell research. It's because, as we've already admitted, we're just not very good at developing and executing political strategies. As a result, we latch onto any *fear-based* theory that we can if it will help us retain our base. The stem-cell issue is just an example.

We really don't think some nut case is going to secretly clone an army of ruthless mercenaries to take over the world. Besides, we saw the movie, and we *win* in the end. No, our opposition is tied to the abortion issue. The *"Sanctity of Life"* card is a little like the *"Race"* card; you can't pick it back up once you've played it.

We believe medicines and treatments should be designed to prolong and enhance life, not destroy it. Therefore, federal funds should not be used for drugs that cause the destruction of human life. Furthermore, the Drug Enforcement Administration ban on use of controlled substances for physician-assisted suicide should be restored.

Now, if we could be assured that testing would be limited to *laboratory rats*, *attorneys* and *Democratic candidates*, we just *might* reconsider. Otherwise, we're against spending Federal money to test drugs for the purpose of committing an act that is illegal under current law. Don't ever say that *we're* not willing to go out on a limb!

PROTECTING RIGHTS OF CONSCIENCE

The health care profession can be both a profession and a calling. No health care professional – doctor, nurse, or pharmacist – or organization should ever be required to perform, provide for, or refer for a health care service against their conscience for any reason. This is especially true of the religious organizations which deliver a major portion of America's health care, a service rooted in the charity of faith communities.

 **Okay. Most of you will see that this is another veiled reference to the abortion issue. *"No health care professional – doctor, nurse, or pharmacist – or organization should ever be required to perform, provide for, or refer for a health care service against their conscience for any reason."* Now, if we can just get enough of them to *refuse treatment* to *registered Democrats* on similar grounds, what a wonderful world it would be.**

MEDICARE

We support the provision of quality and accessible health care options for our nation's seniors and disabled individuals and recognize that in order to meet this goal we must confront the special challenges posed by the growth of Medicare costs. Its projected growth is out of control and threatens to squeeze out other pro-grams, while funding constraints lead to restricted access to treatment for many seniors. There are solutions. Medicare can be a leader for the rest of our health care system by encouraging treatment of the whole patient. Specifically, we should compensate doctors who coordinate care, especially for those with multiple chronic conditions, and eliminate waste and inefficiency. Medicare patients must have more control of their care and choice regarding their doctors, and the benefits of competition must be delivered to the patients themselves if Medicare is to provide quality health care. And Medicare patients must be free to add their own funds, if they choose, to any government benefits, to be assured of unrationed care.

 It's too late now, but we should have worked veterans into the mix with *"our nation's seniors and disabled individuals."* Sure, they're not a direct fit with the Medicare's defined coverage, but older vets are certainly involved ... and they're a huge part of our base. We should try to get as much mileage out of them as we can ... just like the Democrats do with each of their *"oppressed minorities."*

And pay no attention to the fact that we now state, *"we should compensate doctors who coordinate care, especially for those with multiple chronic conditions,"* even though we previously said, *"Providers should be paid for keeping people well."* We can't reconcile the two positions either.

Finally, because it is isolated from the free market forces that encourage innovation, competition, affordability, and expansion of options, Medicare is especially susceptible to fraud and abuse. The program loses tens of billions of dollars annually in erroneous and fraudulent payments. We are determined to root out the fraud and eliminate this assault on the taxpayer.

 *"Medicare is especially susceptible to fraud and abuse ... the program loses tens of billions of dollars annually ... (and) ... we are determined to root out the fraud and eliminate this assault on the taxpayer."* And, by golly, we *mean* it! After all, Medicare was passed in 1965, so it's taken us a little time to get our arms around it; but now, we recognize that it has flaws.

MEDICAID

Our Medicaid obligations will consume $5 trillion over the next ten years. Medicaid now accounts for 20-25 percent of state budgets and threatens to overwhelm state governments for the indefinite future. We can do better while spending less. A first step is to give Medicaid recipients more health care options. Several states have allowed beneficiaries to buy regular health insurance with their Medicaid dollars. This removes the Medicaid "stamp" from people's foreheads, provides beneficiaries with better access to doctors, and saves taxpayers' money. We must ensure that taxpayer money is focused on caring for U.S. citizens and other individuals in our country legally.

 **The truth is … it's getting to the point where health care providers won't accept Medicaid patients. They** *can't***. They'll go bankrupt because the payments approved by Medicaid are so misaligned with reality that no** *rational* **physician can build a practice treating the patients it covers.**

BUILDING A HEALTH CARE SYSTEM FOR FUTURE EMERGENCIES

To protect the American people from the threats we face in the century ahead, we must develop and stockpile medicines and vaccines so we can deliver them where urgently needed. Our health care infra-structure must have the surge capacity to handle large numbers of patients in times of crisis, whether it is a repeat of Hurricane Katrina, a flu pandemic, or a bioterror attack on multiple cities. Republicans will ensure that this infrastructure, including the needed communications capacity, is closely integrated into our homeland security needs.

 **This can create an economic** *boom* **for some of the major pharmaceutical companies that have traditionally contributed to our campaigns. Think about it. Stockpiles of medicines that** *may* **or** *may not* **ever be used; medicines that probably have an expiration date as well. Get the picture? Worst case: the pharmaceutical companies appreciate the windfall profits they derive from manufacturing drugs for a non-existing need. Best case: we get to do the equivalent of a little inside trading by adding their stocks to our portfolios before the government-ordered stockpile significantly impacts their profits. Don't act like you're** *shocked***. How do you think so many of your Congressmen on both sides of the aisle have become multi-millionaires**

while serving in an office that only pays about $150 thousand a year? You can't always make *big* money in PAC payoffs alone!

EDUCATION MEANS A MORE COMPETITIVE AMERICA

Education is a parental right, a state and local responsibility, and a national strategic interest.

Maintaining America's preeminence requires a world-class system of education, with high standards, in which all students can reach their potential. That requires considerable improvement over our current 70 percent high school graduation rate and six-year graduation rate of only 57 percent for colleges.

 *"Our current 70 percent high school graduation rate and six-year graduation rate of only 57 percent for colleges"* **are indictments of our society as well as our educational system. It's just so politically dangerous to do anything that might be considered to be *"politically incorrect."* We've acquiesced to a society in which *all* children must *"pass"* ... lest we scar them for life. As a result, we have fostered a system that generates *embarrassing* result such as these and future generations that will struggle to compete in a global economy. The sense of entitlement of the most recent generations is *staggeringly* disproportionate to their demonstrated ability to contribute. It's almost the equivalent of *our* misplaced sense of entitlement on the Hill.**

Education is essential to competitiveness, but it is more than just training for the work force of the future. It is through education that we ensure the transmission of a culture, a set of values we hold in common. It has prepared generations for responsible citizenship in a free society, and it must continue to do so. Our party is committed to restoring the civic mission of schools envisioned by the founders of the American public school system. Civic education, both in the classroom and through service learning, should be a cornerstone of American public education and should be central to future school reform efforts.

"The civic mission of schools envisioned by the founders of the American public school system" **went out the window when we capitulated to the concept of** *"political correctness."* **We probably should have addressed this in the health care section of our Platform by mandating a restoration of the Congressional body parts that have been removed by the concept of** *"political correctness"* **and have, in effect, rendered us all ...** *political geldings.*

PRINCIPLES FOR ELEMENTARY AND SECONDARY EDUCATION

All children should have access to an excellent education that empowers them to secure their own freedom and contribute to the betterment of our society. We reaffirm the principles that have been the foundation of the nation's educational progress toward that goal: accountability for student academic achievement; periodic testing on the fundamentals of learning, especially math and reading, history and geography; transparency, so parents and the general public know which schools best serve their students; and flexibility and freedom to innovate so schools and districts can best meet the needs of their students.

Of course, this basically reflects what has *failed* **in the past. But we are** *comfortable* **with the past. We are** *"The Party of the Past"* **... which might also explain the present minority we enjoy in the House and the Senate. Come to think of it, that might be a whole new strategy for us. If we can convince people that we are politically**

"oppressed" **under our current circumstance, we will have become an** ***"oppressed minority,"*** **and the Democrats will have no other recourse than to support us.**

We advocate policies and methods that are proven and effective: building on the basics, especially phonics; ending social promotion; merit pay for good teachers; classroom discipline; parental involvement; and strong leadership by principals. We reject a one-size-fits-all approach and support parental options, including home schooling, and local innovations such as schools or classes for boys only or for girls only and alternative and innovative school schedules. We recognize and appreciate the importance of innovative education environments, particularly homeschooling, for stimulating academic achievement. We oppose over-reaching judicial decisions which deny children access to such environments. We support state efforts to build coordination between elementary and secondary education and higher education such as K-16 councils and dual credit programs.

"We ... support parental options, including home schooling, and local innovations such as schools or classes for boys only or for girls only and alternative and innovative school schedules." **The only weakness in our premise is that the current generation of parents actually** *cares.* **Sure, there are parents that care enough to attend an occasional PTA or parent-teacher meeting, and a small minority that are actually willing to assume the challenges associated with home schooling their children, but by and large, a significant percentage of parents have** *abdicated* **their responsibilities in this regard because of the impact that such** *involvement* **would have on their** *social* **lives. They connect with their children more through the social networks that form as the result of extra-curricular activities like soccer, T-ball, marching band and drill team ... activities that have a more pronounced element of adult interaction on the sidelines and partying after the event ... because, after all,** *they* **deserve to have fun too! And if we really understood where the potential collision between parenting and technology exists, we**

might even envision a day when the parent-child relationship is maintained through Twitter.

To ensure that all students will have access to the mainstream of American life, we support the English First approach and oppose divisive programs that limit students' future potential. All students must be literate in English, our common language, to participate in the promise of America.

We think it's tough to argue with requiring that *all* students to learn English. Of course, we predominantly reside in Washington, D.C. where English is still spoken. If our Nation's Capitol were to be relocated to Miami, Florida, or Los Angeles, California, we might have second thoughts. And if *"Sanctuary Cities"* **continue to gain favorable treatment as compared to archaic border States that try to enforce Federal Immigration Law, we might have to completely revisit our position.**

Early Childhood Education

The family is the most powerful influence on a child's ability to succeed. As such, parents are our children's first and foremost teachers. We support family literacy, which improves the literacy, language, and life skills of both parents and children along with the continued improvement of early childhood programs, such as Head Start, from low-income families. We reaffirm our support for the child care tax credit that helps parents choose the care best for their family.

We believe that *"the family is the most powerful influence on a child's ability to succeed."* **We also** *"reaffirm our support for the child care tax credit that helps parents choose the care best for their family."* **So, basically, we think that the family can *best* exert its influence through a third-party ... rather than accepting parental responsibility and scaling back its lifestyle to permit a single income environment or more balanced time with the child.**

Even though we're the self-professed *"Party of the Past,"* we're too afraid to suggest a shift back to the paradigm of *true* parental responsibility. It would be just too much of a threat to our ability to sustain our *"political correctness"* ... even if we legitimately don't mean this in a way that reinforces old sexual stereotypes but rather in a way that just emphasizes that parents should be more involved in their children's lives and make an occasional sacrifice if it would contribute to their child's development in a meaningful way.

<u>Giving Students the Best Teachers</u>

For students to meet world class standards, they must have access to world class teachers, whether in person or through virtual public schools that can bring high-quality instruction into the classroom. School districts must have the authority to recruit, reward, and retain the best and brightest teachers, and principals must have the authority to select and assign teachers without regard to collective bargaining agreements. Because qualified teachers are often not available through traditional routes, we support local efforts to create an adjunct teacher corps of experts from higher education, business, and the military to fill in when needed.

What we'd really like to say is: if you want to attract the bees that can pollinate the minds of our youth, you need to use honey; if you just want to attract flies ..." well, you *know* what attracts flies ... and that's how we view the impact the teacher's union has had on our educational system. It has sacrificed excellence for its ability to broaden the base of mediocrity. Our problem, once again, is our own political ineptness when it comes to communicating this reality to the general public. The unions jump in and *out-spend* us and *out-market* us ... and we lose the elections and ballot issues that could otherwise make a difference.

Teachers must be protected against frivolous litigation and should be able to take reasonable actions to maintain discipline and order in the classroom. We encourage the private-public partnerships and mentoring that can make classroom time more meaningful to students by integrating it with learning beyond school walls. These efforts are crucial to lowering the dropout rate and helping at-risk students realize their potential.

"Teachers must be protected against frivolous litigation and should be able to take reasonable actions to maintain discipline and order in the classroom." **Heck, we're all for corporal punishment. We might even consider applying the death penalty to students who get out of hand.** *"Spare the rod, and spoil the child!"* **There's nothing quite like a good** *"beat down"* **to teach a child a lesson.**

We encourage state efforts to ensure that personnel who interact with children pass thorough background checks and are held to the highest standards of conduct.

This is an area in which we are *really* **firm. We don't think child sex offenders should be allowed to teach elementary and junior high students; high school students ... maybe. And who cares about college students. They're young adults and have to learn to take care of themselves at some point.**

Just don't expect us to be quite as enthusiastic about extending background checks to our *own* **political appointees. We have a hard enough time finding people who want to work with us. If we started screening people, there might not be enough candidates to fill all the useless positions we've created.**

Partnerships between schools and businesses can be especially important in STEM subjects: science, technology, engineering and math. The need to improve secondary education in those fields can be measured by the number of remedial courses now offered at the college level. Our country's reliance upon foreign talent in those areas begins with insufficient emphasis upon them in the high school years. We applaud those who are changing that situation by giving young people real-world experience in the private sector and by providing students with rigorous technical and academic courses that give students the skills and knowledge necessary to be productive members in a competitive American work-force.

We're all in favor of *"STEM subjects: science, technology, engineering and math"* **... as long as they don't lead to** *stem***-cell research. As for our country's** *"reliance upon foreign talent in those areas,"* **it's not like those foreign countries offer greater education opportunities than ours does. We've** *tried* **to figure it out by talking with the** *foreign* **students** *and* **their parents in** *their* **homes ... and by trying to do the same with the biological and multiple step-parents of** *our* **students ... when and where we were** *able* **to find them. We just don't understand the difference. So, we're counting on business, one of our favorite constituencies, to step up and fill the void.**

<u>Asserting Family Rights in Schooling</u>

Parents should be able to decide the learning environment that is best for their child. We support choice in education for all families, especially those with children trapped in dangerous and failing schools, whether through charter schools, vouchers or tax credits for attending faith-based or other non-public schools, or the option of home schooling. We call for the vigilant enforcement of laws designed to protect family rights and privacy in education. We will energetically assert the right of students to engage in voluntary prayer in schools and to have equal access to school facilities for religious purposes. We renew our call for replacing "family planning" programs for teens with increased funding for abstinence education, which teaches abstinence until marriage as the responsible and expected standard of behavior. Abstinence from sexual activity is the only protection that is 100 percent effective against out-of-wedlock pregnancies and sexually transmitted diseases, including HIV/AIDS when transmitted sexually. We oppose school-based clinics that provide referrals, counseling, and related services for abortion and contraception. Schools should not ask children to answer offensive or intrusive personal non-academic questionnaires without parental consent. It is not the role of the teacher or school administration to recommend or require the use of psychotropic medications that must be prescribed by a physician.

 **This area reflects our core values as Republicans. Once again, execution may be another matter.**

"We will energetically assert the right of students to engage in voluntary prayer in schools." We just keep losing the court battles to the ACLU and Federal judges who like to make up law on the fly.

"We renew our call for replacing 'family planning' programs for teens with increased funding for abstinence education." To do this, we know we have to "speak" to teens through the channels to which they listen. In this regard, we've asked Two Live Crew **to write and perform a rap song that expresses the sensitivity of "young love" and the value of abstinence.**

And when it comes to the use of "psychotropic medications," we think that children should be protected against being subjected to an induced state of passive conformance. We firmly believe that the use of such drugs for this purpose should be strictly **reserved for the treatment of the elderly in our nursing homes.**

Reviewing the Federal Role in Primary and Secondary Education

Although the Constitution assigns the federal government no role in local education, Washington's authority over the nation's schools has increased dramatically. In less than a decade, annual federal funding has shot up 41 percent to almost $25 billion, while the regulatory burden on state and local governments has risen by about 6.7 million hours – and added $141 million in costs – during that time. We call for a review of Department of Education programs and administration to identify and eliminate ineffective programs, to respect the role of states, and to better meet state needs.

 **It is an absolute travesty that** *"Washington's authority over the nation's schools has increased dramatically ... in less than a decade."* **This usurpation of power by the Federal government must be stopped! We ask only that you ignore that our figures show how bad the situation has become** *"in less than a decade"* **since** *we* **held a majority in the Senate for 4 of the last 10 years, a majority in the House for 6 of the last 10 years, as well as holding the Presidency for 8 of the past 10 years. We'd still like you to believe that it's been** *strictly* **the Democrats'** *fault* **... well, because that's what the Democrats do!**

To get our schools back to the basics of learning, we support initiatives to block-grant more Department of Education funding to the states, with requirements for state-level standards, assessments, and public reporting to ensure transparency. Local educators must be free to end ineffective programs and reallocate resources where they are most needed.

 **Notice that in the prior paragraph we railed against how** *"in less than a decade ... annual federal funding (for education) has shot up 41 percent to almost $25 billion."* **Notice also how we now** *"support initiatives to block-grant more Department of Education funding to the states."* **Try not to get upset with us!**

<u>Maintaining our Commitment to IDEA</u>

Because a federal mandate on the states must include the promised federal funding, we will fulfill the promise of the Individuals with Disabilities Education Act to cover 40 percent of the costs incurred because of that legislation. We urge preventive efforts in early childhood, especially assistance in gaining pre-reading skills, to help many youngsters move beyond the need for IDEA's protections.

 **Okay, so we're committing to spend Federal dollars on yet *another* educational program. You've got to admit, it's hard to argue with this one. This is an example of how we occasionally extend a hand to an *"oppressed minority"* because we do, in fact, have a heart ... one every bit as strong as Dick Cheney's.**

HIGHER EDUCATION

Our country's system of higher education – public and private, secular and religious, large and small institutions – is unique for its excellence, its diversity, and its accessibility. Learning is a safe-guard of liberty. Post-secondary education not only increases the earnings of individuals but advances economic development. Our colleges and universities drive much of the research that keeps America competitive. We must ensure that our higher education system meet the needs of the 21st century student and economy and remain innovative and accessible.

Meeting College Costs

Students and their parents face formidable challenges in planning for college as costs continue to outpace inflation. Higher education seems immune from market controls and the law of supply and demand. We commend those institutions which are directing a greater proportion of their endowment revenues toward tuition relief.

The Republican vision for expanding access to higher education has led to two major advances, Education Savings Accounts and Section 529 accounts, by which millions of families now save for college. While federal student loans and grants have opened doors to learning for untold numbers of low-and middle-income students, the overall financial aid system, with its daunting forms and confused rationales, is nothing less than Byzantine. It must be simplified. We call for a presidential commission to undertake that task and to review the role of government regulations and policies in the tuition spiral. We affirm our support for the public-private partnership that now offers students and their families a vibrant marketplace in selecting their student loan provider.

 Even though the system of *"federal student loans and grants"* is *"Byzantine"* in its complexity, *"we call for a presidential commission to undertake that task and to review the role of government regulations and policies in the tuition spiral."* Who knows why we think a *"presidential commission,"* comprised of the *same* type of people who have put the *"government regulations and policies"* in place, have any *hope* of resolving the issue. But at least it creates an *illusion* that our expressed concern is real.

<u>Innovation Will Lead to Lifelong Learning</u>

The challenge to American higher education is to make sure students can access education in whatever forms they want. As mobility increases in all aspects of American life, student mobility, from school to school and from campus to campus, will require new approaches to admissions, evaluations, and credentialing. Distance learning propelled by an expanding telecommunications sector and especially broadband, is certain to grow in importance – whether through public or private institutions – and federal law should not discriminate against the latter. Lifelong learning will continue to transform the demographics of higher education, bringing older students and real-world experience to campus.

 We have to concede that technology will have an impact on learning … even though we continue to run candidates who admitted can't even use e-mail. We also think that the *"demographics of higher education"* will continue to shift; *"bringing older students"* onto the campus … but not really because of *"lifelong learning"* … but rather because students are taking a lot more than four *years* to graduate these days.

Community Colleges Continue to Play a Crucial Role

Community colleges are central to the future of higher education, especially as they build bridges between the world of work and the classroom. Many of our returning veterans find community colleges to be welcoming environments where they can develop specific skills for use in the civilian workforce. As the first responders to economic development and retraining of workers, these schools fulfill our national commitment of an affordable and readily accessible education for all.

Finally ... a chance to work one of our constituencies into our Platform! While the Democrats are skilled at working their *"oppressed minorities"* **into virtually every element of their Platform, *we* struggle to even occasionally cite one of our constituencies (veterans in this case). Better late than never!**

Another point we failed to make is that community colleges are going to become increasing important as tuition continues to spiral out of control while our *"presidential committee"* **tries to figure out why that's happening and how to stop it. Community colleges *also* have lower entrance requirements, and with the direction our secondary education programs are going, that's going to become increasingly important.**

Special Challenges in Higher Education

Free speech on college campuses is to be celebrated, but there should be no place in academia for anti-Semitism or racism of any kind. We oppose the hiring, firing, tenure, and promotion practices at universities that discriminate on the basis of political or ideological belief. When federal taxes are used to support such practices, it is inexcusable. We affirm the right of students and faculty to express their views in the face of the leftist dogmatism that dominates many institutions. To preserve the integrity and independence of the nation's colleges, we will continue to ensure alternatives to ideological accrediting systems.

 **This is a highly entertaining area of the debate. Our Democratic colleagues support *"free speech"* as long as the content is *liberal*. *We* support it as long as the content is *conservative*.** Unfortunately, most academicians seem to have a distinctly liberal bias. As a result, they influence college students to *"lean to the left"* in a rather pronounced manner. As a result, these same students tend to support the Democratic agenda ... at least until they graduate, get a real job, and start paying taxes. Then, we've got a shot at converting them.

Because some of the nation's leading universities create or tolerate a hostile atmosphere toward the ROTC, we will rigorously enforce the provision of law, unanimously upheld by the Supreme Court, which denies those institutions federal research grants unless their military students have the full rights and privileges of other students. That must include the right to engage in ROTC activities on their own campus, rather than being segregated elsewhere.

 **"Just to be clear: we're talking about the Reserve Officer's Training Corp as opposed to the *Republican Organization's Training Corp* ... although we feel that the same treatment should be afforded to the latter.**

PROTECTING OUR FAMILIES

Republicans remain the party of vigorous action against crime and the party that empowers the law-abiding by protecting their right to keep and bear arms for self-protection. Our national experience over the past twenty years has shown that vigilance, tough yet fair prosecutors, meaningful sentences, protection of victims' rights, and limits on judicial discretion protect the innocent by keeping criminals off the streets.

Now, we're coming into the home stretch. This is part of our big finish: *"Protecting Our Families."* It's so core to our being the defenders of *"truth, justice, and the American way"* that you can almost see us standing with our hands on our hips, looking skyward in our Superman outfits.

We are the Party of *"Law and Order."* Like we've said before, we even ran one of the series stars as a presidential candidate. That's how *serious* we are about it! Between protecting the Second Amendment and prosecuting and incarcerating criminals, you've pretty much got everything we believe in ... except for defending our Nation by invading other countries on occasion.

STOPPING ONLINE CHILD PREDATORS AND ENDING CHILD PORNOGRAPHY

The Internet must be made safe for children. That's why Republicans have led efforts to increase the funding necessary to track down and jail online predators through the Adam Walsh Act. We commit to do whatever it takes, using all the tools of innovative technology, to thwart those who would prey upon our children. We call on service providers to exercise due care to ensure that the Internet cannot become a safe haven for criminals.

 **While we don't necessarily understand the Internet, we know that predators lurk within it. And wherever there are predators, you'll find Republicans in the wings ... waiting to capture, prosecute and incarcerate them. Did we mention that we're the Party of "*Law and Order?*"**

Child pornography is a hideous form of child abuse. Those who produce it – and those who traffic in it – must be punished to the maximum extent of the law. Because it is an international problem, the Executive branch must carry the fight overseas to where the molesters perpetrate their evil. Congress should expand the range of companies required to report the existence of child pornography, and we congratulate the social networking sites that agree to bar known sex offenders from participation.

 **"*Child pornography is a hideous form of child abuse ... and we congratulate the social networking sites that agree to bar known sex offenders from participation.*" If only we could get *political* figures to leave children alone ... or, at least, get 49 year old Presidents to abstain from trying to convince starry-eyed, 21 year old staffers that oral sex is biblically sanctioned in Genesis 38: 8-10 and does not constitute adultery as defined by Black's Law Dictionary. Then again, that's just a *"liberal"* interpretation of what *"is"* is.**

INTERNET GAMBLING

Millions of Americans suffer from problem or pathological gambling that can destroy families. We support the law prohibiting gambling over the Internet.

 Internet gambling is apparently a *"biggie"* with us. We were going to form a committee and hold a hearing in Las Vegas on the matter when the economy went south. We've put that idea on hold until either the economy recovers or one of us wins the Mega Millions / Powerball Lottery that we all play together. If and when either of these occurs, you can *bet* that we'll go after gambling on the Internet.

RIDDING THE NATION OF CRIMINAL STREET GANGS

Gang violence is a growing problem, not only in urban areas but in many suburbs and rural communities. It has escalated with the rise of gangs composed largely of illegal aliens, most of whose victims are law-abiding members of immigrant communities. We call for stronger enforcement and determined prosecution of gang conspiracies. Illegal alien gang members must be removed from the United States immediately upon arrest or after the completion of any sentence imposed. Aliens convicted of crimes that render them removable from the United States must be removed as soon as possible after the completion of their sentences through the immediate transfer of their custody to Immigration and Customs Enforcement.

 Have we mentioned that we're the Party of *"Law and Order?"* This is a two-for-one opportunity for us since we tie *"gang violence"* to *"illegal aliens."*

Forget the fact that *some* gang violence has *nothing* to do with illegal aliens. The connection is sure to strike *fear* in the hearts of our constituents, which can be leveraged into votes.

True to form, we missed another opportunity. When we said, *"Aliens convicted of crimes that render them removable from the United States must be removed as soon as possible after the completion of their sentences through the immediate transfer of their custody to Immigration and Customs Enforcement,"* it never really occurred to us that entering the country illegally *is* a federal crime subject to deportation.

LOCKING UP CRIMINALS

Criminals behind bars cannot harm the general public. To that end:
- We support mandatory sentencing provisions for gang conspiracy crimes, violent or sexual offenses against children, rape, and assaults resulting in serious bodily injury.
- Gang rape, child rape, and rape committed in the course of another felony deserve, at the least, mandatory life imprisonment.
- We oppose the granting of parole to dangerous or repeat felons.
- Courts must have the option of imposing the death penalty in capital murder cases and other instances of heinous crime, while federal review of those sentences should be streamlined to focus on claims of innocence and to prevent delaying tactics by defense attorneys.
- We encourage the use of advanced technology to monitor nonviolent criminals.

"Criminals behind bars cannot harm the general public." Correspondingly, *dead* criminals *"cannot harm the general public"* either. Our *real* preference would be to issue an order to *"shoot to kill"* in the event of a violent crime. It saves a lot of time and money, and we have a special affinity for the Wild West *"feel"* it brings to the table.

REFORMING PRISONS AND SERVING FAMILIES

Public authorities at all levels must cooperate to regain control of the nation's correctional institutions. It is unacceptable that prison officers should live in fear of the inmates they guard. Similarly, persons jailed for whatever cause should be protected against cruel or degrading treatment by other inmates. We cannot allow correctional facilities to become ethnic or racial battlegrounds.

 What we'd really like to say is that *"prisons should be prisons,"* but we're too afraid of the consequences of being *"politically incorrect."* However, we did slip in one subtle preference. Did you notice that we said, *"persons jailed for whatever cause should be protected against cruel or degrading treatment by other inmates?"* We *didn't* say they *"should be protected against cruel or degrading treatment by prison personnel."* Heck, we support water boarding and think it should be extended to our Federal prison protocols.

Breaking the cycle of crime begins with the children of those who are incarcerated. Deprived of a parent through no fault of their own, these youngsters should be a special concern of our schools, social services, and religious institutions. Government at all levels should work with faith-based institutions that have proven track records in diverting young and first offenders from criminal careers through Second Chance and similar programs. Individuals, including juveniles, who are repeat offenders or who commit serious crimes need to be prosecuted and punished.

 In the old days, families and churches were more naturally inclined to become involved in *"breaking the cycle of crime"* within families. Now, society has shifted to the degree that we think we need to *legislate* it. As for the *"Second Chance"* program, we think it has merit. Of course, if you blow the second chance, we think a public flogging and prolonged incarceration might be in order. And you know where we stand with respect to a *"third strike."* As Frank Sinatra once crooned, *"That's life ... "*

PROTECTING LAW ENFORCEMENT OFFICERS

In solidarity with those who protect us, we call for mandatory prison time for all assaults involving bodily injury to law enforcement officers. Reviews of death sentences imposed for murdering a police officer should be expedited, and a retrial of the penalty Phase of the killer's trial should be allowed in the absence of a unanimous verdict. We support the right of off-duty and retired officers to carry firearms. Criminals should be barred from seeking monetary damages for injuries they incur while committing a crime.

 Truth be told, we really would rather allow the police to have a little more *"latitude"* in resolving these issues privately. If a few *less* violent criminals who have attacked or killed police officers make it into the criminal justice system, what's the harm?

IMPROVING LAW ENFORCEMENT

In recent years, many federal resources for law enforcement have been shifted to the fight against terror. To compensate for that loss of manpower – and with the significant increase in cybercrime, identity theft, and human trafficking – several thousand new FBI agents, U.S. marshals, immigration officers, and Border Patrol agents are needed.

 Our call for *"several thousand new FBI agents, U.S. marshals, immigration officers, and Border Patrol agents"* plays to our *"Law and Order"* constituents. Hopefully, we've created a little *fear* as well by referencing *"the significant increase in cybercrime, identity theft, and human trafficking."*

CONTINUING THE FIGHT AGAINST ILLEGAL DRUGS

The human toll of drug addiction and abuse hits all segments of American society. It is an international problem as well, with most of the narcotics in this country coming from beyond our borders. We will continue the fight against producers, traffickers, and distributors of illegal substances through the collaboration of state, federal, and local law enforcement. We support the work of those who help individuals struggling with addiction, and we support strengthening drug education and prevention programs to avoid addiction. We endorse state and local initiatives, such as Drug Courts, that are trying new approaches to curbing drug abuse and diverting first-time offenders to rehabilitation.

 Back in the '80s, Nancy Reagan came up with the phrase *"Just Say No To Drugs."* We were *hoping* that would take care of the issue, but it seems that the Drug Cartels weren't destroyed by the slogan and that people are still *"using."* So, we know that we need to do more, which plays right into our hope of expanding law enforcement.

Additionally, while we say that *"we support the work of those who help individuals struggling with addiction, and we support strengthening drug education and prevention programs to avoid addiction"* ... just like the Democrats ... the difference is that *we* think the programs should be administered from *inside* our prison system.

PROTECTING THE VICTIMS OF CRIME

Twenty-six years ago, President Reagan's Task Force on Victims of Crime, calling the neglect of crime victims a "national disgrace," proposed a constitutional amendment to secure their formal rights. Today, that disgrace persists in court-rooms across the nation. Innocent victims – battered women, abused children, the loved ones of the murdered – still may not be told when their case is being heard.

They can be excluded from the courtroom even when the defendant and his friends may be present. They have no right to a speedy trial, and a judge or parole board has no obligation to consider their personal safety in making release decisions. In short, the innocent have far fewer rights than the accused. We call on Congress to correct this imbalance by sending to the states for ratification a constitutional amendment to protect the rights of crime victims. In addition, crime victims should be assured of access to legal and social services, and the Crime Victims Fund established under President Reagan should be used solely for that purpose.

 Once again, it's been more that twenty years since President Reagan held office, and we *still* haven't done anything to effectively address victims' rights. As it stands today, *"the innocent (still) have far fewer rights than the accused."* Because we're equally culpable, our best shot is to make it sound like it's been bleeding-heart liberals who have gotten in the way. One thing is for sure: the *"disgrace persists."*

SECURING OUR CIVIL LIBERTIES

Because our Constitution is based on the principles of individual liberty and limited government, we must always ensure that law enforcement respects the civil and constitutional rights of the people. While we wage war on terrorism in foreign lands, it is sometimes necessary for intelligence agencies and law enforcement officials to pursue terrorist threats at home. However, no expansion of governmental powers should occur at the expense of our constitutional liberties.

 When we say that *"no expansion of governmental powers should occur at the expense of our constitutional liberties"* in the case of terrorism, we mean exact that: no expansion of governmental powers should occur at the expense of *OUR* constitutional liberties. When it comes to terrorists, we preferred to believe that *THEY* don't have any constitutional liberties, and we've got a long board and some water that say we're right!

RENEWING NEIGHBORHOODS, BUILDING COMMUNITIES

The two most effective forces in reducing crime and other social ills are strong families and caring communities. Both reinforce constructive conduct and ethical standards by setting examples and providing safe havens from dangerous and destructive behaviors. Given the weight of social science evidence concerning the crucial role played by the traditional family in setting a child's future course, we urge a thoughtful review of governmental policies and programs to ensure that they do not undermine that institution. Decentralized decision-making in the place of official controls empowers individuals and groups to tackle social problems in partnership with government. Bureaucracy is no longer a credible approach to helping those in need. This is especially true in light of alternatives such as faith-based organizations, which tend to have a greater degree of success than others in dealing with problems such as sub-stance abuse and domestic violence. To accomplish their missions, those groups must be able to rely upon people who share their faith; their hiring must not be subjected to government regulation and mandates.

 **While we titled this section *"Renewing Neighborhood, Building Communities,"* we do not endorse that the idea that *"it takes a village."* We do believe that the concepts of *"family"* and *"religion"* are the key to rebuilding our country. Coincidently, people who identify strongly with those two generic elements tend to vote Republican.**

Once we get to Washington, D.C. and become enamored with our own importance, *"family"* and *"religion"* become more distant concepts and our familiarity with them dissipates over time. As a result, we are a bit out of touch with how to go about *reintroducing* both into the culture of the United States. We're *really* hoping that by raising the issue, people will take up the cause on their own or some other organizations will champion it. Besides, we have a photo-op we have to attend.

PRESERVING OUR VALUES

From its founding, America has been an idea as much as a political or geographic entity. It has meant, for untold millions around the world, a set of ideals that speak to the highest aspirations of humanity. From its own beginning, the Republican Party has boldly asserted those ideals, as we now do again, to affirm the rights of the people under the rule of law.

UPHOLDING THE CONSTITUTIONAL RIGHT TO KEEP AND BEAR ARMS

We uphold the right of individual Americans to own firearms, a right which ante-dated the Constitution and was solemnly confirmed by the Second Amendment. We applaud the Supreme Court's decision in Heller affirming that right, and we assert the individual responsibility to safely use and store firearms. We call on the next president to appoint judges who will similarly respect the Constitution. Gun ownership is responsible citizen-ship, enabling Americans to defend themselves, their property, and communities.

Of course, we rather doubt that a Democratic President will appoint judges who will be strongly in favor of the Second Amendment's *"right to bear arms."* **The Democrats are** *more* **likely to present candidates who believe the Second Amendment contains a** *typo* **... and that it** *actually* **was meant to support the right of our citizens** *"to bare arms"* **because it can get really** *hot* **in Washington, D.C. during the summer.**

We, **on the other hand, think** *everybody* **should be a card carrying member of the NRA and should have at least one** handgun and rifle with them at all times. After all, we believe our Founders recognized the need for citizens to organize into a well-armed militia if the government should ever try to usurp our freedom. Of course, *"back in the day,"* handguns and rifles were just about all that the *government* troops had as well, so it would have been a fair fight. Today, we need to expand the Second Amendment to allow ordinary citizens to own a fully-armed F-22 Raptor, a nuclear sub or two, and *at least* one small thermal-nuclear device.

We call for education in constitutional rights in schools, and we support the option of firearms training in federal programs serving senior citizens and women. We urge immediate action to review the automatic denial of gun ownership to returning members of the Armed Forces who have suffered trauma during service to their country. We condemn frivolous lawsuits against firearms manufacturers, which are transparent attempts to deprive citizens of their rights. We oppose federal licensing of law-abiding gun owners and national gun registration as violations of the Second Amendment. We recognize that gun control only affects and penalizes law-abiding citizens, and that such proposals are ineffective at reducing violent crime.

 Don't ask us why we restricted *"firearms training in federal programs"* to *"senior citizens and women"* when we should have extended it to *every* man, woman and child in America like the Democrats do with each of their key issues.

And you could make an argument that it would make more sense to try to identify a *cure* for Post Traumatic Stress Disorder for returning veterans than to *"review the automatic denial of gun ownership to returning members of the Armed Forces who have suffered trauma during service to their country."* We already have enough postal employees without intentionally adding to the problem.

We somewhat boxed ourselves into the argument that *"gun control only affects and penalizes law-abiding citizens, and that such proposals are ineffective at reducing violent crime."*

Sure, we recognize that crimes of passion often result solely because the presence of guns and that children sometimes lose their lives playing with guns, but we *prefer* to take an ostrich's approach to this and bury our heads in the sand rather than try to find a solution that addresses the issue in a way that doesn't trample all over the Second Amendment.

ENSURING EQUAL TREATMENT FOR ALL

Individual rights – and the responsibilities that go with them – are the foundation of a free society. From the time of Lincoln, equality of individuals has been a corner-stone of the Republican Party. Our commitment to equal opportunity extends from landmark school-choice legislation for the students of Washington D.C. to historic appointments at the highest levels of government. We consider discrimination based on sex, race, age, religion, creed, disability, or national origin to be immoral, and we will strongly enforce anti-discrimination statutes. We ask all to join us in rejecting the forces of hatred and bigotry and in denouncing all who practice or promote racism, anti-Semitism, ethnic prejudice, or religious intolerance. As a matter of principle, Republicans oppose any attempts to create race-based governments within the United States, as well as any domestic governments not bound by the Constitution or the Bill of Rights.

The fact that we have to *ask* people to *"join us in rejecting the forces of hatred and bigotry and in denouncing all who practice or promote racism, anti-Semitism, ethnic prejudice, or religious intolerance"* shows how big a PR problem the Democrats have created for us. They've simply done a *fabulous* job of painting us with the broad brush of *"bigotry ... and intolerance,"* and we've been too politically inept to do anything about it. Their senior political leadership can include a former member of the Ku Klux Klan, and they're *still* revered as the saviors of *"oppressed minorities."* We, on the other hand, can order a Black Russian at a bar, and the mainstream press will report that we were

overheard asking a local entrepreneur to participate in slavery and possible spying activities. How stupid are we?

Precisely because we oppose discrimination, we reject preferences, quotas, and set-asides, whether in education or in corporate boardrooms. The government should not make contracts on this basis, and neither should corporations. We support efforts to help low-income individuals get a fair shot based on their potential and merit, and we affirm the common-sense approach of the Chief Justice of the United States: that the way to stop discriminating on the basis of race is to stop discriminating.

 We're afraid to use the term Affirmative Action because it wouldn't be *"politically correct,"* but we're really against the practice. Once again, we just don't know how to make the argument in a way that won't get us *chastised* for being the insensitive thugs people have grow to *expect* us to be.

PROTECTING OUR NATIONAL SYMBOLS

The symbol of our unity, to which we all pledge allegiance, is the flag. By whatever legislative method is most feasible, Old Glory should be given legal protection against desecration. We condemn decisions by activist judges to deny children the opportunity to say the Pledge of Allegiance in public school.

 Flag desecration isn't as big an issue today as it was back in the sixties and early seventies when civil disobedience was ... well, more disobedient. There are flag desecration laws on the books, but the Supreme Court has been somewhat limiting in its support of such laws. We've actually tried to pass a Constitutional Amendment to nail down the issue; but while it's gained the necessary two-thirds majority to get through the House on *eight straight* occasions, it's *failed* to make it through the Senate.

FREEDOM OF SPEECH AND OF THE PRESS

We support freedom of speech and freedom of the press and oppose attempts to violate or weaken those rights, such as reinstatement of the so-called Fairness Doctrine.

 **Currently, we are doing much better on the television and radio airways than our brethren Democrats. As a result, we don't want to have any reinstatement of the Fairness Doctrine that demanded *equal* time be given to *both* parties. Given how inept we are in virtually every *other* area of political communication, we just ask that our *one* stronghold not be diluted.**

MAINTAINING THE SANCTITY AND DIGNITY OF HUMAN LIFE

Faithful to the first guarantee of the Declaration of Independence, we assert the inherent dignity and sanctity of all human life and affirm that the unborn child has a fundamental individual right to life which cannot be infringed. We support a human life amendment to the Constitution, and we endorse legislation to make clear that the Fourteenth Amendment's protections apply to unborn children. We oppose using public revenues to promote or per-form abortion and will not fund organizations which advocate it. We support the appointment of judges who respect traditional family values and the sanctity and dignity of innocent human life.

 **We understand that the abortion issue is controversial and costs us votes in each election, but we're afraid that we'd lose even *more* votes within our right-wing, conservative base if we were to abandon our adamant stance.**

We have made progress. The Supreme Court has upheld prohibitions against the barbaric practice of partial-birth abortion. States are now permitted to extend health-care coverage to children before birth. And the

Born Alive Infants Protection Act has become law; this law ensures that infants who are born alive during an abortion receive all treatment and care that is provided to all newborn infants and are not neglected and left to die. We must protect girls from exploitation and statutory rape through a parental notification requirement. We all have a moral obligation to assist, not to penalize, women struggling with the challenges of an unplanned pregnancy. At its core, abortion is a fundamental assault on the sanctity of innocent human life. Women deserve better than abortion. Every effort should be made to work with women considering abortion to enable and empower them to choose life. We salute those who provide them alternatives, including pregnancy care centers, and we take pride in the tremendous increase in adoptions that has followed Republican legislative initiatives.

It would be nice if we spent as much *time* and *money* figuring out how to *reduce* the number of unwanted pregnancies as we do arguing *against* abortions. It would seem that taking the *need* for an abortion off the table might be the most expeditious way of addressing the issue. However, it's tough to get press coverage for the more mundane subject of prevention than it is to get it for the far more controversial debate that surrounds abortion. And press coverage translates into campaign donations from our more zealous supporters. Besides, this is one of the few areas in which we've been portrayed in a more caring light, and we need all the help we can get in that arena.

Respect for life requires efforts to include persons with disabilities in education, employment, the justice system, and civic participation. In keeping with that commitment, we oppose the non-consensual withholding of care or treatment from people with disabilities, as well as the elderly and infirm, just as we oppose euthanasia and assisted suicide, which endanger especially those on the margins of society. Because government should set a positive standard in hiring and contracting for the services of persons with disabilities, we need to update the statutory authority for the AbilityOne program, the main avenue by which those productive members of our society can offer high quality services at the best possible value.

THE LEFT ISN'T RIGHT

BY

T. J. O'HARA

TELEMACHUS PRESS

If you purchased this book without a cover you should be aware that this book is stolen property. It was reported as "unsold and destroyed" to the publisher and neither the author nor the publisher has received any payment for this "stripped book."

This book is a work of satire. As such it is meant as a humorous yet thought-provoking look at the Platform of the 2008 Democratic Party, *Renewing America's Promise*. With the exception of the text of the Democratic Party Platform, the opinions expressed within this book are solely those of the author.

THE LEFT ISN'T RIGHT
Copyright © 2010 by T. J. O'Hara. All rights reserved, including the right to reproduce this book, or portions thereof, in any form. No part of this text may be reproduced, transmitted, downloaded, decompiled, reverse engineered, or stored in or introduced into any information storage and retrieval system, in any form or by any means, whether electronic or mechanical without the express written permission of the author. The scanning, uploading, and distribution of this book via the internet or via any other means without the permission of the publisher is illegal and punishable by law. Please purchase only authorized electronic editions, and do not participate in or encourage electronic piracy of copyrighted materials.

This book incorporates the original text of the 2008 Democratic National Platform, *Renewing America's Promise* (Copyright © 2008 by the 2008 Democratic National Convention Committee, Inc.) under the doctrine of Fair Use (17 USC 107).

The publisher does not have any control over and does not assume any responsibility for author or third-party websites or their content.

Cover Art Design: Lorraine Hansen
Cover Photography: Kimberly O'Hara
Cover Art Illustrations:
    Copyright © istockphoto/Mark Stay (8180012)
    Copyright © istockphoto/Mark Stay (1089076)
    Copyright © istockphoto/Bob Ash (8115466)

Interior Art Illustration:
    Copyright © istockphoto/Mr_Vector (2366458)

Visit The Common Sense Czar's website at
http://www.TheCommonSenseCzar.net

Become a "Follower" of The Common Sense Czar's blog at
http://TheCommonSenseCzar.blogspot.com

ISBN: 978-1-935670-28-5 (eBook)
ISBN: 978-1-935670-29-2 (Paperback)

Published by: Telemachus Press, LLC
http://www.telemachuspress.com

Printed in the United States of America

10 9 8 7 6 5 4 3 2 1

THE LEFT ISN'T RIGHT

T. J. O'HARA

Dedication

To my beautiful bride, Kimberly, who inspires and supports me in everything I do … and to the rest of *"the Pack,"* Nikki, London and Chanel, who lay by my side as I write and bring me their toys when they think I need a break.

FOREWORD

In the interest of full disclosure ... or should I say *"complete transparency?"* ... I am the product of a *mixed marriage:* my father was a Republican, and my mother was a Democrat. To add to the complexity: my father was of Irish heritage, and my mother was of Italian heritage; my father was Catholic, and my mother was Protestant; and, my father was a male, and my mother was a female (... I think you have to *specify* that these days).

My father grew up on an Irish-only street. By that I mean, as the son of an Irish immigrant, he was safe ... on *his* street. However, he could not walk through the street that stood only a block away, because *that* was a German street, and he would likely be attacked. In case you haven't seen the movie *The Streets of New York*, suffice it to say that the Irish held a unique status at the time that was somewhere between that of the early colonial slaves ... and pond scum.

My mother was the first-born child of Italian immigrants. Back in those days, Italians enjoyed a higher status that the Irish (... but then, who didn't?) until that nettlesome thing called World War II broke out. Italy, you see, was part of the *Axis of Power* along with Germany and Japan; bad news for Italian descendants living in the United States. Never mind that my grandparents were more proud of their United States citizenship than anyone you can imagine or that my mother never set foot in Italy; they were singled out during WWII, and their home was painted by the apparent progeny of today's *"taggers"* with a less-than-artistic swastika.

To add to the confusion, my father was a blue-collar worker, who worked for the newspaper as a journeyman and served as his union's Secretary/Treasurer. In that latter capacity, my sister and I earned part of our meager allowances by helping him balance the books and write the monthly union report. When technology displaced the need for his craft, my father's union lost its battle with a competing union for jurisdiction. As a result, he became an entrepreneur and started a modest but successful house painting business. He had bravely served as a commando in the Navy during WWII, often hitting the beaches in the South Pacific with the first wave of Marines. It was an experience in his life that he generally chose not to discuss. But I have no doubt, were he alive today and this country's freedom at stake, he would take up arms once again without a moment's hesitation ... for he loved this country that much.

Let me apologize ahead of time for the *"political incorrectness"* of the next statement, but it's the truth: my mother was a *"stay-at-home-mom."* There, I said it! Boy, it was sure hard to get it out, but I feel quite relieved.

My mother was always there for my sister and me when we came home from school; she cared for us when we were ill and was active in anything that she thought might contribute in a meaningful way to our lives (*e.g.*, PTA, Playground Mother's Club, etc.). She was passionate about art and music and made sure that we had an appreciation for both. And Mom was in the audience anytime we spoke, sang, acted or played. She also was a member of the local Civic Association, which was as close as she came to political activism. Yet, she was deeply steeped in the national pride that is so often associated with America's *Greatest Generation* and was further driven by one of her parents' favorite phrases: *"God bless America!"*

So now you know! I take my citizenship *very* seriously. While I was *born* into it and didn't have to traverse an ocean or learn a new language, as both sets of my grandparents did, I have a *profound* respect for what it means. Neither did I have to survive the economic hardships of *The Great Depression* nor defend my country on foreign soil as my parents did. However, perhaps it is through the intensity of my family members' experiences and their devotion to what this Nation stands for that has given birth to my undying *love* for ... and *commitment* to ... the United States of America.

And as far as *"political correctness"* goes ... if that concept is meaningful to you, you may wish to read no further because I have no time for such folly. I was raised to *"tell the truth, the whole truth, and nothing but the truth ... so help me God."* If unvarnished honesty offends you, read no further. If the fact that I choose to occasionally call upon the *"help"* of a higher power offends you, read no further. However, if you can muster the strength to weather those two concepts, I encourage you to read on.

I write *not* to *convince* you … but rather to *entertain* you and to *stimulate your thoughts* so that your opinion, moving forward, is more *informed* and reflects *your* true feelings rather than what *someone else* would have you believe. Brace yourself … and enjoy the journey!

THE LEFT ISN'T RIGHT

INTRODUCTION

*** *If you've already read the Introduction in one of the other books you may skip this chapter* ***

By way of introduction, I am the self-appointed *Common Sense Czar*. With all due respect to Thomas Paine, author of *Common Sense*, I think I deserve the job. Besides, Thomas Paine has been dead for over 200 years ... even though he's still registered to vote in three States according to Acorn.

Being a Czar is really cool. Unlike politicians, you don't have to have to raise money to run; you generally don't have to be vetted in a rigorous way; and you have reasonably unbridled authority ... *plus*, you get to be called *"Czar!"*

As the *Common Sense Czar*, I apply *common sense* to the issues of the day; something that has been missing in our Nation's capital for quite some time. As my first official act, I applied *common sense* to the current glut of Czars and dismissed all of them except for the *Faith-Based Czar*. Personally, I can't imagine why the ACLU hasn't attacked that particular position with its normal zeal. The *issue* would seem to be *obvious*. Maybe it's *Devine intervention*. If that's the case, my *common sense* tells me not to *mess* with it.

As for the rest of the positions, the decisions were easy. The *Guantanamo Closure Czar* was going to lose his job anyway since his position was driven by an Executive Order issued by President Obama on January 22, 2009, to close Gitmo *"no later than one year from now"* to quote the President, and we all know how well that's been going.

The *TARP Czar* and *Stimulus Accountability Czar* were also expendable. On February 25, 2009, just eight days after signing the $787-billion dollar economic stimulus package, President Obama stated that he was putting Vice

President Joe Biden in charge of the *"tough, unprecedented oversight effort"* of the fiscal stimulus plan *"because nobody messes with Joe."* I can't imagine why we would need these two Czars if Vice President Biden has everything under control.

The departure of the *Government Performance Czar* was another easy call given our Government's performance in recent years.

I dumped the *Afghanistan Czar* and the *Sudan Czar* because, the last time I looked, these are independent countries. If we have military or humanitarian initiatives in *any* country, it's Congress' responsibility to address the issues. We don't need Czars for specific countries. If we did, then we should at least start with Russia. They're used to it.

Then, we've got the *Mideast Peace Czar*. Talk about a dead-end job! These countries have been fighting for over 2,000 years. What are the odds that a political appointee in the United States will be able to resolve their differences? That's one more position we can eliminate. And while we're at it, let's eliminate the *Central Region Czar* who is responsible for our policies in, you guessed it, the same part of the world; needless duplication. Gone!

While we're on the subject, we presently have a *Terrorist Czar*. No, not Bill Ayres (although he might be a good choice under the assumption that *"it takes one to know one"*) ... a fellow named John Brennan. This is the same John Brennan who allegedly nixed a plan to kill or capture Osama bin Laden back in 1998. Way to establish job security! Eliminating this position shouldn't exactly create a void.

Staying with the terrorist theme for a moment, I see we have a *Weapons Czar* and a *WMD Policy Czar*. Why differentiate? If the *Weapons Czar* only tackles issues of conventional weaponry (like sling-shots), we don't need him. If there really are *"no weapons of mass destruction,"* we don't need the *WMD Policy Czar* either. Assuming for the moment that weapons of mass destruction are *not* just a figment of former President Bush's imagination, I'll establish the policy. Weapons of mass destruction are bad things; particularly in the hands of unstable people. There you have it ... a *common sense* policy and two more positions eliminated.

Along these same lines, we have an *Intelligence Czar*. Let's just agree that it's an obvious oxymoron and eliminate the position to stop the snickering!

We have a *Border Czar* to protect us from illegal immigration. If you call this Czar's office, press 1 for English, press 2 for Spanish, press 3 for Tagalog, press 4 for Farsi, press 5 for … well, you get the picture. Applying *common sense*: we have immigration laws in place. Enforce them! One more position eliminated.

This same solution can be applied to two more positions: *Domestic Violence Czar* and *Drug Czar*. *Common sense* tells us that domestic violence and the illegal use of drugs are bad. We have laws in place against both negative behaviors. Enforce them! That gets rid of those two Czars.

Next, we have a few positions tied to specific locations within our country. We have a *Great Lakes Czar*. I've been to the Lakes. They're indeed *"Great."* That should cover it. Position eliminated!

We also have a *California Water Czar* … as if there aren't any other problems in that State. Interestingly enough, this particular one is man-made. Last year, California and the surrounding States enjoyed record snowfalls, which created an abundance of water. However in 2007, a Federal judge ruled that endangered smelt might get caught in the pumps. So, the pumps were ordered to be shut down to preserve the habitat for the tiny, silver fish. As a result, taxpayers from San Diego to San Jose have been placed on water allocation and have suffered significant rate hikes; farmers have been threatened with foreclosures and bankruptcies because they can't irrigate their crops; but I'm happy to say that the smelt are enjoying living their lives and being eaten by natural predators. I apologize in advance to environmentalists, but there comes a time when *common sense* must intervene. So, I say open the pumps, restore the agrarian economy, fish fry at my house, and eliminate this position.

Since I've already offended my fellow environmentalists, let's take a look at three other unnecessary positions: *Climate Czar*, *Energy and Environment Czar*, and *Green Jobs Czar*. If we accept the premise of Global Warming (as established by world-renowned scientist and inventor of the Internet, Al Gore), our climate would seem to be a legitimate issue. Luckily, the Federal and State governments have authority to create laws that make us better *"citizens of the planet."* Unfortunately, we have no authority to legislate what China, India and the rest of the world do. So, the *Climate Czar* can step down.

Similarly, we don't have a need for an *Energy and Environment Czar*. The environmental element is repetitive and, as for energy, I can set the policy: eliminate our dependence on foreign oil; cultivate our natural resources in a responsible way (which doesn't mean *"rape the earth"* any more than it means that accessing them will destroy the world as we know it); and develop new and better alternative fuels.

This brings us to the *Green Job Czar*, but I need not address this one. Apparently, the White House has already excused him when it was discovered that he took the whole Czar thing a little too literally and pledged allegiance to Stalin. Besides, the title evokes a theme of racial discrimination.

Speaking of jobs, I find it interesting that we don't have a *Jobs Czar*. No problem … I can handle it. We do have an *Economic Czar*, so maybe there's some overlap. Paul Volcker headed the Federal Reserve during the latter stages of the Carter Administration and through the Reagan years. The good news is that he is credited with helping our Nation overcome *"stagflation."* The bad news is that he did it by raising the prime lending rate to 21.5% and driving the economy into a deep recession that created a level of unemployment not seen since the Great Depression. I'm eliminating his position because we're already there when it comes to creating a recession and experiencing an untenable level of unemployment.

Correspondingly, I'm going to eliminate the *Regulatory Czar*. I've soured on the self-righteousness of our regulatory agencies ever since the *"anointed one,"* Eliot Spitzer, prostituted his position as Governor of New York after ruling herd over the bastions of Wall Street. I'll only reconsider if Bernie Madoff gets an early parole and assumes the role of Frank Abagnale, Jr. (I hope that reference isn't too esoteric). Besides, the current *Regulatory Czar* apparently wants to *"regulate"* everything including *"free speech"* (of which I am obviously a fan); having called for taxing or censoring conspiracy theories … such as the theory that Global Warming may be a deliberate fraud. He also wants to lobby for the right for animals to bring lawsuits. This would give even more power to the ACLU (America's Crazy Lunatic Unit) to bring "udderly" worthless lawsuits on behalf of sacred cows; barring them from grazing on government property as a violation of the separation of church and state. Gone!

We also have a *Pay Czar*. This is the individual who, like the *Regulatory Czar*, remains ever vigilant over those fat-cat CEOs in high-profile industries we all love to hate. However, I can't help noticing that he hasn't imposed any restrictions on the compensation of the executives at Fannie Mae and Freddie Mac, who have almost single-handedly destroyed the economy. I also don't recall seeing any *"smack downs"* of the union officials who can consistently deliver political votes in volume. *Common sense* tells me he has to go!

While we're talking about unions, I feel compelled to point out that we have two Czars for the automotive industry: a *Car Czar* and an *Auto Recovery Czar*. By now, you know how I feel about redundancy. I'm not sure what either does, but I'm *sure* we don't need two. Under the *Car Czar's* guidance, both General Motors and Chrysler have gone bankrupt. Since I'm reasonably confident they could have accomplished that without him, his position is being eliminated. As for the *Auto Recovery Czar*, I'm not sure if he's vested with the responsibility to help the automotive industry *"recover"* from the bankruptcies the *Car Czar* has overseen, or if his responsibility is to *"recover"* the taxpayer dollars that have been funneled into the industry without any noticeable results. Once again, this is a position we can safely eliminate.

Moving along into the vital science, technology and information sectors, I am happy to say we have a Czar for each one. Our *Science Czar* is a top-flight academic, which means that *common sense* isn't a part of his world. He once proffered the idea of forced abortions, *"compulsory sterilization,"* and the creation of a *"Planetary Regime"* to control human population and natural resources to save the Earth. *"Earth to Science Czar,"* I'll only consider keeping you if the *"compulsory sterilization"* idea begins with Members of our current Congress.

Our *Technology Czar* and *Information Czar* are good friends. Together, they will lead the evolution of Information Technology within our government. You guessed it ... I see this as redundant. Given that the *Information Czar* came first and brought the *Technology Czar* on board, I've got to give the nod to him. Unfortunately, he's been linked to hiring individuals with criminal records to protect our information. Since I'd hate to break up a team, they both have to go.

With healthcare reform on the forefront, we have two Czars that touch upon it: an *AIDS Czar* and a *Health Czar*. The *AIDS Czar* can go. AIDS is a disease. Other than its associated political capital, it does not rank in the top ten causes of death in the United States (which are: (1) Heart Disease; (2) Cancer; (3) Stroke; (4) Chronic Lower Respiratory Diseases; (5) Accidents (unintentional injuries); (6) Diabetes; (7) Alzheimer's disease; (8) Influenza and Pneumonia; (9) Nephritis, Nephrotic Syndrome, and Nephrosis; and (10) Septicemia). Sorry, but until the Top Ten have their own Czars, AIDS doesn't merit one. Because the *Health Czar* hasn't had the *common sense* to recognize this either, she's gone too!

I'm sad to report that we have a comparatively unaccomplished *Urban Affairs Czar*. Why settle? This is America. We have John Edwards, Bill Clinton, Mark Sanford and, most recently, Tiger Woods. Now, *these* men clearly know how to have urban affairs! If none of them will step up to embrace their civic duty, let's just eliminate this position.

So, with that task completed, let's get to work!

Premise

We may be disenchanted with our politicians, but it's not necessarily fair to blame the inmates for the way they run the asylum. After all, they do *warn* us … particularly in Presidential election years when they author National Platforms that define their positions. Yet, few of us ever take the time to *read* those documents to truly understand each Party's position … even though their positions and underlying beliefs will drive the decisions that dictate the direction in which our country will *be headed* … or should that be spelled *"beheaded?"* Shame on us!

Instead, we tend to take the easy way out and just listen to their speeches and debates (at least as much of them as we can stand); we watch their negative ads (positive ones went away a generation ago); and we let politically jaded wolves, who like to parade around in the sheep's clothing of *"reporting the news"* (once an honored profession), deliver thinly veiled versions of their personal opinions and beliefs. As the *Common Sense Czar*, I say we take a new approach: *let's read the words the Parties have committed to writing and for which we can hold them accountable.*

Now, I know this is a challenging suggestion because Party Platforms are always filled with political platitudes to their own greatness, grossly exaggerated vilifications of the *"Opposition,"* and a tediously repetitive casting of the same old drivel in hopes of gaining a vote. Well, as the *Common Sense Czar*, I've decided to make the endeavor far more entertaining, informative, and worthy of your time … and completely devoid of *"political correctness!"*

In hopes of getting you to actually *read* what the two major Parties have written, I've *"channeled"* them (in two separate books) … not only providing you with the *exact* transcript of their Platforms (misspellings and grammatical errors included) ... but my own satirical interpretation of what they were *actually thinking* at the time. <u>The Left isn't Right</u> has fun with the Democratic National Platform; <u>The Right is Wrong</u> has fun with the Republican National Platform; and the third book, <u>The National Platform of Common Sense</u>, provides a satirical look at how the Parties *could* have structured their Platforms if they had paid attention to the *Declaration of Independence*, the *Constitution*, and the *Bill of Rights* ... and applied some *"common sense."*

As far as trilogies go, this one is devoid of magical rings, wizards, and diminutive beings, but I strongly encourage you to read *all* three books. At the end of the day, regardless of your Party affiliation, you'll have a far better understanding of *both* of our major political Parties' philosophies ... and a *"common sense"* appreciation of our country and the Republic *"for which it stands."*

WHAT YOU NEED TO KNOW BEFORE YOU START

This book incorporates the original text of the 2008 Democratic National Platform, *Renewing America's Promise* (Copyright © 2008 by the 2008 Democratic National Convention Committee, Inc.) under the doctrine of Fair Use (17 USC 107) to maintain the accuracy of the Platform, and it distinguishes its satirical comments, criticisms, and research clearly to avoid any confusion. Its purpose is to stimulate political thought and promote a more informed electorate. The DNC does not endorse any of the views or opinions expressed by the book's author, and the author recommends that you visit www.scribd.com/doc/5580817/2008-Democratic-Party-Platform-Renewing-Americas-Promise for a downloadable, full-color copy of *Renewing America's Promise*.

The *Common Sense Czar's* satirical comments, criticisms, and research start with the *Common Sense Czar's* very own *"idea"* light bulb. They are further distinguished by their indentation and bolded text (with this section serving as an example).

To fully appreciate the satirical nature of the comments, read them *as if* they are being expressed *by* the Party ... but in the end, remember that they are just meant to be entertaining comments that stimulate thought.

When the indentation and bolded text end, so do the *Common Sense Czar's* embellishments and you are returned to the Democratic National Platform's original text.

PREAMBLE

We come together at a defining moment in the history of our nation – the nation that led the 20th century, built a thriving middle class, defeated fascism and communism, and provided bountiful opportunity to many.

 **So obviously, we need to change things in a radical way!**

We Democrats have a special commitment to this promise of America. We believe that every American, whatever their background or station in life, should have the chance to get a good education, to work at a good job with good wages, to raise and provide for a family, to live in safe surroundings, and to retire with dignity and security. We believe that quality and affordable health care is a basic right. We believe that each succeeding generation should have the opportunity, through hard work, service and sacrifice, to enjoy a brighter future than the last.

 **Notice that we said that *every* America should have a *"chance"* ... rather than a *"right"* ... *"to get a good education, to work at a good job with good wages, to raise and provide for a family, to live in safe surroundings, and to retire with dignity and security;"* and they should have an *"opportunity through hard work, service and sacrifice, to enjoy a brighter future than the last."* If it wasn't for the *"right"* to enjoy *"quality and affordable health care,"* we'd all be Republicans.**

But today, we are at a crossroads. As we meet, we are in the sixth year of a two-front war. Our economy is struggling. Our planet is in peril.

 **Just ignore the fact that all of these issues evolved because Congress, which our Party controlled for the last two of those six years, either approved them … or did nothing about them.**
In fact, while we will be complaining a lot about the snail's pace of social reform throughout our Platform, we'd prefer that you ignore the fact that we have had majorities in both the House and Senate for 44 out of the last 66 years; during which time we simultaneously held the Oval Office as well for 22 of those years. We've actually held majorities in the House for 52 of those 66 years and in the Senate for 46 of those 66 years. Still, you can rely on one other fact: we'll blame the Republicans!

A great nation now demands that its leaders abandon the politics of partisan division and find creative solutions to promote the common good. A people that prizes candor, accountability, and fairness insists that a government of the people must level with them and champion the interests of all American families. A land of historic resourcefulness has lost its patience with elected officials who have failed to lead.

It is time for a change. We can do better.

And so, Democrats – through the most open platform process in history – are reaching out today to Republicans, Independents, and all Americans who hunger for a new direction a reason to hope. Today, at a defining moment in our history, the Democratic Party resolves to renew America's promise.

 **Okay, brace yourself: even though the** *"nation demands that its leaders abandon the politics of partisan division and find creative solutions to promote the common good,"* **we're about to eviscerate the Republicans and blame them for everything bad that's** *ever* **happened. And try to stop laughing at the comment**

about how our Party *"prizes candor, accountability, and fairness"* and will create the *"most open platform in history."* We all know where that pledge will wind up. We legislate behind closed doors, cut deals to get votes, and offer candidates other federal jobs if they'll drop out of the race. Heck, we wouldn't even release a simple birth certificate to prove that our Presidential Candidate was actually qualified to run for the office. However, you can't disagree: *"it's time for change,"* and *"we can do better!"*

Over the past eight years, our nation's leaders have failed us. Sometimes they invited calamity, rushing us into an ill-considered war in Iraq. But other times, when calamity arrived in the form of hurricanes or financial storms, they sat back, doing too little too late, and too poorly. The list of failures of this Administration is historic.

 **Again, please ignore that our Party was in control of both the House and the Senate during the last two years of that time frame, held a majority in the Senate for two more of the years, and that the Republicans held very narrow majorities in the rest of those years. Essentially, the President could not act without our tacit approval.**

The American Dream is at risk. Incomes are down and foreclosures are up. Millions of our fellow citizens have no health insurance while families working longer hours are pressed for time to care for their children and aging parents. Gas and home heating costs are squeezing seniors and working families alike. We are less secure and less respected in the world. After September 11, we could have built the foundation for a new American century, but instead we instigated an unnecessary war in Iraq before finishing a necessary war in Afghanistan. Careless policies, inept stewardship and the broken politics of this Administration have taken their toll on our economy, our security and our reputation.

 Our legislative assistance to Fannie Mae and Freddie Mac helped drive the foreclosures as did our infatuation with Acorn and other community organizations that pressured the banking industry to approve loans that never should have been made. We've done *nothing* with our Congressional majority to impact energy concerns. And while we haven't been attacked on our soil for the past eight years, we're pretty sure that if someone had tried, their underwear and car bombs wouldn't have gone off because ... well, we're just *lucky* that way! We also believe that if we bow to the rest of the world (and particularly to royalty in the Middle East), they'll stop resenting us for our success, and we'll finally become everyone's friend!

But even worse than the conditions we find ourselves in are the false promises that brought us here. The Republican leadership said they would keep us safe, but they overextended our military and failed to respond to new challenges. They said they would be compassionate conservatives, but they failed to rescue our citizens from the rooftops of New Orleans, neglected our veterans, and denied health insurance to children. They promised fiscal responsibility but instead gave tax cuts to the wealthy few and squandered almost a trillion dollars in Iraq. They promised reform but allowed the oil companies to write our energy agenda and the credit card companies to write the bankruptcy rules.

These are not just policy failures. They are failures of a broken politics – a politics that rewards self-interest over the common interest and the short-term over the long-term, that puts our government at the service of the powerful. A politics that creates a state-of-the-art system for doling out favors and shuts out the voice of the American people.

 We've never made a false promise, and we're all about *"accountability."* If you need proof, we hold the Republican Party *"accountable"* for everything: from military initiatives we supported in Congress ... to natural disasters that are beyond the control

of mankind. And forget the fact that history has repeatedly demonstrated that tax cuts stimulate economic growth. Why do that when we can use that money to grow government instead? Rather than *"squandering almost a trillion dollars in Iraq"* to fight the war on terrorism *there* rather than in New York City, we have since proven the ability to spend multiple trillions of dollars to create a plethora of new agencies that won't have any positive impact for years to come ... if ever!

So, we come together not only to replace this President and his party – and not only to offer policies that will undo the damage they have wrought. Today, we pledge a return to core moral principles like stewardship, service to others, personal responsibility, shared sacrifice and a fair shot for all –values that emanate from the integrity and optimism of our Founders and generations of Americans since. Today, we Democrats offer leaders – from the White House to the State House – worthy of this country's trust.

 **You can stop laughing now; this wasn't meant to be funny. So what if we can't even staff the Cabinet with people who haven't cheated on their taxes? So what if we refuse to take** *"personal responsibility"* **for any of our past actions (or votes)? And please, just try to ignore the** *"shared sacrifice"* **comment because it's going to get in the way of** *"redistributing the wealth."* **It's just rhetoric. We were on a roll! We really didn't mean that the** *"sacrifice"* **should be shared ... just the fruits of the labor.**

We will start by renewing the American Dream for a new era – with the same new hope and new ideas that propelled Franklin Delano Roosevelt towards the New Deal and John F. Kennedy to the New Frontier. We will provide immediate relief to working people who have lost their jobs, families who are in danger of losing their homes, and those who – no matter how hard they work – are seeing prices go up more than their income. We will invest in America again –in world-class public education, in our infrastructure, and in green technology –so that our economy can generate the good, high-paying jobs of the future. We will end the outrage of unaffordable, unavailable health care, protect Social Security, and help Americans save for retirement. And we will harness American ingenuity to free this nation from the tyranny of oil.

 To accomplish this, we'll tax the rich until they're poor. Then, we'll just print more money. Oh sure, you could argue that this will curb economic expansion and create an inflationary spiral that will push prices beyond almost *anyone's* reach, but don't worry … we'll have created a welfare state by that time, so you'll be able to buy everything with the modern equivalent of food stamps.

The Democratic Party believes that there is no more important priority than renewing American leadership on the world stage. This will require diplomatic skill as capable as our military might. Instead of refusing to confront our most pressing threats, we will use all elements of American power to keep us safe, prosperous, and free. Instead of alienating our nation from the world, we will enable America –once again –to lead.

 Take us at our word: *"there is no more important priority than renewing American leadership on the world stage."* Above all else, *we want to be liked*. Most of us long for the days we served on Student Council and were members of Latin Club in junior high and high school (… the last time we were *really* popular). Oh, but to recapture the essence of those times!

For decades, Americans have been told to act for ourselves, by ourselves, on our own. Democrats reject this recipe for division and failure. Today, we commit to renewing our American community by recognizing that solutions to our greatest challenges can only be rooted in common ground and the strength of our civic life. The American people do not want government to solve all our problems; we know that personal responsibility, character, imagination, diligence, hard work and faith ultimately determine individual achievement. But we also know that at every turning point in our nation's history, we have demonstrated our love of country by uniting to overcome our challenges—whether ending slavery, fighting two world wars for the cause of freedom or sending a man to the moon. Today, America must unite again –to help our most vulnerable residents get back on their feet and to restore the vitality of both urban centers and family farms –because the success of each depends on the success of the other. And America must challenge us again –to serve our country and to meet our responsibilities – whether in our families or local governments; our civic organizations or places of worship.

 **Don't read the last paragraph too closely; particularly if you believe in the value of your own freedom and the power of your personal potential. Our Party's whole strategy is based upon lumping people in groups (Blacks, Hispanics, women, gays, union workers, middle class, poor, etc.); *"minority"* groups comprised of large numbers, so that only a small percentage of you need to show up at the polls to give us a good chance to win.**

By type-casting you and claiming that Republicans are evil people who don't represent your social stereotype's best interests, it's easier to get you to vote for us. Our goal is to make you feel like you're part of a greater whole; an *"oppressed minority"* for whom only the Democrats care. Truth be told, we only care about your vote ... because it represents money and power to us. Oh sure, we talk a good game ... but *"walking the talk"* is an entirely different matter. We have lots of millionaires and billionaires within our party (not to mention celebrities who make more money in a single performance than most of you will accumulate in a lifetime), but we've done an excellent job of positioning the Republicans as the *"fat cats"* who don't care about you. Our money is clean; theirs isn't. It's absolutely vital to our strategy to have you identify yourself with an *"oppressed minority"* we can control, so we can orchestrate your vote through group-directed *fear*.

> **Our greatest concern is that someday you'll wake up and *respect* your own individuality; recognize that you *do* have options and that the choice is *yours*; that you'll begin to compare what we *say* ... to what we *do* ... and vote on an *informed* basis ... rather than vote as *we* tell you to do. So, please, just accept the fact that *we* know better than *you* do and that a larger, *more invasive* government is good for you.**

Americans have been promised change before. And too often we have been disappointed. We believe we must change not just our policies, but our politics as well. We cannot keep doing the same things and expect to get different results. That is why today we come together not only to prevent a third Bush term. Today, we pledge to renew American democracy by promoting the use of new technologies to make it easier for Americans to participate in their government. We will shine a light on government spending and Washington lobbying –so that every American is empowered to be a watchdog and a whistle blower. We are the party of inclusion and respect differences of perspective and belief. And so, even when we disagree, we will work together to move this country forward. There can be no Republican or Democratic ideas, only policies that are smart and right and fair and good for America –and those that aren't. We will form a government as decent, candid, purposeful and compassionate as the American people themselves.

This is the essence of what it means to be a patriot: not only to declare our love of this nation, but to show it –by our deeds, our priorities, and the commitments we keep.

If we choose to change, just imagine what we can do. What makes America great has never been its perfection, but the belief that it can be made better. And that people who love this country can change it. This is the country of Abraham Lincoln, Susan B. Anthony, Martin Luther King Jr., Cesar Chavez, and Rosa Parks – people who had the audacity to believe that their country could be a better place, and the courage to work to make it so. And this Party has always made the biggest difference in the lives of the American people when we summoned the entire nation to a common purpose.

We have a choice to make. We can choose to stay the current failed course. Or we can choose a path that builds upon the best of who and what we are, that reflects our highest values. We can have more of the last eight years, or we can rise together and create a new kind of government. The time for change has come, and America must seize it.

 *"We come together not only to prevent a third Bush term ..."* (since the 22nd Amendment already addressed that issue when Franklin D. Roosevelt nearly became King), but *"to pledge to renew American democracy."* Never mind that the United States Constitution established a *Republic* rather than a *"democracy"* ... and there is a fundamental difference of which the Framers were *profoundly* aware. After all, we're the *"party of inclusion and respect differences of perspective and belief."* We include anyone who votes for us and shares our perspective and belief. Otherwise, we'll ban you from our back room caucuses and vilify you in public; essentially claiming that you are the love-child of Satan ... or a Republican.

I. RENEWING THE AMERICAN DREAM

For months the state of our economy has dominated the headlines–and the news has not been good. The sub-prime lending debacle has sent the housing market into a tailspin, and many Americans have lost their homes. By early August, the economy had shed 463,000 jobs over seven straight months of job loss. Health, gas and food prices are rising dramatically.

 **... And all of this during a time when we controlled *both* the House and the Senate.**

But the problem goes deeper than the current crisis. Families have seen their incomes go down even as they have been working longer hours and as productivity has grown. At the same time, health costs have risen while companies have shed health insurance coverage and pensions. Worse yet, too many Americans have lost confidence in the fundamental American promise that our children will have a better life than we do.

 **On the one hand, we championed *"women's rights"* (they're a minority, right?) and daycare as an alternative to the more traditional roles our society used to embrace, and we trumpeted the importance of unions in protecting workers' rights. On the other hand, now were excoriating the disruption of the family and the expansion of the work day. It must be those insidious**

capitalists' fault ... and you just know they must all be Republicans!

We lobbied for an increase in the minimum wage and higher corporate taxes only to have companies cut back on benefits to try to maintain a sufficient level of profit to either stay in business or to attract capital for expansion. Once again, our best efforts were stymied by those capitalist pigs!

And you could quibble about whether it's a *"promise"* ... or a *"hope"* that our children *"will have a better life than we do,"* but at least we didn't claim that it's a *"right."* Notice, we avoided using our earlier language pertaining to giving them *"the opportunity through hard work, service and sacrifice, to enjoy a brighter future than the last"* lest they come to realize that *they* may have to put some skin in the game.

We are living through an age of fundamental economic transformation. Technology has changed the way we live and the way the world does business. The collapse of the Soviet Union and the advance of capitalism have vanquished old challenges to America's global leadership, but new challenges have emerged. Today, jobs and industries can move to any country with an Internet connection and willing workers.

 **Wow! Can you believe we just admitted that the Soviet Union** *"collapsed"* **and capitalism** *"advanced?"* **Didn't "U.S.S.R." actually stand for the United Soviet** *Socialist* **Republic? Never mind. We'll just have to revise the text books in our public schools.**

And we're okay with capitalism as long as it creates great wealth for a small percentage of people whom we can castigate for their success and portray as evil to the *"oppressed minorities"* we pretend to protect. Besides, we need a *real* minority against whom we can assess a usurious tax to support our rapacious social programs.

As for the migratability of jobs ... weren't we warned by some scrawny little Texan back in the 1990's about the *"giant sucking sound"* we were about to hear when our jobs began moving to Mexico under NAFTA (passed by the Clinton Administration)? On a positive note, at least we've kept our borders open! That has allowed us to *not only* lose our *higher paying jobs* to Mexico, but also attract a lot of *"undocumented workers"* for the *lower paying jobs* here; you know, the ones that ignore the minimum wage legislation we passed. The *real* homerun for us is that Acorn can apparently register these *"undocumented workers"* as Democrats with less effort than it takes to do the same for convicted felons ... or dead people.

Leadership on these issues has been sorely lacking these past eight years. In the 1990s, under Bill Clinton's leadership, employment and incomes grew and we built up a budget surplus. However, our current President pursued misguided policies, missed opportunities, and maintained a rigid, ideological adherence to discredited ideas. Our surplus is now a deficit, and almost a decade into this century, we still have no coherent national strategy to compete in a global economy. The price tag for these failures is being passed on to our families.

During the 1990's, the Internet phenomenon took off and companies no longer actually needed to make money to attract investment capital. The economy grew by leaps and bounds, and it had nothing to do with Clinton's Presidency ... except for the fact that then-Vice Pesident Gore apparently *"invented"* the Internet. Sure, the Republicans attacked his great contribution to technology as *"A Convenient UN-truth,"* but that didn't discourage us because those were the days when *"convenient un-truths"* ruled the day (*i.e.*, *"I did not have sex with that woman ..."*).

But not everything *"sucked"* during the Clinton Administration. He did try to tear down the welfare system ... and with some success. Coupled with the increased tax base generated by the economic surge associated with the Internet, this helped President Clinton bring down the Federal deficit and balance the budget. Of course, his efforts were supported

by a Republican-controlled Congress, but we choose to ignore that.

From the mother working two jobs to pay the bills and the couple struggling to care for young children and aging parents, to the tens of millions of Americans without health insurance and the workers who have seen their jobs shipped overseas, too many Americans have been invisible to our current President and his party for too long. The people who do the work in America have never been invisible to the Democratic Party. It is time to make the American Dream real for them again.

We need a government that stands up for the hopes, values, and interests of working people, and gives everyone willing to work hard the chance to make the most of their God-given potential.

In platform hearings around the country, Americans reaffirmed our belief that this great nation can compete–and succeed–in the 21st century but only if we take a new approach. One that is both innovative and faithful to the basic economic principles that made this country great. We Democrats want–and we hereby pledge–a government led by Barack Obama that looks out for families in the new economy with health care, retirement security, and help, especially in bad times. Investment in our country–in energy, education, infrastructure, science. A ladder of opportunity for all. Democrats see these as the pillars of a more competitive and fair economy that will allow all Americans to take advantage of the opportunities of our new era.

 **It's a good thing that we already stated that our** *"great nation now demands that its leaders abandon the politics of partisan division and find creative solutions to promote the common good,"* **or these last few paragraphs may have sounded like we were trying to turn the country against those rogue Republicans. Most importantly, we pledge** *"a government led by Barack Obama that looks out for families in the new economy with health care, retirement security, and help, especially in bad times."* **The** *"especially in bad times"* **part is** *particularly* **important because, if we keep spending money at our current rate, we'd better get used to** *"bad times"* **... and the debate**

over whether our children will have to worry about having *"a better life"* than ours will be moot ... for generations to come.

JUMPSTART THE ECONOMY AND PROVIDE MIDDLE CLASS AMERICANS IMMEDIATE RELIEF

We will provide an immediate energy rebate to American families struggling with the record price of gasoline and the skyrocketing cost of other necessities – to spend on those basic needs and energy efficient measures. We will devote $50 billion to jumpstarting the economy, helping economic growth, and preventing another one million jobs from being lost. This will include assistance to states and localities to prevent them from having to cut their vital services like education, health care, and infrastructure. We will quickly implement the housing bill recently passed by Congress and ensure that states and localities that have been hard-hit by the housing crisis can avoid cuts in vital services. We support investments in infrastructure to replenish the highway trust fund, invest in road and bridge maintenance and fund new, fast-tracked projects to repair schools. We believe that it is essential to take immediate steps to stem the loss of manufacturing jobs. Taking these immediate measures will provide good jobs and will help the economy today. But generating truly shared prosperity is only possible if we also address our most significant long-run challenges like the rising cost of health care, energy, and education.

If we're giving energy rebates and devoting money to jumpstart the economy, *let's go big!* $50 billion or a trillion ... what's the difference? A "b" versus a "t" can't amount to much. Besides, it's not our money. We'll just tax the rich. Nobody likes them anyway, and they don't vote for us ... except for the *really* rich celebrities and trust-fund socialites who are embarrassed by their luck and assuage their guilt by championing a *"cause"* they can support. That's why most of them gravitate to impoverished countries in Africa because the *photo ops* are more compelling than helping poor and middle class families in America. But hey, as long as they contribute to our campaigns and do free gigs at our fund-raisers and our numerous Presidential Balls, what do we care?

EMPOWERING FAMILIES FOR A NEW ERA

Many Americans once worked 40 hours a week for 40 years for a single employer who provided pay to support a family, health insurance, and a pension. Today, Americans change jobs more frequently than ever and compete against workers around the world for pay and benefits.

 **Ignore the fact that we were at the forefront of the dual-income family movement and we currently support the idea of a global economy (just as long as everyone *likes* us). If you think the revolving door is turning quickly today with respect to jobs, just wait until our U.S.-based businesses become even less competitive internationally as we layer new taxes, regulations, and benefit requirements on them. If you start to hear an even louder *"giant sucking sound,"* at least you'll know what it is.**

The face of America's families is also changing, and so are the challenges they confront. Today, in the majority of families, all parents work. Millions of working Americans are also members of a new "sandwich generation," playing dual roles as working parents and working children, responsible not only for their kids but for their aging mothers and fathers. They are working longer hours than ever, while at the same time having to meet a new and growing set of caregiving responsibilities.

Our government's policies–many designed in the New Deal era–have not kept up with the new economy and the changing nature of people's lives. Democrats believe that it is time for our policies and our expectations to catch up. From health care to pensions, from unemployment insurance to paid leave, we need to modernize our policies in order to provide working Americans the tools they need to meet new realities and challenges.

 We're betting on the fact that most people don't remember the *New Deal* and won't take the time to research it. It wasn't exactly a resounding success even though we had a *New Deal Coalition* in place that dominated most elections from 1933 through the early 1960s. Oh sure, several of the programs were declared unconstitutional and many others were abandoned when they failed miserably, but people forget over time. Through the *New Deal*, we pandered to labor unions, created welfare programs, and fostered Social Security, which helped us dominate the national elections. We also heavily regulated banking and communications as well as transportation (which may be why we never were able to create high speed public transportation like other countries). Who knows: had the last remnants of the *New Deal* not dissipated in the 1970's, Al Gore may never have been inspired to invent the Internet!

While FDR had *The Great Depression* going for him, we've only got a recession ... so it may be harder to create the sense of desperation that people felt back then. Similarly, it's hard to equate our military operations in Iraq and Afganistan with the little skirmish called World War II that served as a galvanizing event back then. But heck, we're willing to *try* because we've become even *more* adept at using emerging media and our control of the mainstream press to spread our ideas successfully. Otherwise, how do you think we could have gotten an inexperienced candidate elected to the highest office in the land. It's all about image, baby!

Affordable, Quality Health Care Coverage for All Americans

If one thing came through in the platform hearings, it was that Democrats are united around a commitment that every American man, woman, and child be guaranteed affordable, comprehensive healthcare. In meeting after meeting, people expressed moral outrage with a health care crisis that leaves millions of Americans–including nine million children–without health insurance and millions more struggling to pay rising costs for poor quality care. Half of all personal bankruptcies in America are caused by medical bills. We spend more on health care than any other country, but we're ranked 47th in life expectancy and 43rd in child mortality. Our nation faces epidemics of obesity and chronic diseases as well as new threats like pandemic flu and bioterrorism. Yet despite all of this, less than four cents of every health care dollar is spent on prevention and public health.

The American people understand that good health is the foundation of individual achievement and economic prosperity. Ensuring quality, affordable health care for every single American is essential to children's education, workers' productivity and businesses' competitiveness. We believe that covering all is not just a moral imperative, but is necessary to making our health system workable and affordable. Doing so would end cost-shifting from the uninsured, promote prevention and wellness, stop insurance discrimination, help eliminate health care disparities, and achieve savings through competition, choice, innovation, and higher quality care. While there are different approaches within the Democratic Party about how best to achieve the commitment of covering every American, with everyone in and no one left out, we stand united to achieve this fundamental objective through the legislative process.

 **Unlike many of the other elements in our Platform, this actually has some merit. Health is a critical element of life; albeit, probably not a Constitutionally protected *"right"* ... but important nevertheless. Our problems with health care reform are two-fold: (1) we don't really understand actuarial tables and aren't very good at math (another reason we may not release our college transcripts); and (2) we tend to forget that we limited our commitment to *"covering every American,"* which many people interpret as being limited to ... well ... actual *Americans*.**

As Democrats, we tend to lump *everyone* in the United States into the term *"Americans."* If they *might* be able to vote (dead or alive) and can somehow be categorized as an

"oppressed minority," we consider them to be *Americans*. Shoot, we even think that *terrorist* should be given the the same Constitutional protections afforded to our citizens. Since we also push for amnesty for *"undocumented workers"* to capture their potential votes, the definition becomes even *more* important because we will immediately incur the costs associated with millions of people who do not contribute to the tax base, and that tab will have to be picked up by *real* citizens for our *"philanthropic"* (and politically motivated) approach.

We therefore oppose those who advocate policies that would thrust millions of Americans out of their current private employer-based coverage without providing them access to an affordable, comprehensive alternative, thereby subjecting them to the kind of insurance discrimination that leads to excessive premiums or coverage denials for older and sicker Americans. We reject those who have steadfastly opposed insurance coverage expansions for millions of our nation's children while they have protected overpayments to insurers and allowed underpayments to our nation's doctors. Our vision of a strengthened and improved health care system for all Americans stands in stark contrast to the Republican Party's and includes:

Hey, it was time to throw in a little *fear-mongering*. By implying that Republicans *don't care* about the average American, the elderly, the sick, and *"our nation's children,"* we're able to reinforce the image of them as *cruel, uncaring people* and *widen* the divide between them and the *"oppressed minorities"* we so zealously solicit as our voting base.

<u>Covering All Americans and Providing Real Choices of Affordable Health Insurance Options.</u>

Families and individuals should have the option of keeping the coverage they have or choosing from a wide array of health insurance plans, including many private health insurance options and a public plan. Coverage should be made affordable for all Americans with subsidies provided through tax credits and other means.

 **This sounds great. Of course, a subsidized public plan could have a huge competitive advantage over private health insurance companies, but we're relying on the fact that we can run it as inefficiently as we have the United States Postal Service, the Social Security Adminstration, and Medicare and Medicaid, so that really shouldn't be a concern. And ignore the language about** *"tax credits and other means"* **to subsidize the costs. We're the government, so we have unlimited funds.**

<u>Shared Responsibility.</u>

Health care should be a shared responsibility between employers, workers, insurers, providers and government. All Americans should have coverage they can afford; employers should have incentives to provide coverage to their workers; insurers and providers should ensure high quality affordable care; and the government should ensure that health insurance is affordable and provides meaningful coverage. As affordable coverage is made available, individuals should purchase health insurance and take steps to lead healthy lives.

 **We're really banking on the concept that all Americans should** *"take steps to lead healthy lives."* **If we** *do* **socialize health care in the U.S. , that may be the** *only* **alternative you have. The delays will be too long to get an appointment with a physician, and the cost will be too high ... given the introduction of additional agencies and their related regulation to** *"oversee"* **the process. You'll** *have* **to take better care of yourself. What a brilliant idea!**

An End to Insurance Discrimination

Health insurance plans should accept all applicants and be prohibited from charging different prices based on pre-existing conditions. They should compete on the cost of providing health care and the quality of that care, not on their ability to avoid or over-charge people who are or may get sick. Premiums collected by insurers should be primarily dedicated to care, not profits.

The premise is good: insurance companies should be required to accept all applicants. The reality is that the risk will be spread uniformly across the group, and those who are fortunate enough to remain "well" will be paying a higher premium to subsidize those who are more chronically "ill."

The real trick here is that this is where we tried to slip in the public health care plan without anyone noticing it. The operative phrase is *"Premiums collected by insurers should be primarily dedicated to care, not profits."* Only non-profit organizations funded by charitable donations and special tax-exemptions (*i.e.*, with costs otherwise subsidized by taxpayers) or a government entity with no accountability for viable business performance need apply. Private-sector companies will neither be able to compete nor attract capital with this type of restriction. But, hey! You know that most of us are Poli-Sci majors who never took a business course, and we've already admitted we aren't very good at math.

Portable Insurance.

No one should have to worry about losing health coverage if they change or lose their job.

Admittedly, many of our delegates thought this meant that you could *physically* carry your policy with you because it would be printed in a

convenient size (*i.e, "portable"*). We didn't try to correct them because this is a good idea anyway.

Meaningful Benefits.

Families should have health insurance coverage similar to what Members of Congress enjoy. They should not be forced to bear the burden of skyrocketing premiums, unaffordable deductibles or benefit limits that leave them at financial risk when they become sick. We will finally achieve long-overdue mental health and addiction treatment parity.

We've had great coverage for years ... just like *we* have a much better retirement program than *you* do ..., and *we* don't have to pay Social Security like *you* do. Notice that we didn't say that you should have the *same* program as we do. You don't deserve it because ... well ... *you're* not *us*. But we do think you should have something *"similar."* The *"mental health and addiction treatment parity"* will be particularly important if we're in control of the White House and Congress for any length of time ... because we will undoubtedly drive you crazy.

An Emphasis on Prevention and Wellness

Chronic diseases account for 70 percent of the nation's overall health care spending. We need to promote healthy lifestyles and disease prevention and management especially with health promotion programs at work and physical education in schools. All Americans should be empowered to promote wellness and have access to preventive services to impede the development of costly chronic conditions, such as obesity, diabetes, heart disease, and hypertension. Chronic-care and behavioral health management should be assured for all Americans who require care coordination. This includes assistance for those recovering from traumatic, life-altering injuries and illnesses as well as those with mental health and substance use disorders. We should promote additional tobacco and substance abuse prevention.

 Our excessive spending on social programs has caught on at the State level. States are teetering on the verge of bankruptcy and have had to cut back on educational budgets. As a result, public schools have reduced or eliminated physical education and organized sports programs. Add to that the pressure of the dual-income lifestyles we've been encouraging since the 60's (which is why *"it takes a village"* to raise a child these days), and you have the root cause of the increase in obesity, diabetes, heart disease, and hypertension in our society and well as the mental health issues and substance abuse disorders propagated by anxiety and other societal stresses.

<u>A Modernized System That Lowers Cost and Improves the Quality of Care.</u>

As Americans struggle with increasing health care costs, we believe a strengthened, uniquely American system should provide the highest-quality, most cost-effective care. This should be advanced by aggressive efforts to cut costs and eliminate waste from our health system, which will save the typical family up to $2,500 per year. These efforts include driving adoption of state-of-the-art health information technology systems, privacy-protected electronic medical records, reimbursement incentives, and an independent organization that reviews drugs, devices, and procedures to ensure that people get the right care at the right time. By working with the medical community to improve quality, these reforms will have the added benefit of reducing the prevalence of lawsuits related to medical errors. We should increase competition in the insurance and drug markets; remove some of the cost burden of catastrophic illness from employers and their employees; and lower drug costs by allowing Medicare to negotiate for lower prices, permitting importation of safe medicines from other developed countries, creating a generic pathway for biologic drugs, and increasing use of generics in public programs.

 **Of course, state-of-the-art technology is not cheap, so you can expect prices to soar in the**

near-term if we ever actually implement this idea. Also, since we are heavily funded by various associations within the legal community, we only wanted to allude tangentially to tort reform. Talk about *laissez-faire*: all we ask you to do is trust attorneys to stop filing lawsuits based upon medical errors ... ethical medical malpractice attorneys like our own former Presidential Candidate, John Edwards.

Then, we'll see a reduction in costs ... insurance costs, catastrophic illness, drugs, etc. ... all from increased competition, Medicare's ability to negotiate lower prices (even though many physician's already refuse to accept Medicare patients because of the economics), and our ability to import medicines from other countries whose FDA-equivalent may be less stringent. What could possibly go wrong with those strategies?

<u>A Strong Health Care Workforce.</u>

Through training and reimbursement incentives, there must be a commitment to sufficient and well-qualified primary care physicians and nurses as well as direct care workers.

We know that we don't have nearly enough *"well-qualified primary care physicians and nurses as well as direct care workers"* to handle the surge in demand that our solution will create, so we'll just provide *"training and reimbursement incentives"* to stimulate the supply. Of course it takes eight years of schooling and residency to qualify as a physician, so it will be several decades before we can effectively address the issue. In the interim, people will just have to learn to be patient (no pun intended). Then there's the whole issue of paying for the *"training and reimbursement incentives,"* but in that regard, we can always increase taxes.

Commitment to the Elimination of Disparities in Health Care.

We must end health care disparities among minorities, American Indians, women, and low-income people through better research and better funded community-based health centers. We will make our health care system culturally sensitive and accessible to those who speak different languages. We will support programs that diversify the health are workforce to ensure culturally effective care. We will also address the social determinants that fuel health disparities, and empower the communities most impacted by providing them the resources and technical assistance to be their own agents of wellness. We will speed up and improve reimbursements by the Indian Health Service.

Remember how we explained our fundamental strategy of segmenting people into classes of "oppressed minorities?" Well, we worked in "minorities" in general with "American Indians, women, and low-income people." Then, we sprinkled in terms like "cultural sensitivity," "accessibility," "social determinant," "health disparities," "empowered communities" and "agents of wellness" to show how much we care. Let's see the Republicans top that!

Public Health and Research.

Health and wellness is a shared responsibility among individuals and families, school systems, employers, the medical and public health workforce and government at all levels. We will ensure that Americans can benefit from healthy environments that allow them to pursue healthy choices. Additionally, as childhood obesity rates have more than doubled in the last 30 years, we will work to ensure healthy environments in our schools.

As we discussed earlier, we're going to pretend that deficit spending and fast food lifestyles haven't contributed *at all* to childhood obesity. The main point we want to get across is that *your*

health is *everyone's* responsibility. Now, you may think that it's actually *your* health, but it's not ... it belongs to all of us. So, we'll collectively decide what you need. As for ensuring that *"Americans can benefit from healthy environments that allow them to pursue healthy choices,"* you really already have the choice to exercise (again, no pun intended) your free will to live a healthy lifestyle. We just think we should create some agencies to regulate your "free choice" *for you*.

We must fight HIV/AIDS in our country and around the world. We support increased funding into research, care and prevention of HIV/AIDS. We support a comprehensive national strategic plan to combat HIV/AIDS and a Ryan White Care Act designed and funded to meet today's epidemic, that ends ADAP waiting lists and that focuses on the communities such as African Americans and Latino Americans who are disproportionately impacted through an expanded and renewed minority HIV/AIDS initiative, and on new epicenters such as the Southern part of our nation. We support providing Medicaid coverage to more low-income HIV-positive Americans.

We know that HIV/AIDS is not even in the Top Ten causes of death in the United States, but many of the other diseases are difficult to align with a particular *"oppressed minority."* Conversely, HIV/AIDS is more readily identified with the gay community, which is an accessible and well organized voting block. So, we're not going to put much effort into mentioning the diseases that are more universal and that represent a bigger threat to the majority of Americans' lives. Why should we when we can capture more votes by spending our time convincing the gay community and then bridging into the African American and Latino American communities as well? Nobody does *"oppressed minority"* marketing like the Democrats!

Health care reform must also provide adequate incentives for innovation to ensure that Americans have access to evidence-based and cost-effective health care. Research should be based on science, not ideology. For the millions of Americans and their families suffering from debilitating physical and emotional effects of disease, time is a precious commodity, and it is running out. Yet, over the past eight years, the current Administration has not only failed to promote biomedical and stem cell research, it has actively stood in the way of that research. We cannot tolerate any further inaction or obstruction. We need to invest in biomedical research and stem cell research, so that we are at the leading edge of prevention and treatment. This includes adequate funding for research into diseases such as heart disease, Alzheimer's disease, Parkinson's disease, multiple sclerosis, breast cancer, diabetes, autism and other common and rare diseases, and disorders. We will increase funding to the National Institutes of Health, the National Science Foundation, and the National Cancer Institutes.

We doubt that anyone will really argue with this part of our program. Of course, embryonic stem cell research may have issues that haven't been widely publicized, but outside of that one exception, this part of our health care initiative may actually make sense.

<u>A Strong Partnership with States, Local Governments, Tribes, and Territories.</u>

Recognizing that considerable progress in health care delivery has been pioneered by state and local governments, necessary nationwide reform should build on successful state models of care.

We only wish there was evidence that this were true. Then, we wouldn't have to create a 2,700+ page document with a *ton* of *pork* in it ... and 159 new agencies ... to establish Health Care Reform. We could just copy a successful health care program that was already in place.

A Strong Safety-Net.

Achieving our health goals requires strengthening the safety-net programs, safety-net providers, and public health infrastructure to fill in gaps and ensure public safety in times of disease outbreak or disaster.

This is important because we just recognized that "stuff happens." Had we noticed that "disease outbreaks" and "disasters" occur on an ongoing basis, we could have done something about it in the past during the *decades* in which we were in control of both the House and the Senate ... and even the Presidency. At least now, we'll create "safety nets" and "fill in the gaps" to "ensure public safety." Just don't ask us to identify what those "safety nets" and "gaps" are. We'll have to create a few hundred new agencies to work on those issues.

Empowerment and Support of Older Americans and People with Disabilities.

Seniors and people with disabilities should have access to quality affordable long-term care services, and those services should be readily available at home and in the community. Americans should not be forced to choose between getting care and living independent and productive lives.

This is our attempt to gain favor with the "oppressed minority" of the elderly population before the Republicans do. In the alternative, we can always claim that the Republicans want to take away Medicare and medication coverage ... or get someone like our Florida Congressman to claim that the Republicans would rather let Americans "die quickly" with their alternative plan. Hey, it's worked in the past. It can work again if we need it.

Reproductive Health Care.

We oppose the current Administration's consistent attempts to undermine a woman's ability to make her own life choices and obtain reproductive health care, including birth control. We will end health insurance discrimination against contraception and provide compassionate care to rape victims. We will never put ideology above women's health.

 If this is where we drew the line, we'd probably have a majority of Americans in agreement. The problem is we often go beyond *contra*-ception and aggressively pursue *post*-conception alternatives with little to no limitations. Apparently, some people have a problem with a *laissez-faire* attitude toward abortion either because of its application to women of tender years or as it's applied to viable fetuses in partial birth abortions. Truth be told, we really don't *care* to enter into a debate about when *"life"* begins. We're much more focused upon the critical issue of identifying the time upon which a person's *voting* preferences can be shaped.

Fiscal Responsibility.

As we improve and strengthen our health care system, we must do so in a fiscally responsible way that ensures that we get value for the dollars that are invested.

 Okay, you're laughing again. We told you that math and business were not our strengths. While we may never have demonstrated the discipline to do anything like this, we really *do* want to be *"fiscally responsible."* We think everything will work out well if we can keep the initial estimates barely under a trillion dollars ... although Vegas puts the over-under at $1.9 trillion. Our fallback position will be that *we'll* take care of the *"fiscal"* part ... and the *Republican's* can be *"responsible"* if it doesn't work.

The Left isn't Right

RETIREMENT AND SOCIAL SECURITY

We will make it a priority to secure for hardworking families the part of the American Dream that includes a secure and healthy retirement. Individuals, employers, and government must all play a role. We will adopt measures to preserve and protect existing public and private pension plans. In the 21st century, Americans also need better ways to save for retirement. We will automatically enroll every worker in a workplace pension plan that can be carried from job to job and we will match savings for working families who need the help. We will make sure that CEOs can't dump workers' pensions with one hand while they line their own pockets with the other. At platform hearings, Americans made it clear they feel that's an outrage, and it's time we had leaders who treat it as an outrage. We will ensure all employees who have company pensions receive annual disclosures about their pension fund's investments, including full details about which projects have been invested in, the performance of those investments and appropriate details about probable future investments strategies. We also will reform corporate bankruptcy laws so that workers' retirements are a priority for funding and workers are not left with worthless IOU's after years of service. Finally, we will eliminate all federal income taxes for seniors making less than $50,000 per year. Lower- and middle-income seniors already have to worry about high health care and energy costs; they should not have to worry about tax burdens as well.

 **We know what you're thinking: we haven't been able to manage Social Security from a fiscal standpoint, so how do we expect to be able to create a portable pension program for every single worker in the country? You might also wonder where the money is coming from to** *"match savings for working families who need help."* **Well, the truth of the matter is ... we** *really* **don't know!**

We could just raise taxes on the rich, but at some point, they're going to run out of money. We could raise taxes on the corporations, but it may drive jobs out of the country as our corporations become less competitive with foreign operations

that aren't burdened by the same level of regulation and taxation.

We actually *understand* that ridiculous pension programs negotiated by major unions have decimated a number of our industries, but those unions contribute a lot of money to our campaigns and serve as a marketing engine to encourage their members to vote for us. We can't just *yield* to the truth! So, even if we don't pull this off, we can still promise it. We've promised *so much* that a miss here or there won't even be remembered. Besides, we've got other *"carrots"* to feed to big labor if they call us on our promise; like turning over controlling interest in General Motors and Chrysler when we nationalized them.

Equally as important: this is just one more opportunity to throw CEOs under the bus. Sure, the vast majority of them are honest, hard working individuals who have made a lot of sacrifices to achieve their level of success; but luckily, there are a few *"scum bags"* who we can single out and *"hang in effigy"* from a political standpoint. Then, we'll just paint *all* CEOs with the same broad brush and claim that they're one and the same with the Republican Party. We just can't lose on this issue!

We reject the notion of the presumptive Republican nominee that Social Security is a disgrace; we believe that it is indispensable. We will fulfill our obligation to strengthen Social Security and to make sure that it provides guaranteed benefits Americans can count on, now and in future generations. We will not privatize it.

 While Democrats and Republicans alike have done a miserable job of managing Social Security, we still like the idea of collecting a sizable portion of everyone's earnings and deciding how to invest it. We think *we* know better (despite our record), and allowing individuals to decide how to invest their *own* money … well, that's just *too much* freedom.

Of course, as Federal employees, we have our own pension program and don't have to pay into Social Security. Forget about the old saying, *"What's good for the goose is good for the gander."* It doesn't apply here. We *deserve* a better system, and we *deserve* to be exempt from the one we administer. After all, we're elected *officials*.

And in case you were wondering, our program is underwritten by AIG ... you know, one of the companies that was *"too big to fail."* We used your tax dollars to provide an $85 billion bailout to it, which then grew to a $182 billion bailout ... but, you know how those things go. In case we didn't mention it before ... thanks for protecting our pension program!

GOOD JOBS WITH GOOD PAY

In the platform hearings, Americans expressed dismay that people who are willing to study and work cannot get a job that pays enough to live on in the current economy. Democrats are committed to an economic policy that produces good jobs with good pay and benefits. That is why we support the right to organize. We know that when unions are allowed to do their job of making sure that workers get their fair share, they pull people out of poverty and create a stronger middle class. We will strengthen the ability of workers to organize unions and fight to pass the Employee Free Choice Act. We will restore pro-worker voices to the National Labor Relations Board and the National Mediation Board and we support overturning the NLRB's and NMB's many harmful decisions that undermine the collective bargaining rights of millions of workers. We will ensure that federal employees, including public safety officers who put their lives on the line every day, have the right to bargain collectively, and we will fix the broken bargaining process at the Federal Aviation Administration. We will fight to ban the permanent replacement of striking workers, so that workers can stand up for themselves without worrying about losing their livelihoods. We will continue to vigorously oppose "Right-to-Work" Laws and "paycheck protection" efforts whenever they are proposed. Suspending labor protections during national emergencies compounds the devastation from the emergency. We opposed suspension of Davis-Bacon following Hurricane Katrina, and we support broad application of

Davis-Bacon worker protections to all federal projects. We will stop the abuse of privatization of government jobs. We will end the exploitative practice of employers wrongly misclassifying workers as independent contractors.

The Bush Administration Department of Labor has failed in its obligation to stand up and protect American workers. Our Department of Labor will restore and expand overtime rights for millions of Americans, and will actively enforce wage and hour laws. The Bush Administration is the only administration that has never voluntarily issued a significant final standard for workplace safety. Our Occupational Safety and Health Administration will adopt and enforce comprehensive safety standards. Right now, far too many workers – especially those in the construction and mining industries-risk their lives every day just by going to work.

In America, if someone is willing to work, he or she should be able to make ends meet and have the opportunity to prosper. To that end, we will raise the minimum wage and index it to inflation, and increase the Earned Income Tax Credit so that workers can support themselves and their families. We will modernize the unemployment insurance program to close gaps and extend benefits to the workers who now fall outside it.

We owe big labor *a lot!* So, we *always* emphasize our support of unions. Back in the days of Company Towns, etc., unions actually had a viable role in our society. Today, they've grown into *"mini-governments"* that, in some cases, mandate membership ... or the loss of employment (within union shops). This is the epitome of *freedom of choice* as we see it: join the union within 90 days or lose your job.

And don't forget how the *really big* unions have helped the economy. By creating severe economic pressure on companies through strikes, they have dramatically escalated salaries and benefits for their members. Heck, they've even negotiated programs that pay full salaries to employees who have been laid-off because of downturns in demand, etc. Consider the positive impact that has on the rest of the country. Labor costs soar; driving businesses to move manufacturing and support services off-shore to remain competitive. Prices to

consumers increase significantly to cover the costs, and if the price increases demonstrate elasticity, margins are spread for foreign competitors as well. This isn't all bad; because if consumers continue to pay higher prices, sales tax revenue increases at the State-level and Gross Domestic Product (GDP) increases as well. The later is important because the Federal Deficit is often measured against GDP, so the bigger the number ... the better we look.

Bottom line: big labor contributes heavily to our campaigns in the form of money and delivering votes. We can ill-afford to separate ourselves from unions. And witness the support we get from them when we have to organize a rally or protest of any kind ... or try to disrupt one that the Tea Party is holding.

In addition, big labor understands our *"oppressed minority"* strategy. After all, it plays the same hand of cards: creating and maintaining a *"We vs. They"* tension between employees and management so the *"oppressed"* workers will follow the union party-line.

Just as an aside: it's funny how we get the unions to back our *"oppressed minority"* strategy when it comes to immigration. We claim that we're *"committed to an economic policy that produces good jobs with good pay and benefits,"* yet we support the infusion of *"undocumented workers"* into the country who take jobs away from our citizens and do so at a wage level that we otherwise have deemed to be illegal. Then, we use taxpayers' money to support the *"undocumented workers"* and their families with respect to public schools, public assistance, health care, etc. even though they don't pay taxes. For some reason, the unions don't seem to find it odd that we choose to ignore Federal Immigration Law and implicitly endorse this form of business corruption when the effect is to take potential jobs away from *their* union members. We just hope they continue to ignore it.

WORK AND FAMILY

Over the last few decades, fundamental changes in the way we work and live have trapped too many American families between an economy that's gone global and a government that's gone AWOL. It's time we stop just talking about family values, and start pursuing policies that truly value families. We will expand the Family and Medical Leave Act to reach millions more workers than are currently covered, and we will enable workers to take leave to care for an elderly parent, address domestic violence and sexual assault, or attend a parent-teacher conference. Today 78 percent of the workers who are eligible for leave cannot take it because it's unpaid, so we will work with states and make leave paid. We will also ensure that every American worker is able earn up to seven paid sick days to care for themselves or an ill family member. And we will encourage employers to provide flexible work arrangements—with the federal government leading by example. We will expand the childcare tax credit, provide every child access to quality, affordable early childhood education, and double funding for after-school and summer learning opportunities for children. We will provide assistance to those who need long-term care and to the working men and women of this country who do the heroic job of providing care for their aging relatives. All Americans who are working hard and taking responsibility deserve the chance to do right by their loved ones. That's the America we believe in.

This is our Party at its very best! We offer *everything* for FREE to *everyone*. While we complain about executive compensation, excess profits, etc., we have no problem promising that *everyone* should be paid for *not* working. Throw a couple of "oppressed minority" categories into the mix (*e.g.,* children, elderly, and everyone in between; childcare, after- school, and summer learning opportunities; victims of domestic violence and sexual assault, etc.) and you've got the perfect Democratic program. And how are we going to fund it? Don't ask. You already know. We're either going to tax the rich or place the burden on the companies to make them eve*n less* competitive. This may not appear to make long-term sense to you, but remember ... we have a great pension program, and we'll all be retired before anything hits the fan!

The kicker is that *"we will encourage employers to provide flexible work arrangements — with the federal government leading by example."* We hardly work now, but wait until you see how *little* we can do when we *really* put our minds to it!

POVERTY

When Bobby Kennedy saw the shacks and poverty along the Mississippi Delta, he asked, "How can a country like this allow it?" Forty years later, we're still asking that question. The most American answer we can give is: "We won't allow it." One in eight Americans lives in poverty today all across our country, in our cities, in our suburbs, and in our rural communities. Most of these people work but still can't pay the bills. Nearly thirteen million of the poor are children. We can't allow this kind of suffering and hopelessness to exist in our country. It's not who we are.

Working together, we can cut poverty in half within ten years. We will provide all our children a world-class education, from early childhood through college. We will develop innovative transitional job programs that place unemployed people into temporary jobs and train them for permanent ones. To help workers share in our country's productivity, we'll expand the Earned Income Tax Credit, and raise the minimum wage and index it to inflation. The majority of adults in poverty are women, and to combat poverty we must work for fair pay, support for mothers, and policies that promote responsible fatherhood. We'll start letting our unions do what they do best again—organize and lift up our workers. We'll make sure that every American has affordable health care that stays with them no matter what happens. We will assist American Indian communities, since 10 of the 20 poorest counties in the United States are on Indian lands. We'll bring businesses back to our inner-cities, increase the supply of affordable housing, and establish "promise neighborhoods" that provide comprehensive services in areas of concentrated poverty. These will be based on proven models, such as the Harlem Children's Zone in New York City, which seeks to engage all residents with tangible goals such as attendance at parenting schools, retention of meaningful employment, college for every participating student, and strong physical and mental health outcomes for children. The Democratic Party believes that the fight against poverty must be national priority. Eradicating poverty will require the sustained commitment of the President of the United States, and we believe that the White House must offer leadership and resources to advance this agenda.

 Notice how we integrated women, unions, American Indians and the Black community (indirectly through the Harlem Children's Zone reference) to reach our *"oppressed minority"* quota for this part of our Platform. Then we invoke the hallowed name of Bobby Kennedy for its emotional value.

Seriously though, poverty in the United States *is* unacceptable. We suggest solving the problem by empowering unions to negotiate higher wages that may, in turn, reduce the number of jobs that companies can offer. We call for higher minimum wages, yet fight hard for amnesty for *"undocumented workers"* who circumvent the system. And finally, we pledge to *"provide all our children a world-class education, from early childhood through college,"* and to *"develop innovative transitional job programs that place unemployed people into temporary jobs and train them for permanent ones."* Of course, these last two promises take money and expertise we don't have.

What we *don't* pledge to do is to create a *primary focus* on improving living conditions for citizens of the United States. Instead, we *will* continue to demonstrate our *"good will"* by writing checks and donating food, product, services and other resources to foreign countries ... particularly those who hate us ... currently to the tune of about $26 billion per year. Remember when we said earlier that *"there is no more important priority than renewing American leadership on the world stage?"* We *meant* that, and we'll spend as much time and money as necessary to become more popular ... because we're politicians; and for politicians, popularity is *everything*. The funny thing is that these people can't even *vote* for us, yet we'll

spend every bit as much time currying *their* favor as we will trying to resolve poverty for our *own* citizens.

OPPORTUNITY FOR WOMEN

We, the Democratic Party, are the party that has produced more women Governors, Senators, and Members of Congress than any other. We have produced the first woman Secretary of State, the first woman Speaker of the House of Representatives, and, in 2008, Hillary Rodham Clinton, the first woman in American history to win presidential primaries in our nation. We believe that our daughters should have the same opportunities as our sons; our party is proud that we have put eighteen million cracks in the highest glass ceiling. We know that when America extends its promise to women, the result is increased opportunity for families, communities, and aspiring people everywhere.

When women still earn 76 cents for every dollar that a man earns, it doesn't just hurt women; it hurts families and children. We will pass the "Lilly Ledbetter" Act, which will make it easier to combat pay discrimination; we will pass the Fair Pay Act; and we will modernize the Equal Pay Act. We will invest in women-owned small businesses and remove the capital gains tax on start-up small businesses. We will support women in math and science, increasing American competitiveness by retaining the best workers in these fields, regardless of gender. We recognize that women still carry the majority of childrearing responsibilities, so we have created a comprehensive work and family agenda. We recognize that women are the majority of adults who make the minimum wage, and are particularly hard-hit by recession and poverty; we will protect Social Security, increase the minimum wage, and expand programs to combat poverty and improve education so that parents and children can lift themselves out of poverty. We will work to combat violence against women.

We believe that standing up for our country means standing up against sexism and all intolerance. Demeaning portrayals of women cheapen our debates, dampen the dreams of our daughters, and deny us the contributions of too many. Responsibility lies with us all.

 No one can argue with the importance of creating equality for women ... or for any other group we choose to identify. *All* citizens should be treated equally. In this day and age, it is a travesty that it even merits mention. Of course, we do it to cement our relationship with that particular voting block. If we can't make women identify themselves with some form of *"oppression,"* we may not be able to count on their votes!

INVESTING IN AMERICAN COMPETITIVENESS

At a critical moment of transition like this one, Americans understand that, more than anything else, success will depend on the dynamism, determination, and innovation of the American people. But success also depends on national leadership that can move this country forward with confidence and a common purpose. In platform hearings, Americans called on their government to "invest back" in them and their country. That's what Lincoln did when he pushed for a transcontinental railroad, incorporated our National Academy of Sciences, passed the Homestead Act and created the land grant colleges. That's what Franklin Delano Roosevelt did in creating the Tennessee Valley Authority, electrifying rural America and investing in an Arsenal of Democracy. That's the kind of leadership we intend to provide.

 This is the second time we've cited Abraham Lincoln, who was a Republican, along with Franklin D. Roosevelt, as role models of leadership. Of course, they also had something else in common. Lincoln was President during the Civil War, and Roosevelt was President during World War II. Those were galvanizing events. Oh, how we long for a good Civil or World War to pull our country together. Just kidding!

NEW AMERICAN ENERGY

In the local platform hearings, Americans talked about the importance of energy to the economy, to national security, and to the health of our planet. Speaking loud and clear, they said that America needs a new bold and sustainable energy policy to meet the challenges of our time. In the past, America has been stirred to action when faced with new threats to our national security, or new competitive conditions that undercut our economic leadership. The energy threat we face today may be less immediate than threats from dictators, but it is as real and as dangerous. The dangers are eclipsed only by the opportunities that would come with change. We know that the jobs of the 21st century will be created in developing new energy solutions. The question is whether these jobs will be created in America, or abroad. We should use government procurement policies to incentivize domestic production of clean and renewable energy. Already, we've seen countries like Germany, Spain and Brazil reap the benefits of economic growth from clean energy. But we are decades behind in confronting this challenge.

It is an embarrassment that our country isn't leap-years ahead in the development of clean energy. While we really don't think *"government procurement policies"* **will efficiently** *"incentivize domestic production of clean and renewable energy,"* **it makes it sound like we should be involved in the process.**

For the sake of our security–and for every American family that is paying the price at the pump– we will break our addiction to foreign oil. In platform hearings around the country, Americans called for a Manhattan or Apollo Project-level commitment to achieve energy independence. We hear that call and we Democrats commit to fast-track investment of billions of dollars over the next ten years to establish a green energy sector that will create up to five million jobs. Good jobs, like those in Pennsylvania where workers manufacture wind turbines, the ones in the factory in Nevada producing components for solar energy generation plants, or the jobs that will be created when plug-in hybrids start rolling off the assembly line in Michigan. This transition to a clean-energy industry will also benefit low-income communities: we'll create an energy-focused youth job program to give disadvantaged youth job skills for this emerging industry.

We know we will spend *"billions of dollars over the next ten years"* because, let's face it, we always do! The *"5 million jobs"* number came from *"atmospheric extraction"* ... we just pulled it out of thin air. With all of the other regulations, taxes, fines and operating burdens we're putting on the business sector in general, you could realistically expect these jobs to move offshore in fairly rapid order. At least we can control when *"plug-in hybrids start rolling off the assembly line in Michigan"* ... since we nationalized General Motors and Chrysler.

And when was the last time you heard of a youth movement (outside of Germany) that would organize an *"oppressed"* segment of our youth into a well-oiled (no pun intended) part of our energy strategy? You've got to admit ... we're good at this!

It will not be easy, but neither was getting to the moon. We know we can't drill our way to energy independence and so we must summon all of our ingenuity and legendary hard work and we must invest in research and development, and deployment of renewable energy technologies—such as solar, wind, geothermal, as well as technologies to store energy through advanced batteries and clean up our coal plants. And we will call on businesses, government, and the American people to make America 50 percent more energy efficient by 2030, because we know that the most energy efficient economy will also gain the competitive edge for new manufacturing and jobs that stay here at home. We will help pay for all of it by dedicating a portion of the revenues generated by an economy-wide cap and trade program- a step that will also dramatically reduce our greenhouse gas emissions and jumpstart billions in private capital investment in a new energy economy.

 Actually, we really could *"drill our way to energy independence"* because we have sufficient, *known* oil deposits within the United States to do it, but it wouldn't please the environmental groups that tend to vote "Democrat." We're not sure how to get you to *"make America 50 percent more energy efficient by 2030,"* but you can count on the fact that taxes and fines will be part of the process ... with *"Cap and Trade"* leading the way.

As an interesting side note, we created the Department of Energy on August 4, 1977 under the Carter Administration for the express purpose of lessening our Nation's dependence on foreign oil. The DOE now has grown to about 16,000 full time employees and 100,000 contract workers with an annual operating budget of approximately $25 billion. We hope this will give you better insight into our competence at delivering what we promise.

We'll dramatically increase the fuel efficiency of automobiles, and we'll help auto manufacturers and parts suppliers convert to build the cars and trucks of the future and their key components in the United States. And we will help workers learn the skills they need to compete in the green economy. We are committed to getting at least 25 percent of our electricity from renewable sources by 2025. Building on the innovative efforts of the private sector, states, cities, and tribes across the country, we will create new federal-local partnerships to scale the success and deployment of new energy solutions, install a smarter grid, build more efficient buildings, and use the power of federal and military purchasing programs to jumpstart promising new markets and technologies. We'll invest in advanced biofuels like cellulosic ethanol which will provide American-grown fuel and help free us from the tyranny of oil. We will use innovative measures to dramatically improve the energy efficiency of buildings.

 We know what you're thinking. If we keep imposing regulations, raising corporate taxes, and establishing new hurdles for businesses to

overcome, how can we possibly *maintain*, much less *move* the manufacturing of automobiles and their components into the United States? Simple! Since we have effectively nationalized them and turned them over to our ever-supportive unions, we'll just exempt them and show you how competitive American industry can be when the government doesn't interfere ... but don't quote us on that!

It was difficult to work a prerequisite *"oppressed minority"* into this section, but we did it. We used the word *"tribe."* If we can bring this same level of creativity to establishing renewable energy sources and advancing biofuels, we should have no problem escaping *"the tyranny of oil,"* which today provides jobs for hundreds of thousands of workers and contributes significantly to the GDP and tax base of the United States.

To lower the price of gasoline, we will crack down on speculators who are driving up prices beyond the natural market rate. We will direct the Federal Trade Commission and Department of Justice to vigorously investigate and prosecute market manipulation in oil futures. And we will help those who are hit hardest by high energy prices by increasing funding for low-income heating assistance and weatherization programs, and by providing energy assistance to help middle-class families make ends meet in this time of inflated energy prices.

 To support the *"fear factor"* strategy that works so well with our *"oppressed minorities"* strategy, we occasionally throw in a *sacrificial lamb* that no one minds seeing slaughtered: in this case, Wall Street. At the same time, we weave low-income and middle-class Americans into the rhetoric to solidify the *"We vs. They"* paradigm we like to maintain.

This plan will safeguard our economy, our country, and the future of our planet. This plan will create good jobs that pay well and can't be outsourced. With these policies, we will protect our country from the national security threats created by reliance on foreign oil and global insecurity due to climate change. And this is how we'll solve the problem of four-dollar-a-gallon gas—with a comprehensive plan and investment in clean energy.

 We had to work *"climate change"* into this somehow to satisfy our environmentalist supporters, not to mention Al Gore, *Father of the Internet and Inconvenient Truths* ... and creator of an enormous, personal carbon footprint while traveling the globe in his private jet to warn the rest of us. We're inspired by how important his *massage* is to him ... uh ... we *meant* to say, his *"message"* is to him! Sorry for the Freudian slip.

A WORLD CLASS EDUCATION FOR EVERY CHILD

In the 21st century, where the most valuable skill is knowledge, countries that out-educate us today will out-compete us tomorrow. In the platform hearings, Americans made it clear that it is morally and economically unacceptable that our high-schoolers continue to score lower on math and science tests than most other students in the world and continue to drop-out at higher rates than their peers in other industrialized nations. We cannot accept the persistent achievement gap between minority and white students or the harmful disparities that exist between different schools within a state or even a district. Americans know we can and should do better.

 Notice that we were able to work in a *minority vs. white theme* to remain consistent with our core strategy. Good, huh?

With respect to the actual issue, please understand how difficult it is for us in our quest to maintain *"political correctness"* to transition our students into individuals who can compete academically at the international level. We've worked so hard to give everyone good grades to build up their self-esteem and to award trophies to everyone who participates. It will be a challenge to move to more of a *merit* basis when it comes to honoring achievement. And that applies to our teachers as well, who up to now have been

instructed by their union advisors to be adamantly opposed to any form of meritocracy that militates against the protection of the archaic practice of tenure.

The Democratic Party firmly believes that graduation from a quality public school and the opportunity to succeed in college must be the birthright of every child–not the privilege of the few. We must prepare all our students with the 21st century skills they need to succeed by progressing to a new era of mutual responsibility in education. We must set high standards for our children, but we must also hold ourselves accountable–our schools, our teachers, our parents, business leaders, our community and our elected leaders. And we must come together, form partnerships, and commit to providing the resources and reforms necessary to help every child reach their full potential.

This is another difficult area of reconciliation for us. While we want to see our children do better, we think that it's their *"birthright"* to graduate from *"a quality public school"* and to *"succeed in college."* This is at odds with one of our original statements (*i.e.*, that each generation should have *"the opportunity through hard work, service and sacrifice, to enjoy a brighter future than the last"*), but it feels so … well … Democratic! How can we *ever* ask them to work hard when success is their *"birthright?"* After all, this is *"a new era of mutual responsibility in education,"* so it must be *our* responsibility to *graduate* them … and *their* responsibility to go through the motions.

Early Childhood

We will make quality, affordable early childhood care and education available to every American child from the day he or she is born. Our Children's First Agenda, including increases in Head Start and Early Head Start, and investments in high-quality Pre-K, will improve quality and provide learning and support to families with children ages zero to five. Our Presidential Early Learning Council will coordinate these efforts.

 **This will allow us to begin indoctrinating children at an early age:** *the government will care for you ... the government will care for you.* **Forget that we lamented earlier about how dual-income families featured parents that didn't have the opportunity to spend quality time with their children. Besides, past generations were wrong:** *it takes a village* **to raise a child. If only we can eliminate "One Nation under God" and replace it with ♪ "Mmm ... mmm ... mmm, Barack Hussein Obama" ♪ ... we'll be just fine!**

<u>K-12</u>

We must ensure that every student has a high-quality teacher and an effective principal. That starts with recruiting a new generation of teacher and principals by making this pledge–if you commit your life to teaching, America will commit to paying for your college education. We'll provide better preparation, mentoring and career ladders. Where there are teachers who are still struggling and underperforming we should provide them with individual help and support. And if they're still underperforming after that, we should find a quick and fair way—consistent with due process— to put another teacher in that classroom.

 **Now, we're promising** *real* **tenure ... just for committing to a particular profession.** *We'll* **pay for your education, and** *you'll* **have a career for life.** *Finally*, **Registered Offenders will have a career path that is in alignment with their beliefs. Okay, that could be a problem, but we'll address it if it arises. In the near term, all you have to do is sign on the dotted line to teach what** *we* **tell you to teach. What could possibly go wrong with that?**

To reward our teachers, we will follow the lead of school districts and educators that have pioneered innovative ways to increase teacher pay that are developed with teachers, not imposed on them. We will make an unprecedented national investment to provide teachers with better pay and better support to improve their skills, and their students' learning. We'll reward effective teachers who teach in underserved areas, take on added responsibilities like mentoring new teachers, or consistently excel in the classroom.

We will fix the failures and broken promises of No Child Left Behind—while holding to the goal of providing every child access to a world-class education, raising standards, and ensuring accountability for closing the achievement gap. We will end the practice of labeling a school and its students as failures and then throwing our hands up and walking away from them without having provided the resources and supports these students need. But this alone is not an education policy. It's just a starting point. We will work with our nation's governors and educators to create and use assessments that will improve student learning and success in school districts all across America by including the kinds of critical thinking, communication, and problem-solving skills that our children will need. We will address the dropout crisis by investing in intervention strategies in middle schools and high schools and we will invest in after-school programs, summer school, alternative education programs, and youth jobs.

We will promote innovation within our public schools—because research shows that resources alone will not create the schools that we need to help our children succeed. We need to adapt curricula and the school calendar to the needs of the 21st century; reform the schools of education that produce most of our teachers; promote public charter schools that are accountable; and streamline the certification process for those with valuable skills who want to shift careers and teach.

 **Most of this makes sense. If you're wondering why we threw in the comment about *"No Child Left Behind,"* it's because it was a program started by the Bush Administration to accomplish very similar goals. We felt obligated to bash it so it didn't appear that we were just continuing a Bush program that made sense.**

We will also meet our commitment to special education and to students who are English Language Learners. We support full funding of the Individuals with Disabilities Education Act. We also support transitional bilingual education and will help Limited English Proficient students get ahead by supporting and funding English Language Learner classes. We support teaching students second languages, as well as contributing through education to the revitalization of American Indian languages.

You probably recognized that it was time to work in some *"oppressed minorities,"* and no one can challenge the emotion pull of evoking those with disabilities. We threw in American Indians just for the heck of it.

While we support Spanish as a primary language when we campaign in Hispanic communities, we are walking a tight rope here when we profess to support English as our Nation's language. Of course, if push came to shove and votes were on the line, we'd default back to a position of *"political correctness"* and claim that those who tried to force others to *"give up their culture"* were just racists or ... worse yet ... Republicans!

We know that there is no program and no policy that can substitute for parents who are involved in their children's education from day one–who make sure their children are in school on time, help them with their homework, and attend those parent-teacher conferences; who are willing to turn off the TV once in a while, put away the video games, and read to their children. Responsibility for our children's education has to start at home. We have to set high standards for them, and spend time with them, and love them. We have to hold ourselves accountable.

Our first draft said, *"If you don't abort the little bastards, you have to take care of them,"* but some of our *less-progressive* constituents thought that it might offend independent moderates whose votes we would like to capture ... so we amended the language accordingly.

Higher Education

We believe that our universities, community colleges, and other institutions of higher learning must foster among their graduates the skills needed to enhance economic competitiveness. We will work with institutions of higher learning to produce highly skilled graduates in science, technology, engineering, and math disciplines who will become innovative workers prepared for the 21st century economy.

 **We recognize that this will be tough to do while retaining our commitment to everyone's *"birthright"* to graduate and be successful in college. Since most of us were Poli-Sci majors in college, we also haven't got a clue of what *"science, technology, engineering, and math disciplines"* require.**

At community colleges and training programs across the country, we will invest in short-term accelerated training and technical certifications for the unemployed and under-employed to speed their transition to careers in high-demand occupations and emerging industries. We will reward successful community colleges with grants so they can continue their good work. We support education delivery that makes it possible for non-traditional students to receive support and encouragement to obtain a college education, including Internet, distance education, and night and weekend programs.

 **This has some real merit. But honestly, we hope these students don't exert too much academic effort. Our union brothers will need a continuing flow of factory workers to organize in the future. Besides, we have no idea how to fund the grants we're promising ... other than by raising taxes of course!**

We must also invest in training and education to prepare incumbent job-holders with skills to meet the rigors of the new economic environment and provide them access to the broad knowledge and concrete tools offered by apprenticeships, internships, and postsecondary education. We need to fully fund joint labor-management apprenticeship programs and reinvigorate our industrial crafts programs to train the next generation of skilled American craft workers.

 **Forget the perennial funding question; the real issue here is that we don't want people to feel like they *need* to take *any* personal responsibility for their future. If we promise to spoon-feed them everything from the day they enter pre-school to the day they die, they'll become *completely* dependent on us. We're the government. We know better! And the sooner they learn that, the more secure *our* jobs and lifestyles will be. We'd start the process *in the womb* if we could. Why do you thing *embryonic* stem cell research has our support?**

We recognize the special value and importance of our Historically Black Colleges and Universities and other minority serving institutions in meeting the needs of our increasingly diverse society and will work to ensure their viability and growth. We will make college affordable for all Americans by creating a new American Opportunity Tax Credit to ensure that the first $4,000 of a college education is completely free for most Americans. In exchange for the credit, students will be expected to perform community service. We will continue to support programs, especially the Pell Grant program, that open the doors of college opportunity to low-income Americans. We will enable families to apply for financial aid simply by checking a box on their tax form.

 **Surely, you've caught on by now ... it's *"oppressed minority"* time! Let's see: Blacks? Check! ... Generic minorities? Check! ... Low-income? Check!**

As for the *"new American Opportunity Tax Credit to ensure that the first $4,000 of a college education is completely free for most Americans"* ... Let's see: there about 3 million freshman entering college each year even *before* we ordain that *everyone* has the right to attend. At $4,000 a pop, that's $12 billion.

That's just round-off error in terms of our propensity to spend. We'll just tax the rich!

Our institutions of higher education are also the economic engines of today and tomorrow. We will partner with them to translate new ideas into innovative products, processes and services.

SCIENCE, TECHNOLOGY AND INNOVATION

America has long led the world in innovation. But this Administration's hostility to science has taken a toll. At a time when technology helps shape our future, we devote a smaller and smaller share of our national resources to research and development.

It is time again to lead. We took a critical step with the America Competes Act and we will start by implementing that Act —then we will do more. We will make science, technology, engineering, and math education a national priority. We will double federal funding for basic research, invest in a strong and inspirational vision for space exploration, and make the Research and Development Tax Credit permanent. We will invest in the next generation of transformative energy technologies and health IT and we will renew the defense R&D system. We will lift the current Administration's ban on using federal funding for embryonic stem cells– cells that would have otherwise have been discarded and lost forever–for research that could save lives. We will ensure that our patent laws protect legitimate rights while not stifling innovation and creativity. We will end the Bush Administration's war on science, restore scientific integrity, and return to evidence-based decision-making.

In sum, we will strengthen our system, treat science and technology as crucial investments, and use these forces to ensure a future of economic leadership, health well-being and national security.

And what time is it? Altogether now: *"It's Bush-bashing time."* You see, "W" pretty much abdicated the Presidency during his second term once we became the Majority Party in both the House and the Senate. Talk about your *"Party of No"* ... we *perfected* it! He couldn't get anything passed, so he apparently just gave up. That's why his second term was so ineffective. Since we've turned public sentiment against him with the help of the mainstream press, it doesn't *matter* whether our ideas are believable ... just as long as we position them as *anti-Bush*. While we won't admit to the legitimacy of a *"war on terrorism,"* we have no problem referencing the Bush Administration's purported *"war on science."*

We think we can continue to get traction out of the anti-Bush sentiment for *at least* a year or two. In fact, we intend to tie every problem we face to the Bush Administration for *as long* as we can, and we encourage *all* Democrats to reference *any* challenges that arise as *"problems we inherited."* That's what we call *true leadership* and *taking responsibility*.

INVEST IN MANUFACTURING AND OUR MANUFACTURING COMMUNITIES

We will invest in American jobs and finally end the tax breaks that ship jobs overseas. We will create an Advanced Manufacturing Fund to provide for our next generation of innovators and job creators; we will expand the Manufacturing Extension Partnerships and create new job training programs for clean technologies. We will bring together government, private industry, workers, and academia to turn around the manufacturing sector of the U.S. economy and provide assistance to automakers and parts companies to encourage retooling of facilities in this country to produce advanced technology vehicles and their key components. We will support efforts like the recently proposed Senate Appropriations measure that gives manufacturers access to low-interest loans to help convert factories to build more fuel-efficient vehicles. And we will invest in a clean energy economy to create up to five million new green-collar jobs.

This is our attempt to subtly take a shot at big business while supporting unions without being too overt about it. Yes, by taking away tax breaks, we'll undoubtedly encourage businesses to keep jobs in the United States where they can be subject to our ever

increasing regulation and our unions' pursuit of higher wages and extravagant benefits and pension programs.

We seriously believe that we can create *"our next generation of innovators and job creators"* by just creating *"an Advanced Manufacturing Fund."* And the only two industries we really care about are the automobile and clean energy sectors. We basically own the one along with the UAW, and you can bet we're all privately investing in the other. Remember, we can basically *legislate* enough tax breaks and deregulation for our favorite industries to create near-monopolistic business environments for them. At least, that's our hope.

Our manufacturing communities need immediate relief. And we will help states and localities whose budgets are strained in times of need. We will modernize and expand Trade Adjustment Assistance. We will help workers build a safety net, with health care, retirement security, and a way to stay out of crippling debt. We will partner with community colleges and other higher education institutions, so that we're training workers to meet the demands of local industry, including environmentally-friendly technology.

This is all a bit repetitive, but we were running out of *real* ideas to make this a substantive Platform. Again, everything is geared toward placating our constituencies without a clue of how we're to pay for all of our promises. The biggest challenge we face is that *rich people* might run out of money before *we* run out of new programs. You do have to smile though when we say that we're going to help workers *"stay out of crippling debt,"* when *creating* crippling debt is what we do best.

CREATING NEW JOBS BY REBUILDING AMERICAN INFRASTRUCTURE

A century ago, Teddy Roosevelt called together leaders from business and government to develop a plan for the next century's infrastructure. It falls to us to do the same. Right now, we are spending less than at any time in recent history and far less than our international competitors on this critical component of our nation's strength. We will start a National Infrastructure Reinvestment Bank that can leverage private investment in infrastructure improvements, and create nearly two million new good jobs. We will undertake projects that maximize our safety and security and ability to compete, which we will fund as we bring the war in Iraq to a responsible close. We will modernize our power grid, which will help conservation and spur the development and distribution of clean energy. We need a national transportation policy, including high-speed rail and light rail. We can invest in our bridges, roads, and public transportation so that people have choices in how they get to work. We will ensure every American has access to highspeed broadband and we will take on special interests in order to unleash the power of the wireless spectrum

 **Now, we call upon the leadership of yet another Republican (although not a particularly good one), Teddy Roosevelt. Once again, using atmospheric extraction, we pull** *"two million new jobs"* **out of the air as the** *result* **of starting a** *"National Infrastructure Reinvestment Bank."* **Truth be told, we'll create another 2 million jobs within the new agencies that we'll undoubtedly decide we need to regulate it.**

At least we've identified how we're going to *pay* **for this program. We're going to** *"bring the war in Iraq to a responsible close."* **No problem! We'll end the war in Iraq on schedule ... just like we'll close Gitmo no later than January 1, 2009.**

As for public transportation, we'll create policies. We're not sure how many people can actually be transported by *policies***, but we'll cross that bridge when we come to it (no pun intended). And in the interest of clean energy, we intend to propose that all** *new* **highways** *run downhill* **to conserve fuel and lessen our dependence on foreign oil.**

A CONNECTED AMERICA

In the 21st century, our world is more intertwined than at any time in human history. This new connectedness presents us with untold opportunities for innovation, but also new challenges. We will protect the Internet's traditional openness and ensure that it remains a dynamic platform for free speech, innovation, and creativity. We will implement a national broadband strategy (especially in rural areas, and our reservations and territories) that enables every American household, school, library, and hospital to connect to a world-class communications infrastructure. We will rededicate our nation to ensuring that all Americans have access to broadband and the skills to use it effectively. In an increasingly technology-rich, knowledge-based economy, we understand that connectivity is a key part of the solution to many of our most important challenges: job creation, economic growth, energy, health care, and education. We will establish a Chief Technology Officer for the nation, to ensure we use technology to enhance the functioning, transparency, and expertise of government, including establishing a national interoperable public safety communications network to help first responders at the local, state and national level communicate with one another during a crisis.

We will toughen penalties, increase enforcement resources, and spur private sector cooperation with law enforcement to identify and prosecute those who exploit the Internet to try to harm children. We will encourage more educational content on the Web and in our media. We will give parents the tools and information they need to manage what their children see on television and the Internet – in ways fully consistent with the First Amendment. We will strengthen privacy protections in the digital age and will harness the power of technology to hold government and business accountable for violations of personal privacy. We will encourage diversity in the ownership of broadcast media, promote the development of new media outlets for expression of diverse viewpoints, and clarify the public interest obligations of broadcasters who occupy the nation's spectrum.

Hey, dude, it's the Internet! We're wild about this media since it helps us beat the white-haired, old men the Republicans run against us who don't even know how to turn on a computer. Governor Blagojevich aside, most of us at least know how to do *that*. If you work in the SEC, you have to know how to download graphics ... and we do mean *graphics!* And some of our our

employees in the Department of Interior can even tell you which porn sites go best with crystal meth.

We want to bring the Internet to *everyone* ... even the one in eight Americans who live in poverty that we described earlier. Oh sure, some of them may prefer food and clothing, but in this technology age, we have to equip them to *compete*! Perhaps a bigger challenge that extends beyond poverty is the problem of illiteracy in America. It's pointless to give Internet access to someone who's illiterate ... unless they work for the SEC or the Department of the Interior. Then, pictures will do.

SUPPORT SMALL BUSINESS AND ENTREPRENEURSHIP

Encouraging new industry and creating jobs means giving more support to American entrepreneurs. We will exempt all start-up companies from capital gains taxes and provide them a tax credit for health insurance. We will provide a new tax credit for small businesses that offer quality health insurance to their employees. We will help small businesses facing high energy costs. We will work to remove bureaucratic barriers for small and start-up businesses—for example, by making the patent process more efficient and reliable. Our Small Business Administration will recognize the importance of small business to women, people of color, tribes, and rural America and will work to help nurture entrepreneurship. We will create a national network of public-private business incubators and technical support.

 While our actions speak louder than our words, we *do* recognize that small business drives our economy. If we're to have any hope of stimulating job growth, it will have to come from small business. For political reasons, we have to appear to be concerned about *"the little guy"* even though we'd rather spend our time harassing big business. That being said, we saw this as an opportunity to reintroduce *"oppressed minorities"* into the discussion by referencing *"women, people of color, tribes, and rural America"* in a totally meaningless way.

REAL LEADERSHIP FOR RURAL AMERICA

Rural America is home to 60 million Americans. The agricultural sector is critical to the rural economy and to all Americans. We depend on those in agriculture to produce the food, feed, fiber, and fuel that support our society. Thankfully, American farmers possess an unrivaled capacity to produce an abundance of these high-quality products.

In return, we will provide a strong safety net for family farms, a permanent disaster relief program, expansion of agriculture research, and an emphasis on agricultural trade. We will promote economic development in rural and tribal communities by investing in renewable energy, which will transform the rural economy and create millions of new jobs, by upgrading technological and physical infrastructure, by addressing the challenges faced by public schools in rural areas, including forest county schools, supporting higher education opportunities and by attracting quality teachers, doctors and nurses through loan forgiveness programs and other incentive programs. All Americans, urban and rural, hold a shared interest in preserving and increasing the economic vitality of family farms. We will continue to develop and advance policies that promote sustainable and local agriculture, including funding for soil and water conservation programs.

We really don't care about *"rural"* America, but we at least have to pay lip service to it. We're not even sure what *"rural"* means. We think it's a synonym for *"farmer."* Have you ever looked at a map that shows where our voter base is located? It's almost *exclusively* in big cities. You know: where *welfare programs* and *social services* are king. People outside of New York City, Los Angeles, Chicago, San Francisco, etc. ... who aren't *dependent* upon us ... just don't *vote* for us.

ECONOMIC STEWARDSHIP

Since the time of our Founders, we have struggled to balance the same forces that confronted Alexander Hamilton and Thomas Jefferson–self-interest and community; markets and democracy; the concentration of wealth and power, and the necessity of transparency and opportunity for each and every American. Throughout our history, Americans have pursued their dreams within a free market that has been the engine of America's progress. It's a market that has created a prosperity that is the envy of the world, and opportunity for generations of Americans. A market that has provided great rewards to the innovators and risk-takers who have made America a beacon for science, technology, and discovery.

Honestly, if this was a multiple choice question, we would have picked *"self-interest"* and *"power."* It galls us that the *"free market"* has *"provided great rewards to the innovators and risk-takers who have made America a beacon for science, technology, and discovery"* because it isn't compliant with *our* need for big government. So, now we have to spend some time *justifying* our self-righteous importance.

But the American experiment has worked in large part because we have guided the market's invisible hand with a higher principle. Our free market was never meant to be a free license to take whatever you can get, however you can get it. That is why we have put in place rules of the road to make competition fair, open, and honest. We have done this not to stifle–but rather to advance – prosperity and liberty.

Truth be told, we've done this because it empowers us. What we really believe is that the *"free market"* was never meant to be *"free."* We think that *everything* should be regulated ... by us!

In this time of economic transformation and crisis, we must be stewards of this economy more than ever before. We will maintain fiscal responsibility, so that we do not mortgage our children's future on a mountain of debt. We can do this at the same time that we invest in our future. We will restore fairness and responsibility to our tax code. We will bring balance back to the housing markets, so that people do not have to lose their homes. And we will encourage personal savings, so that our economy remains strong and Americans can live well in their retirements.

 Why are you shaking your head in disbelief? We really believe this! We really think that we can *"maintain fiscal responsibility, so that we do not mortgage our children's future on a mountain of debt."* Taking our lead from former-President Clinton, *"it depends on what your definition of 'mountain' is."* While we ran on the premise that the irresponsible Bush Administration's deficit was the largest in history, watch as we almost instantly triple it; creating a deficit that exceeds the *cumulative* amount of *every* prior Administration ... and we're just getting started. However, we prefer to look at this as a *"very large hill;"* perhaps one of epic proportions, but we refuse to call it a *"mountain."*

Then, there's the definitional essence of what we mean when we say *"we will restore fairness and responsibility to our tax code."* Clearly, what we mean is that we think it's *"fair"* if only a *small* segment of our society shoulders the tax burden for the rest of us and that they should take *"responsibility"* for whatever programs we put in place to secure the votes of the masses. It's an application of our classic *"We vs. They"* strategy.

And how do you like our *"we will bring balance back to the housing markets, so that people do not have to lose their homes"* comment? Never mind that it was legislation that we sponsored and pushed through that essentially *caused* the crisis. We provided unlimited funds to Fannie Mae and Freddie Mac to back loans that should *never* have been approved, and we funded Acorn to pressure legitimate banks into making those loans. Then, when Fannie Mae's senior executives bilked the company for millions of dollars, we didn't reprimand them for being greedy CEOs because, after all, they were *our* CEOs!

Notice that we *"encourage personal savings, so that our economy remains strong and Americans can live well in their retirements."* While savings really don't contribute to the economy until they're spent or the money is loaned to others, it's *"politically correct"* to endorse savings. And don't let the tie to retirement confuse you ... even though we already *promised* to provide retirement accounts for *everyone*. Again, it's a required protocol of *"political correctness."*

RESTORING FAIRNESS TO OUR TAX CODE

We must reform our tax code. It's thousands of pages long, a monstrosity that high-priced lobbyists have rigged with page after page of special interest loopholes and tax shelters. We will shut down the corporate loopholes and tax havens and use the money so that we can provide an immediate middle-class tax cut that will offer relief to workers and their families. We'll eliminate federal income taxes for millions of retirees, because all seniors deserve to live out their lives with dignity and respect. We will not increase taxes on any family earning under $250,000 and we will offer additional tax cuts for middle class families. For families making more than $250,000, we'll ask them to give back a portion of the Bush tax cuts to invest in health care and other key priorities. We will end the penalty within the current Social Security system for public service that exists in several states. We will expand the Earned Income Tax Credit, and dramatically simplify tax filings so that millions of Americans can do their taxes in less than five minutes.

 **What we really mean to say is that we must skew our tax code even more disproportionately than we already have. We use terms like** *"high-priced lobbyists,"* *"rigged,"* *"corporate loopholes,"* **and** *"tax haven"* **to strike fear and a sense of injustice in the hearts and minds of the masses. Then, we promise to shift the related funds to the** *"middle-class"* **to** *"offer relief to workers and their families."* **When we combine our** *"fear factor"* **strategy with our** *"We vs. They"* **strategy like this, it's called the** *"Robin Hood"* **strategy. Get it? Take from the rich and give to the poor.** *"Oppressed minorities"* **love this stuff!**

We also say that *"We'll eliminate federal income taxes for millions of retirees, because all seniors deserve to live out their lives with dignity and respect."* **Now, we know that well in excess**

of 40% of our citizens don't pay *any* income tax, but this still resonates with those that *do*. Even though we promise to *"dramatically simplify tax filings so that millions of Americans can do their taxes in less than five minutes,"* it really can't get much easier for the tens of millions of citizens that don't pay *any* income tax. And if we're really going to reduce taxes for 95 percent of Americans as Barrack Obama has promised *and* create all the new entitlement programs we keep inventing, you have to wonder when we're going to tax the rich out of existence.

The language about *"end(ing) the penalty within the current Social Security system for public service that exists in several states"* pertains to current legislation: the Government Pension Offset provision (GPO) and the Windfall Elimination Provision (WEP) that prevent government employees from essentially *"double-dipping"* when it comes to retirement funds. GPO and WEP were put into place to create more parity between the average person who *just* receives Social Security and the government employee who may receive a pension funded by taxpayer money *as well as* Social Security. We can't have that because the teacher's unions are against it, and they have a bunch of *high-priced lobbyists* who will … uh … forget that we said that!

HOUSING

The housing crisis has been devastating for many Americans. Minorities have been hit particularly hard—in 2006, more than 40 percent of the home loans made to Hispanic borrowers were subprime, while more than half of those made to African Americans were subprime. We will ensure that the foreclosure prevention program enacted by Congress is implemented quickly and effectively so that at-risk homeowners can get help and hopefully stay in their homes. We will work to reform bankruptcy laws to restore balance between lender and homeowner rights. Because we have an obligation to prevent this crisis from recurring in the future, we will crack down on fraudulent brokers and lenders and invest in financial literacy. We will pass a

Homebuyers Bill of Rights, which will include establishing new lending standards to ensure that loans are affordable and fair, provide adequate remedies to make sure the standards are met, and ensure that homeowners have accurate and complete information about their mortgage options. We will support affordable rental housing, which is now more critical than ever. We will implement the newly created Affordable Housing Trust Fund to ensure that it can start to support the development and preservation of affordable housing in mixed-income neighborhoods throughout the country, restore cuts to public housing operating subsidies, and fully fund the Community Development Block Grant program. We will work with local jurisdictions on the problem of vacant and abandoned housing in our communities. We will work to end housing discrimination and to ensure equal housing opportunity. We will combat homelessness and target homelessness among veterans in particular by expanding proven programs and launching innovative preventive services.

This is a slippery slope for us. We know we created the housing fiasco by cramming subprime lending down the banking industry's throat, but it helped us solidify our voting base among *"oppressed minorities"* like Hispanics and African Americans just to name a few. We need to prevent foreclosures to limit our exposure, but the real trick is in *"investing in financial literacy."* Aside from the fact that we desperately need training in that area *ourselves*, it's really *dangerous* to provide it to the general public. What happens if they begin to make informed decisions ... like realizing that they shouldn't accept a loan that they absolutely cannot pay back? They might start looking into who created the regulations and political pressure to push those loans on an otherwise unsuspecting public whose greed would naturally embrace this *"too good to be true"* opportunity. Nancy, Harry, Chris, Barney ... what do we *do* if they find out how we've been *using* them? What? You say make it a homeless issue and tie it to veterans. Brilliant!

And don't worry about the debt associated with *"the newly created Affordable Housing Trust Fund"* that will *"support*

the development and preservation of affordable housing in mixed-income neighborhoods throughout the country, restore cuts to public housing operating subsidies, and fully fund the Community Development Block Grant program." How much can it be? We've already begun conditioning the public to become numb to the phrase *"a trillion,"* so whatever the debt, it won't be seen as a *"mountain."*

REFORMING FINANCIAL REGULATION AND CORPORATE GOVERNANCE

We have failed to guard against practices that all too often rewarded financial manipulation instead of productivity and sound business practices. We have let the special interests put their thumbs on the economic scales. We do not believe that government should stand in the way of innovation, or turn back the clock to an older era of regulation. But we do believe that government has a role to play in advancing our common prosperity: by providing stable macroeconomic and financial conditions for sustained growth; by demanding transparency; and by ensuring fair competition in the marketplace. We will reform and modernize our regulatory structures and will work to promote a shift in the cultures of our financial institutions and our regulatory agencies. We will ensure shareholders have an advisory vote on executive compensation, in order to spur increased transparency and public debate over pay packages. To make our communities stronger and more livable, and to meet the challenges of increasing global competitiveness, America will lead innovation in corporate responsibility to create jobs and leverage our private sector entrepreneurial leadership to help build a better world.

 Seriously, it's hard for us to say this with a straight face. As Eldridge Cleaver once said, *"If you're not part of the solution, you're part of the problem."* ... and we've clearly been part of the problem. We let *"special interests put their thumbs on the economic scales"* all the time. We just don't want the Republicans to let *their* special interests do it.

We sprinkled in a few phrases like *"macroeconomics"* and *"sustained growth"* for effect even though we're really not sure what they mean. Then we added *"transparency"* for good measure. In all fairness, we should disclose that *"transparency,"* in our lexicon, means *"opaque."*

The reformation and modernization of regulatory structures will be where the rubber meets the road. Normally, this would suggest contraction and the establishment of efficient and effective regulatory agencies; not exactly our demonstrated *forte*. Our new Health Care Reform Bill created 159 new agencies. Just imagine how many we'll have to create when we try to reform the *entire* economy!

We *think* that executive compensation has gotten out of hand, but we *know* that whatever government regulation we propose will be invasive and ineffective. If we were serious about fixing the problem, we would encourage the mainstream press to do some *real* investigative reporting to inform shareholders of how valuable it would be if some of this excess compensation was redirected to create new jobs, stimulate innovation, and improve service. Maybe you could even get someone to answer your support call in English. Naaaah! We'd rather have the press spend it's time justifying its support of our social reform ideas including the redistribution of wealth.

Consumer Protection

We will establish a Credit Card Bill of Rights to protect consumers and a Credit Card Rating System to improve disclosure. Americans need to pay what they owe, but they should pay what's fair. We'll reform our bankruptcy laws to give Americans in debt a second chance. If people can demonstrate that they went bankrupt because of medical expenses, they will be able to relieve that debt and get back on their feet. We will ban executive bonuses for bankrupt companies. We will crack down on predatory lenders and make it easier for low-income families to buy homes. We will require all non-home-based child care facilities to be lead-safe within five years. We must guarantee that consumer products coming in from other countries are truly safe, and will call on the Federal Trade Commission to ensure vulnerable consumer populations, such as seniors, are addressed.

 Too bad Ralph Nader has gone off the deep end. We could have used him on this one. Instead, we're stuck with *"reform(ing) our bankruptcy laws to give Americans in debt a second chance."* We think the American public will respond well to having the opportunity to go bankrupt twice!

We know our approach is pretty weak, so we threw in a few *"oppressed minority"* themes like the *"medical expenses," "low-income," "child care," "seniors,"* etc. to take the focus away from our lack of sophistication ... and we included the word *"predatory"* to create a sense of fear. Then, we finished things off by referencing *"consumer products coming in from other countries"* since we can't mention U.S. products without risking the ire of our friendly unions. After all, as long as people *think* we're protecting them from *something*, they'll probably vote for us.

Savings

The personal saving rate is at its lowest since the Great Depression. Currently, 75 million working Americans—roughly half the workforce—lack employer-based retirement plans. That's why we will create automatic workplace pensions. People can add to their pension, or can opt out at any time; the savings account will be easily transferred between jobs; and people can control it themselves if they become self-employed. We will ensure savings incentives are fair to all workers by matching half of the initial $1000 of savings for families that need help; and employers will have an easy opportunity to match employee savings. We believe this program will increase the saving participation rate for low- and middle-income workers from its current 15 percent to 80 percent. We support good pensions, and will adopt measures to preserve and protect existing public and private pension plans. We will require that employees who have company pensions receive annual disclosures about their pension fund's investments. This will put a secure retirement within reach for millions of working families.

 Personal savings are at their lowest levels since the Great Depression because we've legislated our way into a similarly bleak economy. Our solution: to spend even more to prop up people until they become *fully dependent* upon the government. Republicans have the nerve to suggest that people aren't saving money because they don't *have* any, but we know that it's because they just need more social programs. So, we'll continue to borrow from China, and print more money if we have to, with total disregard to the inflation it may cause down the road. Heck, inflation probably only impacts the rich anyway!

Now, earlier in our platform, we said that we would *"match savings for working families who need the help."* We're going to back off that a little bit by saying now that we'll match *"half of the initial $1000 of savings for families that need help."* Luckily, *"employers will have an easy opportunity to match employee savings."* We're not really sure how they'll do that, but it sounds good and it shifts the responsibility to *them*.

And you may have noticed that we're hedging a bit on our earlier promise to *"automatically enroll every worker in a workplace pension plan that can be carried from job to job and we will match savings for working families who need the help."* Now, we're just going to *"put a secure retirement within reach for millions of working families."* Don't worry! Nobody is going to read our Platform that closely anyway.

Smart, Strong, and Fair Trade Policies

We believe that trade should strengthen the American economy and create more American jobs, while also laying a foundation for democratic, equitable, and sustainable growth around the world. Trade has been a cornerstone of our growth and global development, but we will not be able to sustain this growth if it favors the few rather than the many. We must build on the wealth that open markets have created, and share its benefits more equitably.

Trade policy must be an integral part of an overall national economic strategy that delivers on the promise of good jobs at home and shared prosperity abroad. We will enforce trade laws and safeguard our workers, businesses, and farmers from unfair trade practices–including currency manipulation, lax consumer standards, illegal subsidies, and violations of workers' rights and environmental standards. We must also show leadership at the World Trade Organization to improve transparency and accountability, and to ensure it acts effectively to stop countries from continuing unfair government subsidies to foreign exporters and non-tariff barriers on U.S. exports.

 **This is another area in which we obviously don't have a lot of experience, so we throw out terms like *"transparency"* and *"accountability"* to project a positive image. We do know that it's important *"to stop countries from continuing unfair government subsidies to foreign exporters and non-tariff barriers on U.S. exports."* We would never subsidize a U.S. exporter like General Motors or Chrysler, and we think that foreign countries should just impose regular tariffs rather than trying to be *"politically correct."* They should leave *"political correctness"* to us. After all, we invented it!**

We need tougher negotiators on our side of the table–to strike bargains that are good not just for Wall Street, but also for Main Street. We will negotiate bilateral trade agreements that open markets to U.S. exports and include enforceable international labor and environmental standards; we pledge to enforce those standards consistently and fairly. We will not negotiate bilateral trade agreements that stop the government from protecting the environment, food safety, or the health of its citizens; give greater rights to foreign investors than to U.S. investors; require the privatization of our vital public services; or prevent developing country governments from adopting humanitarian licensing policies to improve access to life-saving medications. We will stand firm against bilateral agreements that fail to live up to these important benchmarks, and will strive to achieve them in the multilateral framework. We will work with Canada and Mexico to amend the North American Free Trade Agreement so that it works better for all three North American countries. We will work together with other countries to achieve a successful completion of the Doha Round Agreement that would increase U.S. exports, support good jobs in America, protect worker rights and the environment, benefit our businesses and our farms, strengthen the rules-based multilateral system, and advance development of the world's poorest countries.

This was our first opportunity to work the *"Wall Street vs. Main Street"* **rhetoric into our Platform that we use so successfully in our campaigns. It's an extremely effective demonstration of our** *"Robin Hood"* **strategy. Notice how we weave in ominous terms like** *"bilateral trade agreements," "enforceable international labor and environmental standards," "privatization of our vital public services," "humanitarian licensing policies," "multilateral framework,"* **to build a sense of fear, inject** *"environment, food, safety, (and) health,"* **to make it of personal interest, and finish it off by working** *"oppressed minorities"* **into it (e.g.,** *"workers," "farms,"* **and** *"poorest countries"*). **This is our Party at its finest!**

Just as important, we will invest in a world-class infrastructure, skilled workforce, and cutting-edge technology so that we can compete successfully on high-value-added products, not sweatshop wages and conditions. We will end tax breaks for companies that ship American jobs overseas, and provide incentives for companies that keep and maintain good jobs here in the United States. We will also provide access to affordable health insurance and enhance retirement security, and we will update and expand Trade Adjustment Assistance to help workers in industries vulnerable to international competition, as well as service sector and public sector workers impacted by trade, and we will improve TAA's health care benefits. The United States should renew its own commitment to respect for workers' fundamental human rights, and at the same time strengthen the ILO's ability to promote workers' rights abroad through technical assistance and capacity building.

Next, we promise to invest in good things (e.g., *"world-class infrastructure," "skilled workforce,"*

"cutting-edge technology," and *"high-value-added products"*) while rejecting the bad (*e.g.*, *"sweatshop wages and conditions"*). Who can argue with that?

We repeat our pledge to *"provide access to affordable health care and enhance retirement security"* even though neither really has anything to do with foreign trade. Then, we promise to *"update and expand Trade Adjustment Assistance to help workers in industries vulnerable to international competition."* You see, even though we criticized *"unfair government subsidies to foreign exporters and non-tariff barriers on U.S. exports"* just a few sentences ago, those are only *"unfair"* when they impact *our* ability to export.

Fiscal Responsibility

Our agenda is ambitious–particularly in light of the current Administration's policies that have run up the national debt to over $4 trillion. Just as America cannot afford to continue to run up huge deficits, so too can we not afford to short-change investments. The key is to make the tough choices, in particular enforcing pay-as-you-go budgeting rules. We will honor these rules by our plan to end the Iraq war responsibly, eliminate waste in existing government programs, generate revenue by charging polluters for the greenhouse gases they are releasing, and put an end to the reckless, special interest driven corporate loopholes and tax cuts for the wealthy that have been the centerpiece of the Bush Administration's economic policy. We will not raise taxes on people making less than $250,000, and we will eliminate federal income taxes for seniors making less than $50,000. We recognize that Social Security is not in crisis and we should do everything we can to strengthen this vital program, including asking those making over $250,000 to pay a bit more. The real long-run fiscal challenge is rooted in the rising spending on health care, but we cannot address this in a way that puts our most vulnerable families in jeopardy. Instead, we must strengthen our public programs by bringing down the cost of health care and reducing waste while making strategic investments that emphasize quality, efficiency, and prevention. In the name of our children, we reject the proposals of those who want to continue George Bush's disastrous economic policies.

The Left isn't Right

 Okay ... we *told* you we weren't very good at math. We act like a $4 trillion national debt is a big deal. Then, we'll more than triple it in only a year. And like the old song says, ♫ *"We've Only Just Begun."* ♫

You're already aware of all the special deals we cut (at a cost of billions of dollars) to get the votes we needed to pass a 2,700+ page Health Care Reform Bill that *none* of us *understood ....or even had the time to read*. As bad as they were, the Bush Administration's *"disastrous economic policies"* pale in comparison to ours. However, we think we *still* have traction with blaming everything on Bush. As long as we can say we *"inherited"* it ... and you buy off on it ... we'll keep playing that card. Our fear is that you'll only fall for that line so long. *Then,* how are we going to explain the mess we've gotten ourselves into? Rest assured, we'll figure out a way to make it the Republicans' fault.

II. RENEWING AMERICAN LEADERSHIP

At moments of great peril in the last century, American leaders such as Franklin Roosevelt, Harry Truman, and John F. Kennedy managed both to protect the American people and to expand opportunity for the next generation. They ensured that America, by deed and example, led and lifted the world–that we stood for and fought for the freedoms sought by billions of people beyond our borders. They used our strengths to show people everywhere America at its best. Just as John Kennedy said that after Hoover we needed Franklin Roosevelt, so too after our experience of the last eight years we need Barack Obama.

 World War II (Roosevelt), the Korean War (Truman), Viet Nam (Kennedy) ... yes, there's nothing like a good *war* to *"show people everywhere America at its best."*

Today, we are again called to provide visionary leadership. This century's threats are at least as dangerous as, and in some ways more complex than, those we have confronted in the past. They come from weapons that can kill on a mass scale and from violent extremists who exploit alienation and perceived injustice to spread terror. They come from rogue states allied to terrorists and from rising powers that could challenge both America and the international foundation of liberal democracy. They come from weak states that cannot control their territory or provide for their people. They come from an addiction to oil that helps fund the extremism we must fight and empowers repressive regimes. And they come from a warming planet that will spur new diseases, spawn more devastating natural disasters, and catalyze deadly conflicts.

 We're just *"building the fear"* here. You know the drill by now. We threw in global warming for good measure. Our only mistake was to imply that *"a warming planet"* may *"spawn more devastating natural disasters."* We were a little careless here because we already worked so hard to establish that *all* natural disasters (like Katrina) were *really* orchestrated by President Bush in an effort to affect the genocide of an *"oppressed minority."* If anyone reads this far, we may have blown that argument!

We will confront these threats head on while working with our allies and restoring our standing in the world. We will pursue a tough, smart, and principled national security strategy. It is a strategy that recognizes that we have interests not just in Baghdad, but in Kandahar and Karachi, in Beijing, Berlin, Brasilia and Bamako. It is a strategy that contends with the many disparate forces shaping this century, including: the fundamentalist challenge to freedom; the emergence of new powers like China, India, Russia, and a united Europe; the spread of lethal weapons; uncertain supplies of energy, food, and water; the persistence of poverty and the growing gap between rich and poor; and extraordinary new technologies that send people, ideas, and money across the globe at ever faster speeds.

 Our *"tough, smart, and principled national security strategy"* that will *"restore our standing in the world"* will begin and end with apologizing for our *"bad behavior"* in the past: such as *littering foreign countries' soil with our fallen soldiers who died to free their people and to defend our freedom; sending millions of tons of food, medical aid, and supplies to those around the world who were in desperate need; and setting such a horrible example of what life can be like that people from all over the*

world still flock to our shores as immigrants striving to experience the *atrocity* of living in the United States for themselves. Please forgive us!

Barack Obama will focus this strategy on seven goals: (i) ending the war in Iraq responsibly; (ii) defeating Al Qaeda and combating violent extremism; (iii) securing nuclear weapons and materials from terrorists; (iv) revitalizing and supporting our military; (v) renewing our partnerships to promote our common security; (vi) advancing democracy and development; and (vii) protecting our planet by achieving energy security and combating climate change.

 **You've heard of the *Seven Deadly Sins*; these are what we jokingly refer to as the *Seven Dreadful Whims*.**

i. *"Ending the war in Iraq responsibly"* or irresponsibly if we think we can get away with it;
ii. *"Defeating Al Qaeda and combating violent extremism"* using skillful diplomacy;
iii. *"Securing nuclear weapons and materials from terrorists"* by asking really politely (twice if necessary);
iv. *"Revitalizing and supporting our military"* by voting against Defense funding or by court marshaling military personnel if they are accused of punching a terrorist (by the terrorist);
v. *"Renewing our partnerships to promote our common security"* by unilaterally surrendering some of our capability to defend NATO, essentially abandoning Israel, and releasing terrorists from Gitmo whenever possible.
vi. *"Advancing democracy and development"* by bowing to royalty and paying deference to the leaders of countries who think *"human rights"* are merely an archaic remnant of the Conservative movement, and
vii. *"Protecting our planet by achieving energy security and combating climate change"* because we *know* we can legislate Nature (outside of the *inconvenient truth* that is occasionally established by a volcanic eruption, etc.).

ENDING THE WAR IN IRAQ

To renew American leadership in the world, we must first bring the Iraq war to a responsible end. Our men and women in uniform have performed admirably while sacrificing immeasurably. Our civilian leaders have failed them. Iraq was a diversion from the fight against the terrorists who struck us on 9-11, and incompetent prosecution of the war by civilian leaders compounded the strategic blunder of choosing to wage it in the first place.

 **Please ignore the fact that we voted in favor of the War in Iraq on multiple occasions and controlled both the House and the Senate during the last two years of the Bush Administration.**

We will re-center American foreign policy by responsibly redeploying our combat forces from Iraq and refocusing them on urgent missions. We will give our military a new mission: ending this war and giving Iraq back to its people. We will be as careful getting out of Iraq as we were careless getting in. We can safely remove our combat brigades at the pace of one to two per month and expect to complete redeployment within sixteen months. After this redeployment, we will keep a residual force in Iraq to perform specific missions: targeting terrorists; protecting our embassy and civil personnel; and advising and supporting Iraq's Security Forces, provided the Iraqis make political progress.

 **Don't look now, but *"sixteen months"* have come and gone. We should *know* not to put promises like this in print ... or to even speak them. At least we closed Gitmo on time. Oops!**

At the same time, we will provide generous assistance to Iraqi refugees and internally displaced persons. We will launch a comprehensive regional and international diplomatic surge to help broker a lasting political settlement in Iraq, which is the only path to a sustainable peace. We will make clear that we seek no permanent bases in Iraq. We will encourage Iraq's government to devote its oil revenues and budget surplus to reconstruction and development. This is the future the American people want. This is the future that Iraqis want. This is what our common interests demand.

 This region has always responded well to a *"diplomatic surge."* It's surprising they've been at war for the past 2000 years given their propensity to listen to reason.

DEFEATING AL QAEDA AND COMBATING TERRORISM

The central front in the war on terror is not Iraq, and it never was. We will defeat Al Qaeda in Afghanistan and Pakistan, where those who actually attacked us on 9-11 reside and are resurgent.

 Let's hope Al Qaeda knows that it's only allowed to operate in Afghanistan and Pakistan and chooses to respect that restriction. It would blow our whole strategy if they were clever enough to develop terrorist cells in other countries or proselytize Jihad through radicalized individuals. If that ever happen, we could have terrorist trying to blow up planes with underwear bombs ... or blow up cars in Times Square ... or even murdering soldiers on a military base on U.S. soil.

Win in Afghanistan

Our troops are performing heroically in Afghanistan, but as countless military commanders and the Chairman of the Joint Chiefs of Staff acknowledge, we lack the resources to finish the job because of our commitment to Iraq. We will finally make the fight against Al Qaeda and the Taliban the top priority that it should be.

We will send at least two additional combat brigades to Afghanistan, and use this commitment to seek greater contributions–with fewer restrictions–from our NATO allies. We will focus on building up our special forces and intelligence capacity, training, equipping and advising Afghan security forces, building Afghan governmental capacity, and promoting the rule of law. We will bolster our State Department's Provincial Reconstruction Teams and our other government agencies helping the Afghan people. We will help Afghans educate their children, including their girls, provide basic human services to their population, and grow their economy from the bottom up, with an additional $1 billion in non-military assistance each year–including investments in alternative livelihoods to poppy-growing for Afghan farmers–just as we crack down on trafficking and corruption. Afghanistan must not be lost to a future of narco-terrorism–or become again a haven for terrorists.

We're serious about this. That's why it only took us a little over two months to decide to send half as many troops to Afghanistan as our U.S. Commander there requested. What does he know? He's too busy fighting to have an appreciation for the broader picture. We watched *Charlie Wilson's War!*

And while we pointed out that *"one in eight Americans lives in poverty today,"* we can still promise to *"help Afghans educate their children, including their girls, provide basic human services to their population, and grow their economy from the bottom up, with an additional $1 billion in non-military assistance each year–including investments in alternative livelihoods to poppy-growing for Afghan farmers."* Besides, they'll never know we made the promise and no one *here* will care if we actually do it.

We do believe that *"Afghanistan must not be lost to a future of narco-terrorism–or become again a haven for terrorists."* The drug isssue is particularly relevant to us since we choose to do nothing about protecting our borders. We're confident that if we shift the poppy-growing Afghan farmers to hemp (so they can make homespun thread from which to weave *real* afghans), our drug problems will go away.

<u>Seek a New Partnership with Pakistan</u>

The greatest threat to the security of the Afghan people–and the American people–lies in the tribal regions of Pakistan, where terrorists train, plot attacks, and strike into Afghanistan and move back across the border. We cannot tolerate a sanctuary for Al Qaeda. We need a stronger and sustained partnership between Afghanistan, Pakistan, and NATO–including necessary assets like satellites and predator drones–to better secure the border, to take out terrorist camps, and to crack down on cross-border insurgents. We must help Pakistan develop its own counter-terrorism and counter-insurgency capacity. We will invest in the long-term development of the Pashtun border region, so that the extremists' program of hate is met with an agenda of hope.

We will ask more of the Pakistani government, rather than offer a blank check to an undemocratic President. We will significantly increase non-military aid to the Pakistani people and sustain it for a decade, while ensuring that the military assistance we provide is actually used to fight extremists. We must move beyond an alliance built on individual leaders, or we will face mounting opposition in a nuclear-armed nation at the nexus of terror, extremism, and the instability wrought by autocracy.

"We will significantly increase non-military aid to the Pakistani people and sustain it for a decade, while ensuring that the military assistance we provide is actually used to fight extremists." **In 2009, we provided $798 million in foreign aid to Pakistan. As promised,** *"we will significantly increase non-military aid to the Pakistani people and sustain it for a decade."* **By the way ... in the past decade they voted against us on United Nations' resolutions about 86% of the time (and about 91% of the time on UN resolutions that we deemed to be** *"important"***). But trust us ... we know what were doing!**

<u>Combat Terrorism</u>

Beyond Afghanistan and Pakistan, we must forge a more effective global response to terrorism. There must be no safe haven for those who plot to kill Americans. We need a comprehensive strategy to defeat global terrorists–one that draws on the full range of American power, including but not limited to our military might. We will create a properly resourced Shared Security Partnership to enhance counter-terrorism cooperation with countries around the world, including through information sharing as well as funding for training, operations, border security, anti-corruption programs, technology, and targeting terrorist financing.

We will pursue policies to undermine extremism, recognizing that this contest is also between two competing ideas and visions of the future. A crucial debate is occurring within Islam. The vast majority of Muslims believe in a future of peace, tolerance, development, and democratization. A small minority embrace a rigid and violent intolerance of personal liberty and the world at large. To empower forces of moderation, America must live up to our values, respect civil liberties, reject torture, and lead by example. We will make every effort to export hope and opportunity–access to education, that opens minds to tolerance, not extremism; secure food and water supplies; and health care, trade, capital, and investment. We will provide steady support for political reformers, democratic institutions, and civil society that is necessary to uphold human rights and build respect for the rule of law.

 **At the crux of our strategy, *"we will pursue policies to undermine extremism, recognizing that this contest is also between two competing ideas and visions of the future."* Even though we say that other countries don't respect us, we believe that they will listen to us and respond to reason.**

First, we must close Gitmo so as not to incite them. Then, we must demonstrate our compassion and sense of fair play by giving captured terrorists high-profile coverage in cases tried in our finest courts while affording them all of the rights and privileges otherwise reserved for citizens who pledge their allegiance to our country.

If they persist in being hostile toward us, we will rely on blind *luck* and their inability to construct a bomb that will actually detonate. When captured, we will read them their Miranda rights (which none of our citizens even understand) and then subject them to serious, but *personable* questioning before they *"lawyer-up."* And the Republicans say we're soft!

"*We will make every effort to export hope and opportunity– access to education, that opens minds to tolerance, not*

extremism; secure food and water supplies; and health care, trade, capital, and investment" because we've done such a good job at home that only 14.3% of our citizens live in poverty and only about 15% suffer from illiteracy. And *"we will provide steady support for political reformers, democratic institutions, and civil society that is necessary to uphold human rights and build respect for the rule of law'* ... unless China says otherwise since we owe them so much money.

Secure the Homeland

Here at home, we will strengthen our security and protect the critical infrastructure on which the entire world depends. We will fully fund and implement the recommendations of the bipartisan 9-11 Commission. We will spend homeland security dollars on the basis of risk. This means investing more resources to defend mass transit, closing the gaps in our aviation security by screening all cargo on passenger airliners and checking all passengers against a reliable and comprehensive watch list, and upgrading plant security and port security by ensuring that cargo is screened for radiation. To ensure that resources are targeted, we will establish a Quadrennial Review at the Department of Homeland Security to undertake a top to bottom assessment of the threats we face and our ability to confront them. And we will develop a comprehensive National Infrastructure Protection Plan that draws on both local know-how and national priorities. We will ensure direct coordination with state, local, and tribal jurisdictions so that first responders are always resourced and prepared.

 **This shows the speed with which we are capable of reacting. It's only been nearly a decade since the attack on September 11, 2001, and we're *just* about ready to *"fully fund and implement the recommendations of the bipartisan 9-11 Commission."* That's got to give you a warm and fuzzy feeling.**

Pursue Intelligence Reform

To succeed, our homeland security and counter-terrorism actions must be linked to an intelligence community that deals effectively with the threats we face. Today, we rely largely on the same institutions and practices that were in place before 9-11. Barack Obama will depoliticize intelligence by appointing a Director of National Intelligence with a fixed term, create a bipartisan Consultative Group of congressional leaders on national security, and establish a National Declassification Center to ensure openness. To keep pace with highly adaptable enemies, we need technologies and practices that enable us to efficiently collect and share information within and across our intelligence agencies. We must invest still more in human intelligence and deploy additional trained operatives with specialized knowledge of local cultures and languages. And we will institutionalize the practice of developing competitive assessments of critical threats and strengthen our methodologies of analysis.

**To help change the process, we've appointed people to key positions within the intelligence community who have absolutely *no* experience in that area. We think it will create a fresh perspective; similar to electing a President who otherwise wouldn't have the experience to qualify for a mid-level management position in a Fortune 500 company.**

To further alleviate your concerns, we recognize that intelligence operatives in foreign countries should have a *"specialized knowledge of local cultures and languages"* rather than just try to guess what the residents are saying or doing. We didn't even have to form a committee or agency to explore this issue. That's the type of unique competence we bring to the table!

PREVENTING THE SPREAD AND USE OF WEAPONS OF MASS DESTRUCTION

We will urgently seek to reduce dramatically the risks from three potentially catastrophic threats: nuclear weapons, biological attacks, and cyber warfare. In an age of terrorism, these dangers take on new dimensions. Nuclear, biological, and cyber attacks all pose the potential for large-scale damage and destruction to our people, to our economy and to our way of life. The capacity to inflict such damage is spreading not only to other countries, but also potentially to terrorist groups.

This is *"forward thinking"* at its finest. One of our ideas is to develop step-by-step instructions for building nuclear and biological weapons as well as providing a *"how-to"* guide for launching cyber attacks and then publishing the information on the Internet. The more people who know what such things look like ... the greater the chance that someone will recognize it when they see it and then call us to tell us about it. How's that for a plan?

<u>A World Without Nuclear Weapons</u>

America will seek a world with no nuclear weapons and take concrete actions to move in this direction. We face the growing threat of terrorists acquiring nuclear weapons or the materials to make them, as more countries seek nuclear weapons and nuclear materials remain unsecured in too many places. As George Shultz, Bill Perry, Henry Kissinger, and Sam Nunn have warned, current measures are not adequate to address these dangers. We will maintain a strong and reliable deterrent as long as nuclear weapons exist, but America will be safer in a world that is reducing reliance on nuclear weapons and ultimately eliminates all of them. We will make the goal of eliminating nuclear weapons worldwide a central element of U.S. nuclear weapons policy.

We believe *the pen is mightier than the sword*, so we'll probably just dismantle our nuclear arsenal first ... to set a good example. We think that other world leaders will be embarrassed and quickly follow suit. Small countries like Iran and North Korea will undoubtedly want to emulate our behavior to elevate the status with which they are viewed by other countries.

The Left isn't Right

Secure Nuclear Weapons and the Materials to Make Them

We will work with other nations to secure, eliminate, and stop the spread of nuclear weapons and materials to dramatically reduce the dangers to our nation and the world. There are nuclear weapons materials in 40 countries, and we will lead a global effort to work with other countries to secure all nuclear weapons material at vulnerable sites within four years. We will work with nations to increase security for nuclear weapons. We will convene a summit in 2009 (and regularly thereafter) of leaders of Permanent Members of the U.N. Security Council and other key countries to agree on implementing many of these measures on a global basis.

A summit ... that's all we need. We just have to *ask* law abiding countries to abandon their nuclear weapons. Diplomacy *always* works! We'll even make them take an oath that they really *did* turn in every weapons-grade material they had in their possession. Then, we'll tell the world where these materials are being stored so everyone can rest safely.

End the Production of Fissile Material

We will negotiate a verifiable global ban on the production of fissile material for nuclear weapons. We will work to prevent the spread of nuclear weapons technology so that countries cannot build–or come to the brink of building–a weapons program under the guise of developing peaceful nuclear power. We will seek to double the International Atomic Energy Agency's budget, support the creation of an IAEA-controlled nuclear fuel bank to guarantee fuel supply to countries that do not build enrichment facilities, and work to strengthen the Nuclear Non-Proliferation Treaty.

We'll probably need another summit for this, but maybe if we *"double the International Atomic Energy Agency's budget, support the creation of an IAEA-controlled nuclear fuel bank to guarantee fuel supply to countries that do not build enrichment facilities, and*

work to strengthen the Nuclear Non-Proliferation Treaty," everyone will just comply. Countries like Iran and North Korea will welcome inspectors with open arms and cease wasting time and money in attempting to become nuclear powers. Even terrorist groups will have no other option than to comply with our ideas or risk being ostracized by all civilized societies.

End Cold War Nuclear Postures

To enhance our security and help meet our commitments under the Non-Proliferation Treaty, we will seek deep, verifiable reductions in United States and Russian nuclear weapons and work with other nuclear powers to reduce global stockpiles dramatically. We will work with Russia to take as many weapons as possible off Cold War, quick-launch status, and extend key provisions of the START Treaty, including its essential monitoring and verification requirements. We will not develop new nuclear weapons, and will work to create a bipartisan consensus to support ratification of the Comprehensive Nuclear Test Ban Treaty, which will strengthen the NPT and aid international monitoring of nuclear activities.

 **We think we've already addressed this concern with our diplomatic supremacy.**

Prevent Iran from Acquiring Nuclear Weapons

The world must prevent Iran from acquiring nuclear weapons. That starts with tougher sanctions and aggressive, principled, and direct high-level diplomacy, without preconditions. We will pursue this strengthened diplomacy alongside our European allies, and with no illusions about the Iranian regime. We will present Iran with a clear choice: if you abandon your nuclear weapons program, support for terror, and threats to Israel, you will receive meaningful incentives; so long as you refuse, the United States and the international community will further ratchet up the pressure, with stronger unilateral sanctions; stronger multilateral sanctions inside and outside the U.N. Security Council, and sustained action to isolate the Iranian regime. The Iranian people and the international community must know that it is Iran, not the United States, choosing isolation over cooperation. By going the extra diplomatic mile, while keeping all options on the table, we make it more likely the rest of the world will stand with us to increase pressure on Iran, if diplomacy is failing.

 Even though we believe Iran will fall into line, we are willing to bribe …uh… we mean *incent* them to comply. After all, diplomacy *always* works when dealing with *rational* leadership. They just want to *belong*.

And right after we get them to capitulate to our wishes, we'll start trying to get them to admit that there may be evidence that the Holocaust *actually* did happen. By the way, Iran used to be known as Persia. Its name was changed in 1935. The name "Iran" is a modern cognate of "Aryan" meaning *"the Land of Aryans."* It is said to have been made upon recommendation of Persia's Ambassador to Germany, who had become enamored with the influence of the Nazi movement. Oh well … forgive and forget! As the late Senator Byrd once said after failing to renew his membership in the Ku Klux Klan, "Anyone can make a little mistake."

De-Nuclearize North Korea

We support the belated diplomatic effort to secure a verifiable end to North Korea's nuclear weapons program and to fully account for and secure any fissile material or weapons North Korea has produced to date. We will continue direct diplomacy and are committed to working with our partners through the six-party talks to ensure that all agreements are fully implemented in the effort to achieve a verifiably nuclear-free Korean peninsula.

 We believe diplomacy will work as long as South Korea doesn't run out of warships before North Korea runs out of torpedoes. Again, diplomacy

always **rules the day when working with** *rational* **leaders. How many times do we need to say this?**

Biological and Chemical Weapons

We will strengthen U.S. intelligence collection overseas to identify and interdict would-be bioterrorists before they strike. We will also build greater capacity to mitigate the consequences of bio-terror attacks, ensuring that the federal government does all it can to get citizens the information and resources they need to help protect themselves and their families. We will accelerate the development of new medicines, vaccines, and production capabilities, and lead an international effort to detect and diminish the impact of major infectious disease epidemics. And we will fully fund our contribution to the Organization for the Prohibition of Chemical Weapons and work to ensure that remaining stockpiles of chemical weapons are destroyed swiftly, safely, and securely.

 **Maybe Bush-orchestrated hurricanes can bring us to our knees, but no biological or chemical attack could possibly overwhelm our resources. That's why we haven't bothered to develop a cogent plan at the Federal level to address such an attack. If one ever did occur, we would undoubtedly develop antidotes as quickly and effectively as we have for all the pandemics that have supposedly plagued our country in recent years. In the mean time, we'll just donate more money to** *"the Organization for the Prohibition of Chemical Weapons and work to ensure that remaining stockpiles of chemical weapons are destroyed swiftly, safely, and securely."*

Stronger Cyber-Security

We will work with private industry, the research community and our citizens, to build a trustworthy and accountable cyber-infrastructure that is resilient, protects America's competitive advantage, and advances our national and homeland security.

 **This is assuming we can get our government employees to stop watching porn long enough to work on the issue.**

REVITALIZING AND SUPPORTING THE MILITARY, KEEPING FAITH WITH VETERANS

To renew American leadership in the world, we must revitalize our military. A strong military is, more than anything, necessary to sustain peace.

Ending the war in Iraq will be the beginning, but not the end, of addressing our defense challenges. We will use this moment both to rebuild our military and to prepare it for the missions of the future. We must retain the capacity to swiftly defeat any conventional threat to our country and our vital interests. But we must also become better prepared to take on foes that fight asymmetrical and highly adaptive campaigns on a global scale.

We will not hesitate to use force to protect the American people or our vital interests whenever we are attacked or imminently threatened. But we will use our armed forces wisely, with others when we can, unilaterally when we must. When we send our men and women into harm's way, we must clearly define the mission, listen to the advice of our military commanders, objectively evaluate intelligence, and ensure that our troops have the strategy, resources, and support they need to prevail.

We believe we must also be willing to consider using military force in circumstances beyond self-defense in order to provide for the common security that underpins global stability–to support friends, participate in stability and reconstruction operations, or confront mass atrocities. But when we do use force in situations other than self-defense, we should make every effort to garner the clear support and participation of others. The consequences of forgetting that lesson in the context of the current conflict in Iraq have been grave.

 **While this is somewhat of a "given," we threw it in just to be able to take another shot at the Bush Administration. Never mind that we supported the War in Iraq with our votes ... or we wouldn't be there today. It's still fun to kick the ex-President whenever**

we get the chance. Dragging the opposition through the mud is how we intend to build bipartisan support. It's only divisive if the Republicans do it.

Expand the Armed Forces

We support plans to increase the size of the Army by 65,000 troops and the Marines by 27,000 troops. Increasing our end strength will help units retrain and re-equip properly between deployments and decrease the strain on military families.

 **We've got so many people out of work; we figure the military is their *only* viable option.**

Recruit and Retain

A nation of 300 million people should not struggle to find additional qualified personnel to serve. Recruitment and retention problems have been swept under the rug, including by applying inconsistent standards and using the "Stop Loss" program to keep our servicemen and women in the force after their enlistment has expired. We will reach out to youth, as well as to the parents, teachers, coaches, and community and religious leaders who influence them, and make it an imperative to restore the ethic of public service, whether it be serving their local communities in such roles as teachers or first responders, or serving in the military and reserve forces or diplomatic corps that keep our nation free and safe.

 As we said before, with our unemployment rate verging on the obscene, this shouldn't be a problem. However, with *"a nation of 300 million people,"* you would think we could find far more qualified people to run for President, the House of Representatives, and the United States Senate as well, but that *obviously* hasn't been the case.

Rebuild the Military for 21st-Century Tasks

We will rebuild our armed forces to meet the full spectrum needs of the new century. We will strongly support efforts to: build up our special operations forces, civil affairs, information operations, engineers, foreign area officers, and other units and capabilities that remain in chronic short supply; invest in foreign language training, cultural awareness, human intelligence, and other needed counter-insurgency and stabilization skill sets; and create a specialized military advisor corps, which will enable us to better build up local allies' capacities to take on mutual threats. We also will ensure that military personnel have sufficient training time before they are sent into battle. This is not the case at the moment, when American forces are being rushed to Iraq and Afghanistan, often with less individual and unit training than is required.

 **Special Ops might be a problem if we keep court marshaling them for doing their job. Former President Clinton and Presidential Candidate John Edwards have both patriotically volunteered to head up any effort involving civil** *affairs.* **We're also still hoping to lure Jack Bauer out of retirement to head up our counter-terrorism initiative, but he's adamant about being allowed to use water boarding in lieu of diplomatic alternatives.**

Develop Civilian Capacity to Promote Global Stability and Improve Emergency Response

We will build the capacity of U.S. civilian agencies to deploy personnel and area experts where they are needed, so that we no longer have to ask our men and women in uniform to perform non-military functions. The creation of a volunteer Civilian Assistance Corps of skilled experts (e.g., doctors, lawyers, engineers, city planners, agriculture specialists, police) who are pre-trained and willing to aid in emergencies will involve more Americans in public service and provide our nation with a pool of talent to assist America in times of need at home and abroad.

 **We used to call people like this mercenaries, but in this case, they won't get to kill anyone. Again, because of unemployment, we should be able to find people who are *desperate* enough to staff these positions in the *wonderful* environments in which they will be required to serve.**

Do Right by Our Veterans and Their Families

We believe that every servicemember is a hero who deserves our respect and gratitude, not just on Veterans Day or Memorial Day, but every day. When they put on their uniforms, these servicemembers all become all of our daughters and all of our sons, and it is time we started treating them as such. As the shameful events at Walter Reed hospital and the recent reports on growing numbers of homeless and unemployed veterans show, this Administration that has asked so much of them has not repaid their sacrifice.

We will build a 21st century Department of Veterans Affairs that reflects the reality of America's all volunteer military and has the resources, without returning every year to fight the same battles, to uphold America's sacred trust with our veterans. We will make sure that members of our Armed Forces have a fair shot at the American Dream by implementing the new GI Bill. We will ensure that every veteran has access to quality health care for injuries both physical and mental, and we will require that health professionals screen all servicemembers upon their return from combat. We will aggressively address Post-Traumatic Stress Disorder and Traumatic Brain Injury. We will work to ensure that every veteran receives the benefits he or she has earned and the assistance he or she needs by making the disability benefits process more fair, efficient, and equitable. We will dramatically reduce the backlog of disability claims. We will combat homelessness, unemployment, and underemployment among veterans and improve the transition for servicemen between the Departments of Defense and Veterans Affairs. We will continue to honor our promises to all veterans, including the Filipino veterans, especially with regards to citizenship and family reunification.

 **Maybe we'll even stop prosecuting our military personnel in the name of *"political correctness."* We actually could have begun treating military personnel with respect decades ago, but most members of our Party were too involved in protesting the Vietnam War and treating returning veterans as if they were criminals. Now, we've come full circle. We're even thinking of offering the position of Secretary of Defense or the Director of Veterans Affairs to Jane Fonda if she'll promise not to run against one of our Congressional incumbents.**

Lift Burdens on Our Troops and Their Families

We must better support those families of whom we are asking so much. We will create a Military Families Advisory Board to help identify and develop practical policies to ease the burden on spouses and families.

We will protect our military families from losing their homes to foreclosure. We will work for pay parity so that compensation for military service is more in line with that of the private sector. We will end the stop-loss and reserve recall policies that allow an individual to be forced to remain on active duty well after his or her enlistment has expired, and we will establish regularity in deployments so that active duty and reserve troops know what they must expect and their families can plan for it.

 **We believe that forming Boards, Agencies or Committees is the way to resolve *all* problems. *Otherwise*, we'd only have to appoint one or two people who had the intelligence and integrity to do the right thing and vest them with the responsibility and authority to get it done. That's almost un-American, and it wouldn't take nearly enough time or money to qualify as a government initiative. Forget we even mentioned it.**

Support the Readiness of the Guard and Reserve

Democrats will provide the National Guard with the equipment it needs for foreign and domestic emergencies and provide time and support to restore and refit between deployments. We will also ensure that reservists and Guard members are treated fairly when it comes to employment, health, education benefits, deployment, and reintegration. We will do this by adequately funding reintegration programs to assist returning service members and by enforcing the Service Members Civil Relief Act and the Uniformed Service Employment Rights and Readjustment Act, laws too often observed in the breach today. To ensure that the concerns of our citizen soldiers reach the level they mandate, Democrats will elevate the Chief of the National Guard to be a member of the Joint Chiefs of Staff.

Since we've already promised to provide these same benefits to *all* Americans (beyond the *"support to restore and refit between deployments"*), it would seem inappropriate to deny them to members of the National Guard. Additionally, *"elevat(ing) the Chief of the National Guard to be a member of the Joint Chiefs of Staff"* is an important step as it will provide us with one more position to offer up-and-coming individuals to withdraw from Congressional races if they start to challenge the *"old guard"* (no pun intended).

Allow All Americans to Serve

We will also put national security above divisive politics. More than 12,500 service men and women have been discharged on the basis of sexual orientation since the "Don't Ask, Don't Tell" policy was implemented, at a cost of over $360 million. Many of those forced out had special skills in high demand, such as translators, engineers, and pilots. At a time when the military is having a tough time recruiting and retaining troops, it is wrong to deny our country the service of brave, qualified people. We support the repeal of "Don't Ask Don't Tell" and the implementation of policies to allow qualified men and women to serve openly regardless of sexual orientation.

 Frankly, we don't know why President Clinton ever established the *"Don't Ask, Don't Tell"* policy anyway. It must have been a Bush's fault since President Clinton was bracketed in between them! We believe that everyone should have an equal opportunity to have someone try to kill them.

Southern Democrats, in particular, support the idea of getting to shoot at individuals of a *"non-traditional sexual orientation."* They've even suggested a licensing program for non-military personnel of a similar persuasion; although they do suggests *limits* and recommend restricting the season to only those months whose names contain a vowel.

Reform Contracting Practices and Make Contractors Accountable

We believe taxpayer dollars should be spent to invest in our fighting men and women, not to fatten the pockets of private companies. We will instruct the Defense and State Departments to develop a strategy for determining when contracting makes sense, and when certain functions are "inherently governmental" and should not be contracted out. We will establish the legal status of contractor personnel, making possible prosecution of any abuses committed by private military contractors, and create a system of improved oversight and management, so that government can restore honesty, openness, and efficiency to contracting and procurement.

 Don't try to reconcile this with our proposed *"creation of a volunteer Civilian Assistance Corps of skilled experts (e.g., doctors, lawyers, engineers, city planners, agriculture specialists, police) who are pre-trained and willing to aid in emergencies"* so that *"we no longer have to ask our men and women in uniform to perform non-military functions."* We only mean for this section to apply to large military contractors who do not contribute in a meaningful way to our campaigns. Although if they have a

union in house, rest assured ... they'll be safe from prosecution.

Working for Our Common Security

To renew American leadership in the world, we will rebuild the alliances, partnerships, and institutions necessary to confront common threats and enhance common security. Needed reform of these alliances and institutions will not come by bullying other countries to ratify American demands. It will come when we convince other governments and peoples that they too have a stake in effective partnerships. It is only leadership if others join America in working toward our common security.

Too often, in recent years, we have sent the opposite signal to our international partners. In the case of Europe, we dismissed European reservations about the wisdom and necessity of the Iraq war and their concerns about climate change. In Asia, we belittled South Korean efforts to improve relations with the North. In Latin America, from Mexico to Argentina, we failed to address concerns about immigration and equity and economic growth. In Africa, we have allowed genocide to persist for over five years in Darfur and have not done nearly enough to answer the United Nation's call for more support to stop the killing. Under Barack Obama, we will rebuild our ties to our allies in Europe and Asia and strengthen our partnerships throughout the Americas and Africa.

 **Trust us when we say, *"The Democratic Party believes that there is no more important priority than renewing American leadership on the world stage."*** Getting kudos from other countries is really important to us. President Bush was too opinionated about the United States' preeminence in the world, and he was too adamant about executing his beliefs. Why, it only took President Obama twelve days to win the *Nobel Peace Prize*. That speaks volumes about how far an apologetic tone and obsequious manner will go ... and how politically *unbiased* the Nobel Prize Committee is.

This also gives us an opportunity to slip immigration reform into our Platform in an extremely subtle way. We feel that we should grant amnesty to 13 million illegal aliens in the United States ... or at least those who are willing to register as Democrats. President Obama supports this position as well. Of course, for all we know, he *is* one!

Support Africa's Democratic Development

U.S. engagement with Africa should reflect its vital significance to the U.S. as well as its emerging role in the global economy. We recognize Africa's promise as a trade and investment partner and the importance of policies that can contribute to sustainable economic growth, job creation, and poverty alleviation. We are committed to bringing the full weight of American leadership to bear in unlocking the spirit of entrepreneurship and economic independence that is sweeping across markets of Africa.

We believe that sustainable economic growth and development will mitigate and even help to reverse such chronic and debilitating challenges as poverty, hunger, conflict, and HIV/AIDS. We are committed to bringing the full weight of American leadership to bear to work in partnership with Africa to confront these crises. We will work with the United Nations and Africa's regional organizations to prevent and resolve conflict and to build the capacity of Africa's weak and failing states. We must respond effectively when there is a humanitarian crisis–particularly at this moment in Sudan where genocide persists in Darfur and the Comprehensive Peace Agreement is threatened.

Many African countries have embraced democratization and economic liberalization. We will help strengthen Africa's democratic development and respect for human rights, while encouraging political and economic reforms that result in improved transparency and accountability. We will defend democracy and stand up for rule of law when it is under assault, such as in Zimbabwe.

 **We admit there's a possibility that most African nations would trade food and water for our promise to bring** *"the full weight of American*

leadership to bear in unlocking the spirit of entrepreneurship and economic independence that is sweeping across markets of Africa." And if you've ever been to Africa or seen a documentary, you know how big they are on human rights.

With respect to AIDS, the President's Emergency Plan for AIDS Relief (PEPFAR) has been credited with saving over 10 million lives. Never mind that it was President Bush's Emergency Plan. *We* think it should be credited to President Obama. If he gets to *live* in the White House, he should get credit for any program that *started* in the White House. And besides, we have it on good authority that while on a tour of East Africa in 2006, President Obama took the time to visit his half-brother, George, for only the second time in his life; and he reached into his own pocket and gave his brother a dollar. Try to appreciate the significance of that: it was his *own* dollar ... not taxpayers' money. Now, that's leadership *we can believe in*.

Recommit to an Alliance of the Americas

We recognize that the security and prosperity of the United States is fundamentally tied to the future of the Americas. We believe that in the 21st century, the U.S. must treat Latin America and the Caribbean as full partners, just as our neighbors to the south should reject the bombast of authoritarian bullies. Our relationship with Canada, our long-time ally, should be strengthened and enhanced. An alliance of the Americas will only succeed if it is founded on the bedrock of mutual respect and works to advance democracy, opportunity, and security from the bottom-up. We must turn the page on the arrogance in Washington and the anti-Americanism across the region that stands in the way of progress. We must work with close partners like Mexico, Brazil, and Colombia on issues like ending the drug trade, fighting poverty and inequality, and immigration. We must work with the Caribbean community to help restore stability and the rule of law to Haiti, to improve the lives of its people, and to strengthen its democracy. And we must build ties to the people of Cuba and help advance their liberty by allowing unlimited family visits and remittances to the island, while presenting the Cuban regime with a clear choice: if it takes significant steps toward democracy, beginning with the unconditional release of all political prisoners, we will be prepared to take steps to begin normalizing relations.

 Let us be clear: South America is critical to our success. Otherwise, where can we vacation conveniently and inexpensively? Canada? ... Not so much! In fact, we can just take Canada for granted. But South America? That's a whole different story.

South America's stability is always in a delicate balance. Uncaring dictators, who are only in it for themselves, use insidious tactics to trick the general population into trusting them ... until it's too late. First, they separate the population into readily identifiable groups. Then, they manipulate the groups to get the members to believe that they're oppressed. Next, they create an emotionally charged fear that the "Opposition" doesn't care about these groups. To prove it, they offer each group things for free and promise them all sorts of benefits. Then, they finally execute a *"We vs. They"* strategy by suggesting that the *"freebies"* will continue and that they'll be funded by taxing the rich. It's amazing how *stupid* these people are. They fall for the *same old thing* ... time ... after time ... after time. The only reason they ever get a *new* dictator is because he or she thinks of some *new* bribe with which to tempt the masses. Then, they rise up and depose the old dictator ... and let the *new* one rape their country. We just can't *relate* to this kind of culture ... but we're *obviously* trying.

Lead in Asia

We are committed to U.S. engagement in Asia. This begins with maintaining strong relationships with allies like Japan, Australia, South Korea, Thailand, and the Philippines, and deepening our ties to vital democratic partners, like India, in order to create a stable and prosperous Asia. We must also forge a more effective framework in Asia that goes beyond bilateral agreements, occasional summits, and ad hoc diplomatic arrangements.

We need an open and inclusive infrastructure with the countries in Asia that can promote stability, prosperity, and human rights, and help confront, from terrorist cells in the Philippines to avian flu in Indonesia. We will encourage China to play a responsible role as a growing power–to help lead in addressing the common problems of the 21st century. We are committed to a "One China" policy and the Taiwan Relations Act, and will continue to support a peaceful resolution of cross-Straits issues that is consistent with the wishes and best interests of the people of Taiwan. It's time to engage China on common interests like climate change, trade, and energy, even as we continue to encourage its shift to a more open society and a market-based economy, and promote greater respect for human rights, including freedom of speech, press, assembly, religion, uncensored use of the internet, and Chinese workers' right to freedom of association, as well as the rights of Tibetans.

We strike a good balance here between positive goals (*e.g., "stability, prosperity, and human rights"*) and negative *"transnational threats"* (*i.e., "from terrorist cells in the Philippines to avian flu in Indonesia"*); although you may be a little less concerned with *"avian flu"* than you are with *"terrorist threats."* In any event, it makes us sound like we know what we're talking about.

We also state that *"it's time to engage China on common interests like climate change, trade, and energy, even as we continue to encourage its shift to a more open society and a market-based economy, and promote greater respect for human rights, including freedom of speech, press, assembly, religion, uncensored use of the internet, and Chinese workers' right to freedom of association, as well as the rights of Tibetans."* If this were a stock opportunity, you'd want to sell short. We already owe the Chinese government nearly $800 billion, and the amount is growing every day. It's a check we can't write, so we have about as much leverage with China as Dick Cheney has at a DNC rally.

Strengthen Transatlantic Relations

Europe remains America's indispensable partner. We support the historic project to build a strong European Union that can be an even stronger partner for the United States. NATO has made tremendous strides over the last fifteen years, transforming itself from a Cold War security structure into a partnership for peace. But today, NATO's challenge in Afghanistan has exposed a gap between its missions and its capabilities. To close this gap, we will invest more in NATO's mission in Afghanistan and use that investment to leverage our NATO allies to contribute more resources to collective security operations and to invest more in reconstruction and stabilization capabilities. As we promote democracy and accountability in Russia, we must work with the country in areas of common interest–above all, in making sure that nuclear weapons and materials are secure. We will insist that Russia abide by international law and respect the sovereignty and territorial integrity of its neighbors. We are committed to active Presidential leadership in the full implementation of the Irish Good Friday Agreement and St. Andrews Accords. We will seek to strengthen and broaden our strategic partnership with Turkey, end the division of Cyprus, and continue to support a close U.S. relationship with states that seek to strengthen their ties to NATO and the West, such as Georgia and Ukraine.

 **This should be easy. First, we'll strengthen our bonds with NATO by unilaterally deciding to change our missile defense strategy so we can gain favor with Russia. Then, we'll rely on Russia's long history of** *"abid(ing) by international law and respect(ing) the sovereignty and territorial integrity of its neighbors"* **… just as soon as their tanks finish taking a scenic tour through Georgia.**

Stand with Allies and Pursue Diplomacy in the Middle East

For more than three decades, Israelis, Palestinians, Arab leaders, and the rest of the world have looked to America to lead the effort to build the road to a secure and lasting peace. Our starting point must always be our special relationship with Israel, grounded in shared interests and shared values, and a clear, strong, fundamental commitment to the security of Israel, our strongest ally in the region and its only established democracy. That commitment, which requires us to ensure that Israel retains a qualitative edge for its national security and its right to self-defense, is all the more important as we contend with growing threats in the region–a strengthened Iran, a chaotic Iraq, the resurgence of Al Qaeda, the reinvigoration of Hamas and Hezbollah. We support the implementation of the memorandum of understanding that pledges $30 billion in assistance to Israel over the next decade to enhance and ensure its security.

It is in the best interests of all parties, including the United States, that we take an active role to help secure a lasting settlement of the Israeli-Palestinian conflict with a democratic, viable Palestinian state dedicated to living in peace and security side by side with the Jewish State of Israel. To do so, we must help Israel identify and strengthen those partners who are truly committed to peace, while isolating those who seek conflict and instability, and stand with Israel against those who seek its destruction. The United States and its Quartet partners should continue to isolate Hamas until it renounces terrorism, recognizes Israel's right to exist, and abides by past agreements. Sustained American leadership for peace and security will require patient efforts and the personal commitment of the President of the United States. The creation of a Palestinian state through final status negotiations, together with an international compensation mechanism, should resolve the issue of Palestinian refugees by allowing them to settle there, rather than in Israel. All understand that it is unrealistic to expect the outcome of final status negotiations to be a full and complete return to the armistice lines of 1949. Jerusalem is and will remain the capital of Israel. The parties have agreed that Jerusalem is a matter for final status negotiations. It should remain an undivided city accessible to people of all faiths.

We recognize that *"sustained American leadership for peace and security will require patient efforts and the personal commitment of the President of the United States."* **That's why President Obama has made a concerted effort to reinforce his commitment to Israel … by bowing to the Saudi King, rhetorically**

hypothecating that the United States could be considered to be *"one of the largest Muslim countries in the world,"* and by describing the Arabic call to prayer as *"one of the prettiest sounds on Earth at sunset;"* not to mention how quickly he came to Israel's defense when activist groups (which included known terrorists) attempted to run the Gaza blockade that is designed to prevent weapons from reaching Hamas.

Deepen Ties with Emerging Powers

We also will pursue effective collaboration on pressing global issues among all the major powers–including such newly emerging ones as China, India, Russia, Brazil, Nigeria, and South Africa. With India, we will build on the close partnership developed over the past decade. As two of the world's great, multi-ethnic democracies, the U.S. and India are natural strategic allies, and we must work together to advance our common interests and to combat the common threats of the 21st century. We believe it is in the United States' interest that all of these emerging powers and others assume a greater stake in promoting international peace and respect for human rights, including through their more constructive participation in key global institutions.

We have learned not to be as arrogant as the Bush Administration. That's why we have so generously referred to China, India, Russia, Brazil, Nigeria, and South Africa as *"emerging powers."* We're sure that China, Russia and even India will be appreciative to know that we have *finally* elevated them to a status they surely would *never* have given to themselves. Now, they're right up there with Nigeria and, to a lesser extent, Brazil and South Africa. It must be *exciting* for them. This certainly will make China rethink its stance on human rights issues and look to us for direction.

Revitalize Global Institutions

To enhance global cooperation on issues from weapons proliferation to climate change, we need stronger international institutions. We believe that the United Nations is indispensable but requires far-reaching reform. The U.N. Secretariat's management practices remain inadequate. Peacekeeping operations are overextended. The new U.N. Human Rights Council remains biased and ineffective. Yet none of these problems will be solved unless America rededicates itself to the organization and its mission. We support reforming key global institutions —such as the U.N. Security Council and the G-8—so they will be more reflective of 21ˢᵗ century realities.

 **We are committed to the United Nations. Not only do we provide a home for it; we also are assessed 22% of its regular budget and 27% for its ineffective peacekeeping operations. What a deal!**

In return, we get reprimanded for *our* human rights violations for using drone aircraft to kill terrorists. We're right up there with China, Iran and North Korea. Well, maybe a little below them since Iran was elected to the U.N.'s *Commission on the Status of Women*; a four-year appointment to the influential human rights body. That's the same Iran that operates as a theocratic state in which stoning is enshrined in law and lashings are required for women judged *"immodest."* Good call, U.N.!

Advancing Democracy, Development, and Respect for Human Rights

No country in the world has benefited more from the worldwide expansion of democracy than the United States. Democracies are our best trading partners, our most valuable allies, and the nations with which we share our deepest values. The United States must join with our democratic partners around the world to meet common security challenges and uphold our shared values whenever they are threatened by autocratic practices, coups, human rights abuses, or genocide.

 **Just to be clear: we *know* that we're misusing the word *"democracy."* The Framers of the United States Constitution clearly created a *Republic* that, while fostering open elections (the concept that is most often confused with the term *"democracy"*), was not designed to embrace the *"majority rule"* doctrine of a democracy. No, they wanted to protect against the formation of a democracy, which they had seen fail in the past because *"majority rule"* ultimately decimates the minority ... *because it can*; stripping them of property, rights and liberty until insurrection arises. It's kind of like redistributing the wealth until those who have earned the money just won't put up with it any more. Forget we ever said that!**

We use the word *"democracy"* more liberally and reinforce the misconception that the United States is and always has been a democracy. Part of the reason is that it better serves our purpose and our strategy of rallying theoretically *"oppressed minorities"* into an overwhelming majority so we can tax the rich minority. The other value is pure marketing: we want to subliminally reinforce our *"brand,"* and continually asserting that we are a *"democracy"* gets the job done!

<u>Build Democratic Institutions</u>

The Democratic Party reaffirms its longstanding commitment to support democratic institutions and practices worldwide. A more democratic world is a more peaceful and prosperous place. Yet democracy cannot be imposed by force from the outside; it must be nurtured with moderates on the inside by building democratic institutions.

The United States must be a relentless advocate for democracy and put forward a vision of democracy that goes beyond the ballot box. We will increase our support for strong legislatures, independent judiciaries, free press, vibrant civil society, honest police forces, religious freedom, equality for women and minorities, and the rule of law. In new democracies, we will support the development of civil society and representative institutions that can protect fundamental human rights and improve the quality of life for all citizens, including independent and democratic unions. In non-democratic countries, we pledge to work with international partners to assist the efforts of those struggling to promote peaceful political reforms. Ongoing funding to the National Endowment for Democracy and other U.S. government-funded democracy programs reflects American values and serves our interests.

Here's our brand initiative in action again. But this time, we reinforce it with all sorts of good things: *"our support for strong legislatures, independent judiciaries, free press, vibrant civil society, honest police forces, religious freedom, equality for women and minorities, and the rule of law."* Then, we add our commitment to *"support the development of civil society and representative institutions that can protect fundamental human rights and improve the quality of life for all citizens, including independent and democratic unions."*

This is consistent with the way we market our *internal* programs to induce you to vote for us. We aren't as good at articulating our value at the international level because these people *can't* vote for us ... but we still *desperately* want to earn their approval.

Invest in Our Common Humanity

To renew American leadership in the world, we will strengthen our common security by investing in our common humanity. In countries wracked by poverty and conflict, citizens long to enjoy freedom from want. Because extremely poor societies and weak states provide optimal breeding grounds for terrorism, disease, and conflict, the United States has a direct national security interest in dramatically reducing global poverty and joining with our allies in sharing more of our riches to help those most in need.

Forget about the massive federal deficit we're building or the *"one in eight Americans"* who are living in poverty. Remember, *"the Democratic

Party believes that there is no more important priority than renewing American leadership on the world stage."

It is time to make the U.N. Millennium Development Goals, which aim to cut extreme poverty in half by 2015, America's goals as well. We need to invest in building capable, democratic states that can establish healthy and educated communities, develop markets, and generate wealth.

Such states would also have greater institutional capacities to fight terrorism, halt the spread of deadly weapons, and build health-care infrastructures to prevent, detect, and treat deadly diseases such as HIV/AIDS, malaria, and avian flu.

 **President Bush's program that already addresses this has a generic name, the President's Emergency Plan for AIDS Relief (PEPFAR). Maybe we could just claim we created it. It's been a few years, so who's going to remember?**

We will double our annual investment in meeting these challenges to $50 billion by 2012 and ensure that those new resources are directed toward worthwhile goals. We will work with philanthropic organizations and the private sector to invest in development and poverty reduction. But if America is going to help others build more just and secure societies, our trade deals, debt relief, and foreign aid must not come as blank checks. We will recognize the fragility of small nations in the Caribbean, the Americas, Africa, and Asia and work with them to successfully transition to a new global economy. We will couple our support with an insistent call for reform, to combat the corruption that rots societies and governments from within. As part of this new funding, we will create a $2 billion Global Education Fund that will bring the world together in eliminating the global education deficit with the goal of supporting a free, quality, basic education for every child in the world. Education increases incomes, reduces poverty, strengthens communities, prevents the spread of disease, improves child and maternal health, and empowers women and girls. We cannot hope to shape a world where opportunity outweighs danger unless we ensure that every child everywhere is taught to build and not to destroy.

 At our current rate of spending, our national debt is projected to exceed our Gross Domestic Product by 2012. But don't worry! We'll just print some more money.

The real key factor here is that *"we will couple our support with an insistent call for reform, to combat the corruption that rots societies and governments from within."* We want to try out our theories *somewhere else* ... before we attempt to combat the corruption that's rotting *our* society and government from within. Besides, if we did it here first, we may not be around to govern!

Speaking of which, did you notice that we now have a goal of *"supporting a free, quality, basic education for every child in the world,"* and we're going to put up $2 billion to get the job done. Given the world's population versus our own, this means it's only going to cost a few hundred thousand dollars to educate all of the children in the United States.

Our policies will recognize that human rights are women's rights and that women's rights are human rights. Women make up the majority of the poor in the world. So we will expand access to women's economic development opportunities and seek to expand microcredit. Women produce half of the world's food but only own one percent of the land upon which it is grown. We will work to ensure that women have equal protection under the law and are not denied rights and therefore locked into poverty.

 Stop the presses ... late breaking news! *Women are apparently humans!* We not only recognize that, but since Affirmative Action hasn't exactly been the poster child of success for our African American population, we're now going to extend it to women.

And notice that, once again, our reach is *global*. We're going to make sure that the *world* equates women's rights to human rights. We think that a civil, diplomatic intervention will probably do the trick, so we're going to start with asking that

honor killings and the stoning of women be suspended throughout the world on National Women's Day.

We will modernize our foreign assistance policies, tools, and operations in an elevated, empowered, consolidated, and streamlined U.S. development agency. Development and diplomacy will be reinforced as key pillars of U.S. foreign policy, and our civilian agencies will be staffed, resourced, and equipped to address effectively new global challenges.

American leadership on human rights is essential to making the world safer, more just, and more humane. Such leadership must begin with steps to undo the damage of the Bush years. But we also must go much further. We should work with others to shape human rights institutions and instruments tailored to the 21st century. We must make the United Nations' human rights organs more objective, energetic, and effective. The U.S. must lead global efforts to promote international humanitarian standards and to protect civilians from indiscriminate violence during warfare. We will champion accountability for genocide and war crimes, ending the scourge of impunity for massive human rights abuses. We will stand up for oppressed people from Cuba to North Korea and from Burma to Zimbabwe and Sudan. We will accord greater weight to human rights, including the rights of women and children, in our relationships with other global powers, recognizing that America's long-term strategic interests are more likely to be advanced when our partners are rights-respecting.

Coupled with our position on women's rights, we think the United Nations took a step in the right direction when it appointed Iran to a four-year term on the *Commission on the Status of Women*. We steadfastly deny that the war in Iraq had anything to do with human rights or genocide or we would still be on record as supporting it. It was merely George W. Bush's aggressive, ill-conceived idea ... even though we *voted* for it. Just as there were no weapons of mass destruction to be found, we believe that the accused violations of human rights and the genocide of the Kurds are no more founded on fact than the actual occurrence of the Holocaust!

Democrats will invest in improving global health. It is a human shame that many of the diseases which compound the problem of global poverty are treatable, but they are yet to be treated.

 **You've probably already noticed that we Democrats will pretty much commit to spending money on anything that has the word *"global"* in front of it. We believe *"there is no more important priority than renewing American leadership on the world stage"* ... at any cost.**

The HIV/AIDS pandemic is a massive human tragedy. It is also a security risk of the highest order that threatens to plunge nations into chaos. There are an estimated 33 million people across the planet infected with HIV/AIDS, including more than one million people in the U.S. Nearly 8,000 people die every day of AIDS. We must do more to fight the global HIV/AIDS pandemic, as well as malaria, tuberculosis, and neglected tropical diseases. We will provide $50 billion over five years to strengthen existing U.S. programs and expand them to new regions of the world, including Southeast Asia, India, and parts of Europe, where the HIV/AIDS burden is growing. We will increase U.S. contributions to the Global Fund to ensure that global efforts to fight endemic disease continue to move ahead.

 **Even though HIV/AIDS probably isn't on any countries *"Top Ten Causes of Death"* (it's certainly not one of ours), it's still a *"politically correct"* issue to address, and *we* think it garners votes *whenever* we bring it up.**

We also support the adoption of humanitarian licensing policies that ensure medications developed with the U.S. taxpayer dollars are available off patent in developing countries. We will repeal the global gag rule and reinstate funding to the United Nations Population Fund (UNFPA). We will expand access to health care and nutrition for women and reduce the burden of maternal mortality.

 **Even though we say that health care is a disaster in the United States, we feel comfortable in asserting our ability to improve health care in all *other* nations.**

We will leverage the engagement of the private sector and private philanthropy to launch Health Infrastructure 2020–a global effort to work with developing countries to invest in the full range of infrastructure needed to improve and protect both American and global health.

 **Truth be told, no one around here can remember how this particular suggestion got into our Platform since it relies on the private sector and philanthropy to fund it. Couldn't we have just taxed the rich instead?**

Human Trafficking

We will address human trafficking—both labor and sex trafficking–through strong legislation and enforcement to ensure that trafficking victims are protected and traffickers are brought to justice. We will also address the root causes of human trafficking, including poverty, discrimination, and gender inequality, as well as the demand for prostitution.

 **We will erect a new series of traffic signs ... in multiple languages ... to bring order to human trafficking. You know ... kind of like we do with *"deer crossing"* signs.**
In the interest of full disclosure, we shot down the idea of disbanding Congress and the U.N., even though both ideas would have severely curtailed the demand for prostitution ... at least in the States.

PROTECTING OUR SECURITY AND SAVING OUR PLANET

We must end the tyranny of oil in our time. This immediate danger is eclipsed only by the longer-term threat from climate change, which will lead to devastating weather patterns, terrible storms, drought, conflict, and famine. That means people competing for food and water in the next fifty years in the very places that have known horrific violence in the last fifty: Africa, the Middle East, and South Asia. That could also mean destructive storms on our shores, and the disappearance of our coastline.

Ahhh ... *"the tyranny of oil."* This is the second time we've gotten to raise this phrase in our Platform. It just rolls off your lips.

We love to attack our dependence on oil, even though we haven't done anything about it (other than having spent billions of dollars on our totally ineffective Department of Energy). You see: George Bush is from Texas. He's an *"oil man."* All Texans are! You may have noticed that we're passionately against *anything* associated with the former President. Besides, the issue is *"politically correct,"* and Al Gore has already received a *richly deserved* Nobel Peace Prize, as well as an Oscar, for his tireless work in this area. This is a veritable *oil field* ...uh... we mean *gold mine* of publicity for us.

We understand that climate change is not just an economic issue or an environmental concern– this is a national security crisis.

Luckily, we believe that we can create enough agencies, councils and summits to justifying spending ridiculous sums of money, which will *undoubtedly* overcome Mother Nature ... whom *we* believe ... is a Republican.

Establish Energy Security

Not since the 1970s has America's national security been so threatened by its energy insecurity, and, as we have learned the hard way over the past eight years, achieving energy security in the 21st century requires far more than simply expending our economic and political resources to keep oil flowing steadily out of unstable and even hostile countries and regions.

Rather, energy security requires stemming the flow of money to oil rich regimes that are hostile to America and its allies; it requires combating climate change and preparing for its impacts both at home and abroad; it requires making international energy markets work for us and not against us; it requires standing up to the oil companies that spend hundreds of millions of dollars on lobbying and political contributions; it requires addressing nuclear safety, waste, and proliferation challenges around the world; and more.

As you probably already know, this is more of a political issue than it is an environmental one. We're trying to subtly align the Republicans with the *evil* oil industry on a global level. So, we *"talk tough"* about how we're going to deal with those *evil* entities, which in turn casts a bad light on the Republicans. Get it?

So, when we say we're going to stem *"the flow of money to oil rich regimes that are hostile to America and its allies,"* we *really* don't mean it. How could we, when we've already committed to paying for their health care, their food, their children's education, etc. on a variety of occasions in other parts of our Platform?

Democrats will halt this dangerous trend, and take the necessary steps to achieving energy independence. We will make it a top priority to reduce oil consumption by at least 35 percent, or ten million barrels per day, by 2030. This will more than offset the amount of oil we are expected to import from OPEC nations in 2030.

 Again, ignore the fact that we created the Department of Energy back in 1977 to do this very thing. It's only been a little over 30 years, and these things take time!

Lead to Combat Climate Change

We will lead to defeat the epochal, man-made threat to the planet: climate change. Without dramatic changes, rising sea levels will flood coastal regions around the world. Warmer temperatures and declining rainfall will reduce crop yields, increasing conflict, famine, disease, and poverty. By 2050, famine could displace more than 250 million people worldwide. That means increased instability in some of the most volatile parts of the world.

 This is *"fear mongering"* at it's finest. You've probably noticed that we don't get to use our standard tactics as frequently in these international issues, but the environment is an area in which we can still *"have fun with fear!"*

Forget the fact that scientists can't agree on the meaning of the data; we can claim that it's *"conclusive."* After all, if Al Gore was smart enough to have invented the Internet, he's smart enough to know what's going to happen with the environment ... even if his own experts disagree with him.

Yes, we can say with confidence ... and even glee ... that 'without dramatic changes, rising sea levels will flood coastal regions around the world ... (and) warmer temperatures and declining rainfall will reduce crop yields, increasing conflict, famine, disease, and poverty ... (so, that) by 2050, famine could displace more than 250 million people worldwide." If you thought *Titanic* was a good movie, wait until you see the one that our favorite Oscar winner is conjuring up for you. Besides, none of us will still be in office in 2050, so who cares if we're wrong? In the mean time, we can rant and rave and spend countless billions of dollars trying to overcome Mother Nature.

Never again will we sit on the sidelines, or stand in the way of collective action to tackle this global challenge. Getting our own house in order is only a first step. We will invest in efficient and clean technologies at home while using our assistance policies and export promotions to help developing countries preserve biodiversity, curb deforestation, and leapfrog the carbon-energy-intensive stage of development.

We will reach out to the leaders of the biggest carbon emitting nations and ask them to join a new Global Energy Forum that will lay the foundation for the next generation of climate protocols. China has replaced America as the world's largest emitter of greenhouse gases. Clean energy development must be a central focus in our relationships with major countries in Europe and Asia. We need a global response to climate change that includes binding and enforceable commitments to reducing emissions, especially for those that pollute the most: the United States, China, India, the European Union, and Russia.

"Never again will we sit on the sidelines" **... and we mean it! To do this, we will have to gather our massive personal staffs (as well as our family members) and board our planes to fly to wherever our Global Energy Forums will be held. Then, we'll have to take limousines to-and-from our five-star hotels as well as to-and-from our embassy parties, our press conferences, and our diplomatic sight-seeing tours ... just as we did at the recent (and oft-recurring)** *United Nations' Climate Change Conference.* **Our first order of business will be to overcome our** *own* **carbon-footprints. After that, it should be easy.**

This challenge is massive, but rising to it will also bring new benefits to America. By 2050, global demand for low-carbon energy could create an annual market worth $500 billion. Meeting that demand would open new frontiers for American entrepreneurs and workers.

Normally, we arrive at our numbers through *"atmospheric extraction."* **However, this $500 billion number is so big we had to pull it from a**

far more personal orifice ... from which we first had to remove our heads.

SEIZING THE OPPORTUNITY

It is time for a new generation to tell the next great American story. If we act with boldness and foresight, we will be able to tell our grandchildren that this was the time we confronted climate change and secured the weapons that could destroy the human race. This was the time we defeated global terrorists and brought opportunity to forgotten corners of the world. This was the time when we helped forge peace in the Middle East. This was the time when we renewed the America that has led generations of weary travelers from all over the world to find opportunity and liberty and hope on our doorstep.

 **Our biggest fear is that you'll vote people into office who can actually *do* this, which would leave almost all of *us* unemployed.**

It was not all that long ago that farmers in Venezuela and Indonesia welcomed American doctors to their villages and hung pictures of John F. Kennedy on their living room walls, when millions waited every day for a letter in the mail that would grant them the privilege to come to America to study, work, live, or just be free.

We can be this America again. This is our moment to renew the trust and faith of our people– and all people–in an America that battles immediate evils, promotes an ultimate good, and leads the world once more.

 **We came up with this tag line after watching a rerun of the 1950's Superman show on TV. He protected us in *"the never ending battle for truth, justice and the American way."* As Democrats, we lead an America that *"battles immediate evils, promotes an ultimate good, and leads the world once more."***

And while we reference the Kennedy Administration as a time *"when millions waited every day for a letter in the mail that would grant them the privilege to come to America to study,*

work, live, or just be free," we still haven't been able to shake loose from that dilemma. People are still trying to migrate here by the millions. Luckily, we're trying to eliminate the belief that they need to be willing to *"wait for the letter"* and then *"study"* and *"work"* to achieve the American Dream. We'll just *grant* everybody amnesty ... because it's the only *fair* thing to do.

III. RENEWING THE AMERICAN COMMUNITY

In local platform hearings around the country and the world, Americans talked of the need for compassion, empathy, a commitment to our values, and the importance of being united in order to take on the challenges and opportunities of the new century. They sounded the same themes we have heard since the campaign began, whether in town halls in Nevada, policy roundtables in Philadelphia, or online gatherings held by Democrats Abroad. They said that they valued Barack Obama's message that alongside Americans' famous individualism, there's another ingredient in the American saga: a belief that we are connected to each other. We could all choose to focus on our own concerns and live our lives in a way that tries to keep our individual stories separate from the larger story of America. But that is not who we are. That is not our American story. If there's a child on the south side of Chicago who can't read, that matters to us, even if it's not our child. Similarly, if there's a senior citizen in Elko, Nevada who has to choose between medicine and the rent, that makes our lives poorer, even if it's not our grandmother. Because it is only when we join together in something larger than ourselves that we can write the next great chapter in America's story.

Altogether now, *"We are the world ... We are the people ..."* This is straight out of our *"mom, apple pie, and the girl-we-left-behind"* playbook. It appeals to everyone's sense of *"compassion"* and *"empathy."* Of course, we subtly slip in the thing about a *"commitment to OUR values,"* but most people will read right past it. As long as voters focus on our *message* rather than our *deeds*, we think we'll be okay.

Can you tell that we're running out of steam at this point? We're trying to pad our Platform with everything we can think of to make it *thicker*.

SERVICE

The future of our country will be determined not only by our government and our policies but through the efforts of the American people. That is why we will ask all Americans to be actively involved in meeting the challenges of the new century. In this young century, our military has answered the call to serve, even as that call has come too often. We must now make it possible for all citizens to serve. We will expand AmeriCorps, double the size of the Peace Corps, enable more to serve in the military, create new opportunities for international service, integrate service into primary education, and create new opportunities for experienced and retired persons to serve. And if you invest in America, America will invest in you: we will increase support for service-learning, establish tax incentives for college students who serve, and create scholarships for students who pledge to become teachers. We will use the Internet to better match volunteers to service opportunities. In these ways, we will unleash the power of service to meet America's challenges in a uniquely American way.

"If you invest in America, America will invest in you" is just a rallying cry to try to *"enroll"* our youth into an *"activist"* mode ... so they'll vote Democrat. We've basically already *promised* to give *every* citizen *everything* that they could possibly want. Heck! We've pretty much *promised* to give *everyone in the world* everything they could possibly want. All that really remains is to figure out how to pay for it ... but then, that's why we continue to allow rich people to live.

IMMIGRATION

America has always been a nation of immigrants. Over the years, millions of people have come here in the hope that in America, you can make it if you try. Each successive wave of immigrants has contributed to our country's rich culture, economy and spirit. Like the immigrants that came before them, today's immigrants will shape their own destinies and enrich our country.

 **Unlike the old days, when immigrants brought skills and work ethic to back up their pursuit of the American Dream, we no longer think that should be the case. No, once we discovered that *illegal* immigrants could populate our social programs to make the need self-sustaining *and* that we could finagle voter registration for them (*"from one small acorn, a mighty oak can grow"*), we were convinced that our borders should be open to *everyone*. Oh sure, we'll get the occasional terrorist or two who will cross with members of a drug cartel and a few honest migrant workers, but it's about the *votes* ... and being *"politically correct."* A successful terrorist attack is a small price to pay to fix an election.**

Nonetheless, our current immigration system has been broken for far too long. We need comprehensive immigration reform, not just piecemeal efforts. We must work together to pass immigration reform in a way that unites this country, not in a way that divides us by playing on our worst instincts and fears. We are committed to pursuing tough, practical, and humane immigration reform in the first year of the next administration.

 **At one of our local Platform hearings, someone suggested that we start by reinforcing the fact that there is a *legal* way to immigrate to the United States and an *illegal* one. We threw him out because he either had to be a Republican or a member of the Tea Party.**

We cannot continue to allow people to enter the United States undetected, undocumented, and unchecked. The American people are a welcoming and generous people, but those who enter our country's borders illegally, and those who employ them, disrespect the rule of the law. We need to secure our borders, and support additional personnel, infrastructure, and technology on the border and at our ports of entry. We need additional Customs and Border Protection agents equipped with better technology and real-time intelligence. We need to dismantle human smuggling organizations, combating the crime associated with this trade. We also need to do more to promote economic development in migrant-sending nations, to reduce incentives to come to the United States illegally. And we need to crack down on employers who hire undocumented immigrants. It's a problem when we only enforce our laws against the immigrants themselves, with raids that are ineffective, tear apart families, and leave people detained without adequate access to counsel. We realize that employers need a method to verify whether their employees are legally eligible to work in the United States, and we will ensure that our system is accurate, fair to legal workers, safeguards people's privacy, and cannot be used to discriminate against workers.

We don't really believe any of this because it would cost us votes, but we *have* to say it to try to catch some of the Independent voters as well. It's a tough balancing act since we're so blatant about accusing *anyone* who believes in this of being a *racist*. If we really believed it, we could just start enforcing the laws that we have in place rather than ostracizing States like Arizona for trying to do it *for* us ... while rewarding *"Sanctuary Cities"* like San Francisco for flaunting their ability to *ignore* Federal law.

We must also improve the legal immigration system, and make our nation's naturalization process fair and accessible to the thousands of legal permanent residents who are eager to become full Americans. We should fix the dysfunctional immigration bureaucracy that hampers family reunification, the cornerstone of our immigration policy for years. Given the importance of both keeping families together and supporting American businesses, we will increase the number of immigration visas for family members of people living here and for immigrants who meet the demand for jobs that employers cannot fill, as long as appropriate labor market protections and standards are in place. We will fight discrimination against Americans who have always played by our immigration rules but are sometimes treated as if they had not.

 Yes, we must *"improve the legal immigration system, and make our nation's naturalization process fair and accessible to the thousands of legal permanent residents who are eager to become full Americans."* It's presently unfair. After all, our Naturalization materials and tests are only offered in 14 languages, and Ket (a language spoken by only a few hundred people in Central Siberia) isn't one of them!

You have to smile when we firmly state that *"we should fix the dysfunctional immigration bureaucracy"* considering that we're the people who put it in place. Besides, if you delete the word *"immigration,"* you may truly have the type of *"change"* that all Americans *"can believe in."*

And when it comes to our promise to *"fight discrimination against Americans who have always played by our immigration rules but are sometimes treated as if they had not,"* we realize the hypocrisy of our comment. Whenever we play the *"race card"* with respect to *illegal* aliens, whom we now demand be called *"undocumented workers"* out of respect for how they have chosen to circumvent Federal law, we are in fact inherently discriminating against our naturalized citizens who immigrated legally. So, why do we take the risk? Because we think we can pick up *more* donations and votes from the *illegal* alien community than we will lose among naturalized citizens who are offended. Besides, *"playing the race card"* is a key component of our core *"oppressed minority"* strategy.

For the millions living here illegally but otherwise playing by the rules, we must require them to come out of the shadows and get right with the law. We support a system that requires undocumented immigrants who are in good standing to pay a fine, pay taxes, learn English, and go to the back of the line for the opportunity to become citizens. They are our neighbors, and we can help them become full tax-paying, law-abiding, productive members of society.

 **We do not believe *any* individual should be judged too harshly for a single bad trait. Applying our standard *equally*, we believe that for the thousands of pedophiles and other sociopaths,** who may molest a child or kill people on a serial basis *"but otherwise play by the rules"* ... *"we must require them to come out of the shadows and get right with the law." "We support a system that requires"* **pedophiles and sociopaths** *"who are in good standing to pay a fine (and) pay taxes."* **After all,** *"they are our neighbors, and we can help them become full tax-paying, law-abiding, productive members of society."*

HURRICANE KATRINA

For many in America, Hurricane Katrina conjures up the memory of a time when America's government failed its citizens. When the winds blew and the floodwaters came, we learned that for all of our wealth and power, something wasn't right with Washington. Our government's response during Hurricane Katrina is a national shame–and yet three years later, the government has still failed to keep its promise to rebuild.

 **We're allowed to blame Republican leadership for failing to prevent and respond to a natural disaster. We're Democrats!**
    However, let us be clear: if another natural disaster should happen to a Democratic Administration ... or even one caused by human error (you know, like an oil rig accident offshore) ... then, *all bets are off*. **It would be unfair to criticize** *our* **President and his Administration. Why, Jimmy Carter might even suggest that to do so is racist! No, if we were to suffer such a fate, you may rest assured that we would work feverishly to find a way to blame the Bush Administration.**

Then, once responsibility has been reassigned, we'd look into solving the actual issue that caused the problem to arise in the first place.

The people of New Orleans and the Gulf Coast are heroes for returning and rebuilding, and they shouldn't face these challenges alone. We will partner with the people of the Gulf Coast to assist the victims of Hurricane Katrina and restore the region economically. We will create jobs and training opportunities for returning and displaced workers as well as contracting opportunities for local businesses to help create stronger, safer, and more equitable communities. We will increase funding for affordable housing and home ownership opportunities for returning families, workers, and residents moving out of unsafe trailers. We will reinvest in infrastructure in New Orleans: we will construct levees that work, fight crime by rebuilding local police departments and courthouses, invest in hospitals, and rebuild the public school system.

Next time, we hope the *"heroes"* will actually follow all the warnings they received before the actual disaster struck. When San Diego was threatened a few years ago by wildfires that created a disaster of similar scale and length, there was virtually no loss of life (other than a few people who ignored the warnings that they received) because almost everyone *followed instructions*. Those people even avoided the temptation to rob and rape each other when they were forced by the tens of thousands to seek shelter at *their* football stadium. For this type of *abhorrent* behavior, the citizens of San Diego cannot be called heroes or given any special attention. Besides, while Hispanics and Blacks were displaced by the wildfire, they do not make as visible a majority in the San Diego community as does the African American population in New Orleans, so it would have been harder to reference the wildfires as an intentional act of genocide as we accused the Bush Administration of orchestrating in New Orleans.

We also commit to the rebuilding and restoration of the Iowa communities affected by the floods of 2008.

 Hey, Iowa is a "throw in." We just threw it in because they have a caucus that's been important to us in the past during the primary elections.

<u>Preventing and Responding to Future Catastrophes</u>

We will also work to prevent future catastrophic response failures, whether the emergency comes from hurricanes, earthquakes, floods, tornadoes, wild fires, drought, bridge collapses, or any other natural or man-made disaster. Maintaining our levees and dams is not pork barrel spending—it is an urgent priority. We will fix governmental agencies like the Federal Emergency Management Agency, ensure that they are staffed with professionals, and create integrated communication and response plans. We will reform the Small Business Administration bureaucracy, and develop a real National Response Plan.

We will develop a National Catastrophic Insurance Fund to offer an affordable insurance mechanism for high-risk catastrophes that no single private insurer can cover by itself for fear of bankruptcy. This will allow states and territories to deal comprehensively with the economic dislocation of natural disasters.

 Don't compare *"Maintaining our levees and dams"* to pork barrel spending. We *know* pork barrel spending, and this is *not* pork barrel spending. Have you noticed that we're going to resolve the problems with all the government agencies that are too *stupid* to staff themselves with professionals? We're going to *"FIX government agencies like the Federal Emergency Management Agency"* and *"REFORM the Small Business Administration bureaucracy, and develop a REAL National Response Plan"* ... as opposed to the *FAKE* National Response Plan we rely on today.

And of course, we have to *"develop a National Catastrophic Insurance Fund to offer an affordable insurance mechanism for high-risk catastrophes."* Truth be told, it gives us a chance to nationalize part of the insurance industry. We think the margins could be higher than the States' lotteries; and besides, it will undoubtedly require a bunch of new agencies that won't know how to hire professionals for the new jobs they'll create.

STEWARDSHIP OF OUR PLANET AND NATURAL RESOURCES

Global climate change is the planet's greatest threat, and our response will determine the very future of life on this earth. Despite the efforts of our current Administration to deny the science of climate change and the need to act, we still believe that America can be earth's best hope. We will implement a market-based cap and trade system to reduce carbon emissions by the amount scientists say is necessary to avoid catastrophic change and we will set interim targets along the way to ensure that we meet our goal. We will invest in advanced energy technologies, to build the clean energy economy and create millions of new, good "Green Collar" American jobs. Because the environment is a truly global concern, the United States must be a leader in combating climate change around the world, including exporting climate-friendly technologies to developing countries. We will use innovative measures to dramatically improve the energy efficiency of buildings, including establishing a grant program for early adopters and providing incentives for energy conservation. We will encourage local initiatives, sustainable communities, personal responsibility, and environmental stewardship and education nationwide.

 Remember how we said we could just say the scientific evidence of climate change was *"conclusive"* so we could implement our *"fear strategy?"* Well, here's just one more example of it.

"We will use innovative measures to dramatically improve the energy efficiency of buildings, including establishing a grant

program for early adopters and providing incentives for energy conservation." Now, you may ask: what does *"establishing a grant program for early adopters and providing incentives for energy conservation"* have to do with *"innovative measures (that) dramatically improve the energy efficiency of buildings."* On the surface, the answer would appear to be *nothing!* However, we believe that the walls of these buildings can be insulated with shredded paper from the millions of pages of regulations that our new agencies will print ... but no one will utilize. And besides, we get to spend more money building yet *another* bureaucracy that we'll have to say we'll fix in the next National Platform we have to write.

We will help local communities in the American West preserve water to meet their fast growing needs. We support a comprehensive solution for restoring our national treasures—such as the Great Lakes, Everglades, and Chesapeake Bay—including expanded scientific research and protections for species and habitats there. We will reinvigorate the Environmental Protection Agency so that we can work with communities to reduce air and water pollution and protect our children from environmental toxins, and never sacrifice science to politics. We will protect Nevada and its communities from the high-level nuclear waste dump at Yucca Mountain, which has not been proven to be safe by sound science. We will restore the "polluter pays" principle to fund the cleanup of the most polluted sites, so that those who cause environmental problems pay to fix them.

Right now, we deny water to the communities in the American West to protect the smelt (a tiny little fish that environmentalists fear may get caught in water pumps). As a result, water can no longer be pumped in parts of California. It is a matter of extinction! Oh, not of the *fish* ... but of the *farmers* who have lost *everything* they own because they can no longer irrigate their farms; of the *taxpayer base* that's *moving away* because the government induced crisis is limiting access to water and using the imposed scarcity of resources to justify rate

increases; and of the *competitive price of fruits and wines* that require water to grow. And just for good measure, you can add the Environmental Protection Agency to the list of ineffective agencies we created in the past that we will need to spend massive amounts of money to *"fix."*

<u>Federal Lands</u>

We will create a new vision for conservation that works with local communities to conserve our existing publicly-owned lands while dramatically expanding investments in conserving and restoring forests, grasslands, and wetlands across America for generations to come. Unlike the current Administration, we will reinvest in our nation's forests by providing federal agencies with resources to reduce the threat of wildland fires, promote sustainable forest product industries for rural economic development and ensure that national resources are in place to respond to catastrophic wildland fires. We will treat our national parks with the same respect that millions of families show each year when they visit. We will recognize that our parks are national treasures, and will ensure that they are protected as part of the overall natural system so they are here for generations to come. We are committed to conserving the lands used by hunters and anglers, and we will open millions of new acres of land to public hunting and fishing.

 **This is just one more opportunity to take a meaningless shot at the Bush Administration. Of course, the Federal agencies that haven't seemed to get the job done to our standards are the agencies that *we* created. No problem! We'll just invest even more money in them. Maybe they just haven't hired professionals. There's a lot of that going around these days.**

   As for our concession to conserving lands for public hunting and fishing ... we're going to do that just after we repeal the Second Amendment. Note that the repeal will have *no effect* on those who like to hunt with bows and arrows.

Metropolitan and Urban Policy

We believe that strong cities are the building blocks of strong regions, and strong regions are essential for a strong America. To build vibrant and diverse cities and regions, we support equitable development strategies that create opportunities for those traditionally left behind by economic development efforts.

We also believe that these *"strong"* cities are the building blocks of our voter base as witnessed in every election for the past 100 years. We do *extremely* well in big cities where poverty is high and social services are a way of life ... because that's what our Platform is all about. The more *"oppressed minorities"* we can cram into a city and scare, the easier it is to corral them and bus them to a polling site. We get *crushed* politically *everywhere else* in America.

For the past eight years, the current Administration has ignored urban areas. We look forward to greater partnership with urban America. We will strengthen federal commitment to cities, including by creating a new White House Office on Urban Policy and fully funding the Community Development Block Grant. We support community-based initiatives, such as micro-loans, business assistance centers, community economic development corporations, and community development financial institutions. To help regional business development we will double federal funding for basic research, expand the deployment of broadband technology, increase access to capital for businesses in underserved areas, create a national network of public-private business incubators, and provide grants to support regional innovation clusters. Since businesses can only function when workers can get to their place of employment, we will invest in public transportation including rail, expand transportation options for low-income communities, and strengthen core infrastructure like our roads and bridges. We will provide cities the support they need to perform public safety and national security functions, reinvest in Community Oriented Policing Services, and keep children off the streets by supporting expanded after-school and summer opportunities. Finally, we will work to make cities greener and more livable by training employees to work in skilled clean technologies industries, improving the environmental efficiency of city buildings, and taking smart growth principles into account when designing transportation.

Now, we're getting back into Democratic country ... the area where we can spin give-away programs into votes. A grant program here, a grant program there, and pretty soon we've got the attention of our *"huddled masses."* Yeah, baby! Give us your tired and your poor. Without us, you're going to starve! Stay in those cities because we can help you get to your jobs with public transportation. Look at the great job we've done in Detroit.

Firearms

We recognize that the right to bear arms is an important part of the American tradition, and we will preserve Americans' Second Amendment right to own and use firearms. We believe that the right to own firearms is subject to reasonable regulation, but we know that what works in Chicago may not work in Cheyenne. We can work together to enact and enforce common-sense laws and improvements – like closing the gun show loophole, improving our background check system, and reinstating the assault weapons ban, so that guns do not fall into the hands of terrorists or criminals. Acting responsibly and with respect for differing views on this issue, we can both protect the constitutional right to bear arms and keep our communities and our children safe.

Of course, if we clamped down on illegal immigration and didn't keep releasing prisoners from jails for budgetary reasons, maybe we wouldn't have to worry so much about guns *"fall(ing) into the hands of terrorists or criminals."* In the interim, we'll just keep trying to clamp down on registration because we believe that most terrorists and criminals go through appropriate channels to acquire their weapons.

Faith

We honor the central place of faith in our lives. Like our Founders, we believe that our nation, our communities, and our lives are made vastly stronger and richer by faith and the countless acts of justice and mercy it inspires. We believe that change comes not from the top-down, but from the bottom-up, and that few are closer to the people than our churches, synagogues, temples, and mosques. To face today's challenges–from saving our planet to ending poverty— we need all hands on deck. Faith-based groups are not a replacement for government or secular non-profit programs; rather, they are yet another sector working to meet the challenges of the 21st century. We will empower grassroots faith-based and community groups to help meet challenges like poverty, ex-offender reentry, and illiteracy. At the same time, we can ensure that these partnerships do not endanger First Amendment protections – because there is no conflict between supporting faith-based institutions and respecting our Constitution. We will ensure that public funds are not used to proselytize or discriminate. We will also ensure that taxpayer dollars are only used on programs that actually work.

This is a whole new venue for us since we normally are strict *mis*-constructionists of the First Amendment and usually are the one's trying to take God out of the equation. Of course, we don't necessarily *believe* in God, but we *do* believe in tapping into the *"faith-based institutions."* You just never know where you're going to find individuals like the Reverent Jeremiah Wright or noted cleric, Anwar al-Awlaki, who are willing to do whatever is necessary to *"change"* America.

The Arts

Investment in the arts is an investment in our creativity and cultural heritage, in our diversity, in our communities, and in our humanity. We support art in schools and increased public funding for the National Endowment for the Arts and the National Endowment for the Humanities. We support the cultural exchange of artists around the world, spreading democracy and renewing America's status as a cultural and artistic center.

We usually get the art vote, but we're not taking any chances. The funny thing is that we end up spending a lot of taxpayer money on *"art"* that is fairly vulgar by most people's standards and seemingly without any redeeming social value … which is basically the definition of pornography. But rather than let private artisans fund the *"arts"* like most civilized countries do, we'd rather get the government involved. Besides, we have unlimited funds at our disposal.

AMERICANS WITH DISABILITIES

We will once again reclaim our role as world leaders in protecting the rights of people with disabilities. We will lead the United States in ratifying the U.N. Convention on the Rights of Persons with Disabilities, the first human rights treaty approved in the United Nations in the 21st century. We will ensure there is sufficient funding to empower Americans with disabilities to succeed in school and beyond. We will fully fund and increase staffing for the Equal Employment Opportunity Commission. We will restore dignity for Americans with disabilities by signing the Community Choice Act into law, which will allow them the choice of living in their communities rather than being warehoused in nursing homes or other institutions.

It's funny that we, the protectors of *"political correctness,"* chose to use the term *"disability."* You would have thought we would have chosen something like *"physically or intellectually inconvenienced."* In any event, we prefer to typecast these individuals as *"disabled."* It's just easier to characterize them as an *"oppressed minority"* if they are *"disabled"* even though the label may be *lame* (no pun intended).

CHILDREN AND FAMILIES

If we are to renew America, we must do a better job of investing in the next generation of Americans. For parents, the first and most sacred responsibility is to support our children: setting an example of excellence, turning off the TV, and helping with the homework. But we must also support parents as they strive to raise their children in a new era. We must make it easier for working parents to spend time with their families when they need to. We will make an unprecedented national investment to guarantee that every child has access to high-quality early education, including investments in Pre-K, Head Start, and Early Head Start, and we will help pay for child care. We will ensure that every child has health insurance, invest in playgrounds to promote healthy and active lifestyles, and protect children from lead poisoning in their homes and toys. Improving maternal health also improves, so we will provide access to home visits by medical professionals to low-income expectant first-time mothers. We must protect our most vulnerable children, by supporting and supplementing our struggling foster care system, enhancing adoption programs for all caring parents, and protecting children from violence and neglect. Online and on TV, we will give parents tools to block content they find objectionable. We also must recognize that caring for family members and managing a household is real and valuable work.

You've already heard about our *"unprecedented national investment to guarantee that every child has access to high-quality early education, including investments in Pre-K, Head Start, and Early Head Start, and we will help pay for child care,"* but we hadn't mentioned our idea about getting you to turn off the TV. You really shouldn't have any trouble doing that since your children will be searching the web instead. Remember how we said, *"We will ensure every American has access to highspeed broadband and we will take on special interests in order to unleash the power of the wireless spectrum"*...? Well, that's where your children will be stationed ... in front of their computers instead of their TVs.

That's one of the reasons we're going to *"ensure that every child has health insurance"* **because they won't be using the** *"playgrounds to promote healthy and active lifestyles"* **that we'll be building. Similarly, don't bother worrying about** *"lead paint."* **You'll be living in government housing since you won't be able to afford your own home after we've finished destroying the economy.**

We did manage to work in *"maternal health,"* *"children's health,"* *"low-income expectant first-time mothers,"* *"vulnerable children,"* *"struggling foster care,"* *"protecting children from violence and neglect."* **That should show our good intentions!**

Fatherhood

Too many fathers are missing–missing from too many lives and too many homes. Children who grow up without a father are five times more likely to live in poverty and are more likely to commit crime, drop out of school, abuse drugs, and end up in prison. We need more fathers to realize that responsibility does not end at conception. We need them to understand that what makes a man is not the ability to have a child–it's the courage to raise one. We will support fathers by providing transitional training to get jobs, removing tax penalties on married families, and expanding maternity and paternity leave. We will reward those who are responsibly supporting their children by giving them a tax credit and we will crack down on men who avoid child support payments and ensure those payments go directly to families instead of bureaucracies.

Do you notice how it's still *"politically correct"* *to demean men? Don't you just love it?* *"We need more fathers to realize that responsibility does not end at conception. We need them to understand that what makes a man is not the ability to have a child–it's the courage to raise one."* *Wow! If we substituted the word* *"mothers"* *for* *"fathers"* *and* *"woman"* *for* *"man,"* *we'd have every woman's group in America storming our gates. But, we can get away with this when we're talking about* men *...*

because *men* aren't organized. Sure, there are good and bad fathers, just as there are good and bad mothers, but this is the one time we can be get away with having a pronounced sexual bias.

Oh, we joked in the committee meetings about how, in a lot of cases, children who *end up* in prison *finally* get to meet their fathers. And we discussed how more children would have the opportunity to grow up with their fathers at home if men weren't *"profiled"* for crimes as compared to women. But, obviously, we couldn't make any reference to *those* discussions in our Platform. It wouldn't be *"politically correct!"*

SENIORS

We will protect and strengthen Medicare by cutting costs, protecting seniors from fraud, and fixing Medicare's prescription drug program. We will repeal the prohibition on negotiating prescription drug prices, ban drug companies from paying generic producers to refrain from entering drug markets, and eliminate drug company interference with generic competition–and we will dedicate all of the savings from these measures towards closing the donut hole. We will end special preferences for insurance companies and private plans like Medicare Advantage to force them to compete on a level playing field. We will address the challenges that older Americans who are not yet eligible for Medicare face in finding affordable and quality health insurance.

We will take steps to ensure that our seniors have meaningful long-term care options that are consistent with their individual needs, including the option of home care. We believe that we must pay caregivers a fair wage and train more nurses and health care workers so as to improve the availability and quality of long-term care. We must reform the financing of long-term care to ease the burden on seniors and their families. We will safeguard Social Security. We will develop new retirement plans and pension protections that will give Americans a secure, portable way to save for retirement. We will ensure a safe and dignified retirement. We will work to end abuse of the elderly. We will safeguard from discrimination those who choose to work past the age of 65.

 We like old people. In the past, they've been easier to *scare*. That's one of the reasons we *hate* the Tea Party. It's starting to organize seniors and encourage them to make *informed* decisions. That spells *bad news* for the Democratic Party if we can't get the insurrection under control.

Don't get lost in the logic of what we promise. We know that we say we're going to *lower* the cost of health care by *raising* the compensation for physicians so they'll accept Medicare patients. But remember, most of our health care plan doesn't go into effect for years. Between Alzheimer's and *"natural causes,"* we're hoping that no one will remember what we promised when the time comes.

As for *"end(ing) special preferences for insurance companies and private plans like Medicare Advantage,"* we *mean* it ... except for when we need to cut a side deal that exempts 800,000 seniors in Florida in order to *buy* a Senator's vote to pass Health Care Reform. As Machiavelli would say, *"The end justifies the means."*

CHOICE

The Democratic Party strongly and unequivocally supports *Roe v. Wade* and a woman's right to choose a safe and legal abortion, regardless of ability to pay, and we oppose any and all efforts to weaken or undermine that right.

The Democratic Party also strongly supports access to comprehensive affordable family planning services and age-appropriate sex education which empower people to make informed choices and live healthy lives. We also recognize that such health care and education help reduce the number of unintended pregnancies and thereby also reduce the need for abortions.

The Democratic Party also strongly supports a woman's decision to have a child by ensuring access to and availability of programs for pre- and post-natal health care, parenting skills, income support, and caring adoption programs.

 We won't tell you how many delegates at our Platform hearings thought *Roe v. Wade* was a choice about crossing a river (*i.e., "row v. wade"*). It was embarrassing. But once we got everybody *on board* (no pun intended), we banged out a resolution that will allow the government to begin sex education *in vitro*.

We know there's a bit of a cultural downside to *"support(ing) a woman's decision to have a child by ensuring access to ... income support ...."* In the past, Aid to Dependent Children (ADC) actually provided an economic incentive for women on welfare to bear additional children with or without benefit of wedlock. This, of course, exacerbates the issue of absentee fathers that we pontificated against earlier, but we're caught between a rock and a hard place. We love maintaining a welfare state because it creates *all sorts of* perceived dependencies upon our Party. On the other hand, it flies in the face of our reprimand to fathers. Oh well, men aren't organized, so we'll just bury our heads in the sand on this issue.

CRIMINAL JUSTICE

As Democrats, we are committed to being smart on crime. That means being tough on violent crime, funding strategic, and effective community policing, and holding offenders accountable, and it means getting tough on the root causes of crime by investing in successful crime prevention, including proven initiatives that get youth and nonviolent offenders back on track. We will support communities as they work to save their residents from the violence that plagues our streets. We will reverse the policy of cutting resources for the brave men and women who protect our communities every day. At a time when our nation's officers are being asked both to provide traditional law enforcement services and to help protect the homeland, taking police off of the street is neither tough nor smart; we reject this disastrous approach. We support and will restore funding to our courageous police officers and will ensure that they are equipped with the best technology, equipment, and innovative strategies to prevent and fight crimes.

 Yes, we're the *"tough on crime"* Party as long as it requires *"funding strategic, and effective community policing"* or programs *"that get youth and nonviolent offenders back on track."* We're all about *funding.* Give us a *cause,* and we'll find an *expensive solution* to make it part of the fabric from which our country is woven.

We're tough on crime. We think terrorist should be given their Miranda Rights and then appointed counsel to represent them in multi-million dollar trials (it's good TV); we think recidivists should be given *as many chances as necessary* to be rehabilitated ... no matter *how* many victims they leave in their wake; and we believe that *serious* criminals, doing *serious* time, should have the right to file frivolous appeals *as many times as they want* on the taxpayers' dime. You can't *get* much tougher than that!

We will end the dangerous cycle of violence, especially youth violence, with proven community-based law enforcement programs such as the Community Oriented Policing Services. We will reduce recidivism in our neighborhoods by supporting local prison-to-work programs. We will continue to fight inequalities in our criminal justice system. We believe that the death penalty must not be arbitrary. DNA testing should be used in all appropriate circumstances, defendants should have effective assistance of counsel. In all death row cases, and thorough post-conviction reviews should be available.

 We think programs like the Community Oriented Policing Services *"will end the dangerous cycle of violence, especially youth violence."* Once we establish the service, gangs will disband, drugs will dry up, poverty will go away, and crime will be a thing of the past.

We support *"local prison-to-work programs"* to stop recidivism. Notice that we said *"local"* rather than Federal because we don't want those criminals moving into *our* neighborhoods. Beside, it would be too dangerous to have criminals associate with Congressman. If they were already headed down the wrong path, just *imagine* how they'd end up if they were able to refine their craft under *our* tutelage.

And as for DNA testing, we think it *"should be used in all appropriate circumstances"* ... which, by special request, shall *not* include testing any bodily fluids found on a *particular* blue dress.

We must help state, local, and tribal law enforcement work together to combat and prevent drug crime and drug and alcohol abuse, which are a blight on our communities. We will restore funding for the Byrne Justice Assistance Grant Program and expand the use of drug courts and rehabilitation programs for first-time, non-violent drug offenders.

 Since this issue impacts a lot of our voter base, we'd like to go easy in the enforcement area of drug and alcohol abuse.

We support the rights of victims to be respected, to be heard, and to be compensated.

 There, we said it! That *certainly* differentiates us from any other Party.

Ending violence against women must be a top priority. We will create a special advisor to the president regarding violence against women. We will increase funding to domestic violence and sexual assault prevention programs. We will strengthen sexual assault and domestic violence laws, support the Violence Against Women Act, and provide job security to survivors. Our foreign policy will be sensitive to issues of aggression against women around the world.

 Our society does look upon *"domestic violence and sexual assault"* as particularly vile crimes. It also let's us raise the specter of an *"oppressed minority"* one last time. Sure, you could argue that a civil society should be against *any* type of unjustified violence no matter *who* the victim is; but remember, men aren't organized. Although now that you mention it, we should have put something in our Platform about *"hate crimes."* It would have been a perfect opportunity to work in more *"oppressed minorities."* This is one time that we really *blew it!* At least we're not as inept as the Republicans. They don't know how to generate *any* sympathy among *"oppressed minorities!"*

A More Perfect Union

We believe in the essential American ideal that we are not constrained by the circumstances of birth but can make of our lives what we will. Unfortunately, for too many, that ideal is not a reality. We have more work to do. Democrats will fight to end discrimination based on race, sex, ethnicity, national origin, language, religion, sexual orientation, gender identity, age, and disability in every corner of our country, because that's the America we believe in.

 *"Race, sex, ethnicity, national origin, language, religion, sexual orientation, gender identity, age, and disability;"* there you have it ... the very essence of our *"oppressed minorities"* strategy. We believe we can fit every single person on Earth into one or more of those categories. So if you *"buy what we're selling,"* you're going to vote Democrat!

We all have to do our part to lift up this country, and that means changing hearts and changing minds, and making sure that every American is treated equally under the law. We will restore professionalism over partisanship at the Department of Justice, and staff the civil rights division with civil rights lawyers, not ideologues. We will restore vigorous federal enforcement of civil rights laws in order to provide every American an equal chance at employment, housing, health, contracts, and pay. We are committed to banning racial, ethnic, and religious profiling and requiring federal, state, and local enforcement agencies to take steps to eliminate the practice.

 When we say, *"We will restore professionalism over partisanship at the Department of Justice, and staff the civil rights division with civil rights lawyers, not ideologues,"* we mean that we'll staff these positions with professionals and civil rights lawyers who will follow *our* partisan ideologies like little automatons. You can expect the Department of Justice to prosecute even weak cases that threaten any of our *"oppressed minorities"* while it will avoid prosecuting strong cases that include any of our *"oppressed minorities."* For example, the Department of Justice might prosecute a State for trying to *enforce* Federal Immigration Laws, but it *won't* prosecute *"Sanctuary Cities"* that declare that they *won't* enforce Federal Immigration Laws. Get it?

We also bring up our commitment to ban *"racial, ethnic, and religious profiling"* because it's *"politically correct"* and will garner votes among our base. The reality is that we know that it's illogical to investigate Catholic priests for spousal abuse, but we must give the impression that we have such a high level of integrity that our justice is truly *"blind."* Of course, to rational people, our justice may appear to be *"ignorant"* as well, but our heart is in the right place.

We are committed to ensuring full equality for women: we reaffirm our support for the Equal Rights Amendment, recommit to enforcing Title IX, and will urge passage of the Convention on the Elimination of All Forms of Discrimination Against Women. We will pursue a unified foreign and domestic policy that promotes civil rights and human rights, for women and minorities, at home and abroad. We will pass the Local Law Enforcement Hate Crimes Prevention Act. We will restore and support the White House Initiative on Asian-American and Pacific Islanders, including enforcement on disaggregation of Census data. We will make the Census more culturally sensitive, including outreach, language assistance, and increased confidentiality protections to ensure accurate counting of the growing Latino and Asian American, and Pacific Islander populations, and continue working on efforts to be more inclusive. We will sign the U.N. Convention on the Rights of Persons with Disabilities and restore the original intent of the Americans with Disabilities Act. That is the America we believe in.

Notice how we're trotting out short paragraphs that reaffirm our previously stated positions on our highest profile *"oppressed minorities."* In this one, we reassert our belief in *"equality for women"* and *finally* include *"hate crimes"* (which we missed earlier in our Platform). We even work in *"Asian-American and Pacific Islanders"* to go along with our oft-mentioned Latino population.

We do struggle with whether to go with *"Latino"* versus *"Hispanic."* *"Hispanic"* sounds more sophisticated, but *"Latino"* gives us a grass roots, *La Raza* flair. We're equally perplexed about choosing between *"Black"* versus *"African American"* for much the same reasons; and with respect to our President, we're somewhat in a gray area (no pun intended). We still think *"disabled"* may be our weakest link from a *"politically correct"* basis, but we had already rejected *"handicapped"* and didn't have a suitable replacement. Besides, we already have legislation called the *Americans with Disabilities Act,* and we don't want to have to rename it. Bottom line: we try to be as *"culturally sensitive"* as our Census; and we want the Census to be as *"culturally sensitive"* as possible because we use it to identify demographic shifts in our *"oppressed minorities"* that we can leverage for our *own* political gain.

It is not enough to look back in wonder at how far we have come; those who came before us did not strike a blow against injustice only so that we would allow injustice to fester in our time. That means removing the barriers of prejudice and misunderstanding that still exist in America. We support the full inclusion of all families, including same-sex couples, in the life of our nation, and support equal responsibility, benefits, and protections. We will enact a comprehensive bipartisan employment non-discrimination act. We oppose the Defense of Marriage Act and all attempts to use this issue to divide us.

We had to work in something for the gay community since they vote for us in such high percentages. So, we went with the *"same sex marriage"* issue because our polls show that it's a high priority for them. While we're big on protecting children's rights and caring for their best interests, we will do so only until such time that it infringes on our ability to attract votes from one of our key *"oppressed minorities,"* as it does here. Besides, children can't vote, and we'll have plenty of years to mold their thoughts before they're eligible to register.

But it is no good to be able to ride the bus when you can't afford the bus fare. We will work to provide real opportunities for all Americans suffering from disadvantage; we will pioneer new policies and remedies against poverty and violence that address real human needs and we will close the achievement gap in education and provide every child a world-class education. We support affirmative action, including in federal contracting and higher education, to make sure that those locked out of the doors of opportunity will be able to walk through those doors in the future. As the late Ann Richards said, "We offer a vision where opportunity knows no race, no gender, no color, a glimpse of what can happen in government if we simply open the doors let the people in."

Before we closed out this section, we wanted to work race, poverty, gender and violence in one more time. Forgive us for our repetitiveness. As for *"affirmative action,"* we've chosen to ignore the inherent discrimination it creates, and the biases it reinforces because ... well ... it still sounds *so* Democratic!

IV. RENEWING AMERICAN DEMOCRACY

Americans of every political stripe are hungry for a new kind of government. We want a government that favors common sense over ideology, honesty over spin, that worries less about losing the next election and more about winning the battles we owe to the next generation.

 Unfortunately, that's not what *we* care to offer ... and *we're* in charge. So until then, you're stuck with business as usual: where we promise *everything* to *everybody* and spend *other people's money* with impunity.

The over 30,000 Americans who attended 1645 local platform hearings demonstrated their commitment to reasserting government of, by, and for the people. So too did the millions of Americans who turned out in primaries and caucuses, and the record-breaking number of Americans abroad who participated – including men and the women who serve in our military. Democrats want to continue the momentum of the election. Only by doing so can we bring the change necessary to restore the promise of America.

 If you do the math, that means we attracted about 19 people to each local Platform hearing ... 19 people to decide what *you* need. When you have that small of a turnout, you can expect to attract only those who would be best defined as *"activists,"* and these local Platform hearings *"didn't disappoint."* But hey! If you didn't care enough to get involved, then this is what you get.

By the way, while a record number of people turned out, the winners never really garnered an actual *majority* of the whole population. And as far as military personnel ... they *tried* to vote, but since they generally have to vote by mail, their ballots don't always make it to the polls in time ... no matter how early they seem to mail them. As a matter of fact, about 70 percent of overseas military ballots weren't recorded in 2006, and we just didn't have *time* to correct the problem before the 2008 Presidential election. But don't worry! They tend to vote Republican anyway.

The government we create will open up democracy to the people and protect our civil liberties. We'll invite the service and participation of American citizens, and use the tools of government and technology to lead us into a new era of connectedness, teamwork, and progress. A Barack Obama Administration will make it clear to the special interests that their days of setting the agenda in Washington are over, because the American people are not the problem in the 21st century—they are the solution. We'll make every vote count, because in America, everyone's voice matters in the political process.

 This is our warning to you. We intend to *"create"* a new government. Don't say we didn't *tell* you! We're ushering in a *"new era of correctness"* driven by a strict adherence to the ideologies *we* support.

As for *"mak(ing) every vote count"* and *"everyone's voice matter"* ... well ... actions speak louder than words. We've already locked out the Republicans in Congress and dismissed them as *"the Party of No"* just because they disagree with us, and we've attacked the Tea Party movement as a façade orchestrated by the Republicans that should *not* have *any* voice in America. That's what we call *"open(ing) up democracy."*

OPEN, ACCOUNTABLE, AND ETHICAL GOVERNMENT

In Barack Obama's Administration, we will open up the doors of democracy. We will use technology to make government more transparent, accountable, and inclusive. Rather than obstruct people's use of the Freedom of Information Act, we will require that agencies conduct significant business in public and release all relevant information unless an agency reasonably foresees harm to a protected interest.

Of course, this transparency is not extended to birth certificates, college transcripts, etc. And as far as inclusion goes, it's limited to members of *"oppressed minorities"* who remain faithful to the Democratic Party ... and to politicians who either remain faithful or whose votes can be *bought* with pork barrel amendments or offers of political enrichment. Now, *that's* what *we* mean when we use the term *"buy partisan"* support ... regardless of how *you* may spell it.

We will lift the veil of secret deals in Washington by publishing searchable, online information about federal grants, contracts, earmarks, loans, and lobbyist contacts with government officials. We will make government data available online and will have an online video archive of significant agency meetings. We will put all non-emergency bills that Congress has passed online for five days, to allow the American public to review and comment on them before they are signed into law. We will require Cabinet officials to have periodic national online town hall meetings to discuss issues before their agencies.

We will only conceal our backroom deals and make exceptions to our ban on hiring lobbyists with respect to those *we* choose to put in White House staff positions.
When we say, *"We will make government data available online and will have an online video archive of significant agency meetings,"* we mean it. We'll even include top secret

information about our nuclear arsenal, deep-cover intelligence efforts, etc. in the name of *"transparency."*

And when it comes to *"put(ting) all non-emergency bills online for five days, to allow the American public to review and comment on them before they are signed into law,"* we mean that too. First, because the bills will be so voluminous, *no one will have the ability to read and digest them within that time frame.* And secondly, because we didn't promise to pay any *attention* to any comments that do not support what Congress has already passed.

Implementing our Party's agenda will require running competent, innovative, and efficient public agencies at all levels of government with the resources necessary to get results. We will develop a comprehensive management agenda to prevent operational breakdowns in government and ensure that government provides the level of service that the American people deserve. Because we understand that good government depends on good people, we will work to rebuild and reengage our federal workforce and encourage state and local governments to do the same. We will make government a more attractive place to work. Our hiring will be based only on qualification and experience, and not on ideology or party affiliation. We will pay for our new spending, eliminate waste in government programs, demand, and measure results, and stop funding programs that don't work. We will not privatize public services for the sake of privatizing. We will use carefully crafted guidelines when determining whether to contract out any government service and whether a function is "inherently governmental." We will provide improved accountability, oversight, and management in the contracting process to protect the public.

By definition, *"competent, innovative, and efficient public agencies"* is an oxymoron, but when we pledge to *"make government a more attractive place to work,"* we absolutely mean it. That's why government jobs now offer 46% higher pay than equivalent private sector jobs and have superior benefits as well. And you can take the *"attractive place to work"* literally in the case of Speaker Pelosi's new, *Taj Mahal* of an office that rents for a cool $19,000 a month.

Now, please don't pay any attention to the language that states that *"we will use carefully crafted guidelines when determining whether to contract out any government service and whether a function is "inherently governmental."* We think *everything* should ultimately be defined as *"inherently governmental."* We'd do it today if anyone other than the President and Members of Congress could become wealthy enough to be deemed to be rich. Remember, we *need* the rich ... or there won't be anyone to tax!

We are committed to a participatory government. We will use the most current technology available to improve the quality of government decision-making and make government less beholden to special interest groups and lobbyists. We will enhance the flow of information between citizens and government—in both directions—by involving the public in the work of government agencies. We will not simply solicit opinions, but will also use new technology to tap into the vast expertise of the American citizenry, for the benefit of government and our democracy.

 Stop laughing! Other than the part about *"mak(ing) government less beholden to special interest groups and lobbyists,"* we *meant* what we said. Technology has given us new tools to *manipulate* the masses.

Americans want real reform that will help them pay their medical bills and put the country on the path to energy independence. They are tired of lobbyists standing in their way. So we'll end the abuse of no-bid contracts by requiring nearly all contract orders over $25,000 to be competitively awarded and tell the drug companies and the oil companies and the insurance industry that, while they may get a seat at the table in Washington, they don't get to buy every chair. We will institute a gift ban so that no lobbyist can curry favor with the Administration. We will close the revolving door that has allowed people to use their position in the Administration as a stepping-stone to further their lobbying careers. We support campaign finance reform to reduce the influence of moneyed special interests, including public financing of campaigns combined with free television and radio time. We will have the wisdom to put the public interest above special interests. As a national party, we will not take any contributions from Political Action Committees during this election.

 **Remember: we're being led by an Administration that learned its politics in Chicago. So, when we say we're going to *"clean up"* politics, you can count on it.**

RECLAIMING OUR CONSTITUTION AND OUR LIBERTIES

As we combat terrorism, we must not sacrifice the American values we are fighting to protect. In recent years, we've seen an Administration put forward a false choice between the liberties we cherish and the security we demand. The Democratic Party rejects this dichotomy. We will restore our constitutional traditions, and recover our nation's founding commitment to liberty under law.

 **Shoot, we'll go well beyond *"restor(ing) our constitutional traditions, and recover(ing) our nation's founding commitment to liberty under law."* We'll create entirely new liberties that our Founders never even *considered* and extend them *well beyond* just the actual *citizens* of the United States.**

We support constitutional protections and judicial oversight on any surveillance program involving Americans. We will review the current Administration's warrantless wiretapping program. We reject illegal wiretapping of American citizens, wherever they live.

We reject the use of national security letters to spy on citizens who are not suspected of a crime. We reject the tracking of citizens who do nothing more than protest a misguided war. We reject torture. We reject sweeping claims of "inherent" presidential power. We will revisit the Patriot Act and overturn unconstitutional executive decisions issued during the past eight years. We will not use signing statements to nullify or undermine duly enacted law. And we will ensure that law-abiding Americans of any origin, including Arab-Americans and Muslim-Americans, do not become the scapegoats of national security fears.

We'll get rid of *all* of the nasty, old security measures that were approved by the Bush Administration after 9/11. We will *also* rely on blind luck and continue to hope that for every successful attack (like Ft. Hood) there will be at least two failed attempts (like the Christmas Day Underwear Bomber and the Times Square Bomber). We believe that it is far better to lose a few thousand citizens because of a successful terrorist attack than to aggressively try to protect their lives by potentially invading the privacy of those who are suspected of terrorism. Remember, we want the rest of the world to like us!

We believe that our Constitution, our courts, our institutions, and our traditions work.

We have to say this even though our President is on record as saying that the U.S. has suffered from a *"fundamentally flawed Constitution"* that does not mandate or allow for the redistribution of wealth.

In its operations overseas, while claiming to spread freedom throughout the world, the current Administration has tragically helped give rise to a new generation of potential adversaries who threaten to make America less secure. We will provide our intelligence and law enforcement agencies with the tools to hunt down and take out terrorists without undermining our Constitution, our freedom, and our privacy.

We like to talk tough because it makes us feel *"in charge,"* but the reality is that we didn't pursue

Osama Bin Laden during the Clinton Administration when we had a much better idea of his whereabouts. In all fairness, we were distracted at the time by having to defend certain acts that occurred in the Oval Office that the Republicans portrayed as *"morally incorrect."*

To build a freer and safer world, we will lead in ways that reflect the decency and aspirations of the American people. We will not ship away prisoners in the dead of night to be tortured in far-off countries, or detain without trial or charge prisoners who can and should be brought to justice for their crimes, or maintain a network of secret prisons to jail people beyond the reach of the law. We will respect the time-honored principle of habeas corpus, the seven century-old right of individuals to challenge the terms of their own detention that was recently reaffirmed by our Supreme Court. We will close the detention camp in Guantanamo Bay, the location of so many of the worst constitutional abuses in recent years. With these necessary changes, the attention of the world will be directed where it belongs: on what terrorists have done to us, not on how we treat suspects.

We basically will afford every protection that we provide to our citizens to those individuals who would come from other countries to kill innocent men, women and children in horrific acts of terrorism; the same people who video tape severing the heads of captured Americans while they are still alive and then broadcast the videos to *"send a message to the world."* We believe these individuals are just misguided and lack solid family relationships, free health care, free educational opportunities, etc. We humbly apologize for our transgressions against them and welcome them into our country (psssst ... try the Mexican border ... we don't adequately protect it).

We recognize what leaders on the front lines of the struggle against terrorism have long known: to win this fight, we must maintain the moral high ground. When millions around the world see America living up to its highest ideals, we win friends and allies in this struggle for our safety and our lives, and our enemies lose ground.

 **We believe that if we apologize enough and *"maintain the moral high ground,"* the terrorists will come to respect us and put down their weapons to join us in our quest for world peace. Remember:** *"The Democratic Party believes that there is no more important priority than renewing American leadership on the world stage."*

For our Judiciary, we will select and confirm judges who are men and women of unquestionable talent and character, who firmly respect the rule of law, who listen to and are respectful of different points of view, and who represent the diversity of America. We support the appointment of judges who respect our system of checks and balances and the separation of power among the Executive Branch, Congress, and the Judiciary–and who understand that the Constitution protects not only the powerful, but also the disadvantaged and the powerless.

 **We will appoint people without *any* judicial experience to the highest court in the land to bring a *"fresh perspective"* to it. We will ignore far more qualified justices in order to place individuals from *"oppressed minorities"* on the Supreme Court as well as in other federal positions ... basically confirming why Affirmative Action is a blatant form of discrimination.**

Our Constitution is not a nuisance. It is the foundation of our democracy. It makes freedom and self-governance possible, and helps to protect our security. The Democratic Party will restore our Constitution to its proper place in our government and return our Nation to our best traditions–including our commitment to government by law.

 **And someday, at least one of us is actually going to read it!**

VOTING RIGHTS

Voting rights are fundamental rights because they are protective of all other rights. We will work to fully protect and enforce the fundamental Constitutional right of every American vote—to ensure that the Constitution's promise is fully realized. We will fully fund the Help America Vote Act and work to fulfill the promise of election reform, including fighting to end long lines at voting booths and ensuring that all registration materials, voting materials, polling places, and voting machines are truly accessible to seniors, Americans with disabilities, and citizens with limited English proficiency. We will call for a national standard for voting that includes voter-verified paper ballots. We will ensure that absentee ballots are accessible and accurately counted. We will vigorously enforce our voting rights laws instead of making them tools of partisan political agendas; we oppose laws that require identification in order to vote or register to vote, which create discriminatory barriers to the right to vote and disenfranchise many eligible voters; and we oppose tactics which purge eligible voters from voter rolls. We are committed to passing the Count Every Vote Act. Finally, we will enact legislation that establishes harsh penalties for those who engage in voter intimidation and creates a process for providing accurate information to misinformed voters so they can cast their votes in time.

Because of our *"oppressed minorities"* and *"Robin Hood"* strategies, the numbers are in our favor. The more *uninformed* people we register ... the more *votes* for the Democratic Party. We aren't even particular with respect to whether you're dead or alive, a legal registrant or an illegal one, a convicted felon or a totally fictitious person ... as long as you vote Democrat. We definitely favor the *Count Every Vote Act* ... except maybe for military personnel.

And when it comes to our intent to *"enact legislation that establishes harsh penalties for those who engage in voter intimidation and creates a process for providing accurate information to misinformed voters so they can cast their votes in time,"* we're serious! Of course, if it's an *"oppressed minority"* that's

intimidating non-minority voters with a night stick at a polling place, we won't prosecute the offense with full vigor. And if voters happen to be military personnel stationed overseas (who generally vote Republican), we won't bend over backwards to get *their* votes counted because ... well, they aren't really *"misinformed."* They cast their ballots promptly. We've just set up the system to be a little bit *"inefficient"* when it comes to receiving their votes in time to count them.

PARTNERSHIPS WITH STATES

Given the economic crisis across the country, states, and territories today face serious difficulties. More than half of our states face a combined billions of dollars in shortfalls. As a result, states have had to innovate and take matters into their own hands—and they have done an extraordinary job. Yet they should not have to do it alone. We will provide significant and immediate temporary funding to state and local governments, as well as territories and tribes. We will give these governmental entities a partner in the federal government, and a president who understand that prosperity comes not only from Wall Street and Washington, but from the perseverance of the American people. County and municipal governments, as well as territories and tribes, are also key partners with the federal government. These partnerships need to be revitalized to address their critical needs.

 You don't even have to combine States to get to a billion dollar deficit. Most of the States can get there on their own.

We applaud States that take matters into their own hands ... except for Arizona. We're going to fix everything by *"provid(ing) significant and immediate temporary funding to state and local governments, as well as territories and tribes."* And we understand that *"prosperity comes not only from Wall Street and Washington, but from the perseverance of the American people."* Given where we are today, we think most of you need to *"persevere"* finding a job since so many of you are unemployed.

PARTNERSHIP WITH CIVIC INSTITUTIONS

Social entrepreneurs and leading nonprofit organizations are assisting schools, lifting families out of poverty, filling health care gaps, and inspiring others to lead change in their own communities. To support these results-oriented innovators, we will create a Social Investment Fund Network that invests in ideas that work, tests their impact, and expands the most successful programs.

We will create an office to coordinate government and nonprofit efforts.

Normally, you'd expect *"social entrepreneurs and leading nonprofit organizations"* **to provide funding, but not in our world ... the world of the Democrats; not when we can create yet another Social Investment Fund Network. No initiative will go unfunded under a Democratic Administration. We** *firmly believe* **that asking people to accomplish something on their** *own* **is un-American!**

DISTRICT OF COLUMBIA

Our civil rights leaders and many Americans of every background have sacrificed too much for us to tolerate continuing denial to the nearly 600,000 residents of our nation's capital of the benefits of full citizenship, especially the vote, that are accorded to citizens of every state. We support equal rights to democratic self-government and congressional representation for the citizens of our nation's capital.

Plus, these people overwhelmingly vote Democrat because Washington, D.C. ... beyond the glitz of our Federal structure ... is predominantly a welfare district.

TRIBAL SOVEREIGNTY

American Indian and Alaska Native tribes have always been sovereign, self-governing communities, and we affirm their inherent right to self-government as well as the unique government-to-government relationship they share with the United States. In exchange for millions of acres of land, our nation pledged to provide certain services in perpetuity; we will honor our nation's treaty and trust obligations by increasing resources for economic development, health care, Indian education, and other important services. We will respect American Indian cultural rights and sacred places. We will reexamine the legal framework that allows extreme rates of violent crime in Indian country; we will create a White House advisor on Indian Affairs; and we will host an annual summit with Indian leaders.

Yes, we'll provide another *"advisor"* and *"host an annual summit."* The American Indians and Alaskan Native tribes will undoubtedly be happy with that decision. Maybe we can create a few new agencies as well. In the meantime, we'll just continue to give them beads and seal meat to placate them. And, of course, we'll party at their casinos ... as long as what *happens* in their casinos *stays* in their casinos.

We support the efforts for self-determination and sovereignty of Native Hawaiians, consistent with principles enumerated in the Apology Resolution and the Native Hawaiian Government Reorganization Act. We will increase federal resources for economic development, education, health, and other important services. We will respect Native Hawaiian culture rights and sacred places.

We're on a roll here with inserting last minute *"oppressed minorities."* First, it was *American Indians* and *Alaskan Native* tribes. Now, we throw in *Native Hawaiians*. You may argue, *"Aren't these people just Americans?"* Of course they are. Hello! Anybody home? If we treated all of our citizens the same, we wouldn't be able to split Americans into the *"oppressed minorities"* we need to win.

Puerto Rico, Guam, American Samoa, the Northern Mariana Islands, and the U.S. Virgin Islands

We recognize and honor the contributions and the sacrifices made in service of our country by the people living in Puerto Rico, Guam, American Samoa, the Northern Mariana Islands, and the U.S. Virgin Islands. We believe that the people of Puerto Rico have the right to the political status of their choice, obtained through a fair, neutral, and democratic process of self-determination. The White House and Congress will work with all groups in Puerto Rico to enable the question of Puerto Rico's status to be resolved during the next four years. We also believe that economic conditions in Puerto Rico call for effective and equitable programs to maximize job creation and financial investment. Furthermore, in order to provide fair assistance to those in greatest need, the U.S. citizens in Puerto Rico should receive treatment under federal programs that is comparable to that of citizens in the States. We will phase-out the cap on Medicaid funding and phase-in equal participation in other federal health care assistance programs. Moreover, we will provide equitable treatment to the U.S. citizens in Puerto Rico on programs providing refundable tax credits to working families. We believe that U.S. citizens in Guam, American Samoa, the Northern Mariana Islands, and the U.S. Virgin Islands should receive similar treatment.

We support full self-government and self-determination for the people of Guam, American Samoa, the Northern Mariana Islands, and the Virgin Islands, and their right to decide their future status. We will seek input from Guam on relevant military matters and we acknowledge the unique health care challenges that Pacific Island communities face. For all those who live under our flag, we support strong economic development and fair and equitable treatment under federal programs.

 **And just when you thought we were done, we try to drive the opportunity for statehood for yet more potentially *"oppressed minorities"* (i.e., likely Democrats).** *Puerto Rico, Guam, American*

Samoa, the Northern Mariana Islands, and the U.S. Virgin Islands ... let's make them all States. While there aren't many rich people in any of these countries to tax on a per capita basis, they all offer built in *"oppressed minorities"* we can exploit ... uh ... we mean, *serve!*

Another plus is that this move would create new jobs; particularly if we stretch it over a period of years. People will need new flags. The government will need new flags. As long as we approve statehood for each country with a year or two in between, we'll keep the flag industry in business for years. It is unionized, isn't it? That alone justifies the idea for us ... that and the fact that most of the inhabitants will probably vote Democrat.

Our biggest challenge will be coming up with *"politically correct"* names for each group so that we can make them feel *separate* from the rest of America. But by now, you must be confident in our ability to provide *that* type of leadership.

So there you have it: The Democratic National Platform for 2008. Good for another four years or until the impeachment of a President, whichever comes first.

We've entitled it *Renewing America's Promise*. The first Tuesday in November of every even year, you get to cast your vote for whether you agree with our title or think, in the interest of truth in advertising, we should rename it *Reviling America With Promises.*

 You would think that since euthanasia and assisted suicides are *illegal*, that would be enough. But we feel compelled to go on record against them. Perhaps this is just another sad indictment of today's society.

You've got to admit that it is interesting that we're against Affirmative Action (at least as we have indirectly addressed it), yet we support the AbilityOne program that provides jobs to the disabled. Correspondingly, AbilityOne is an example of the Federal government operating at its *finest* to protect a segment of our society that *needs* it. Sometimes, the issue isn't black and white. Oops we didn't mean to say *"black and white."* Please don't take it out of context. We wouldn't want to be perceived to be *"politically incorrect."*

PRESERVING TRADITIONAL MARRIAGE

Because our children's future is best preserved within the traditional understanding of marriage, we call for a constitutional amendment that fully protects marriage as a union of a man and a woman, so that judges cannot make other arrangements equivalent to it. In the absence of a national amendment, we support the right of the people of the various states to affirm traditional marriage through state initiatives.

 In all honesty, we really don't care who marries whom, but it would decimate our base of right-wing, conservatives, and their campaign contributions would dry up if we were neutral on this issue.

We'd actually rather make the argument that *conception*, in or out of wedlock, should only occur between a man and a woman. We think we could actually *win* on *that* issue. Oh sure, we might lose the support of a few surrogates and a test-tube or two along the way, but on the whole, we think our position would carry the day.

Republicans recognize the importance of having in the home a father and a mother who are married. The two-parent family still provides the best environment of stability, discipline, responsibility, and character. Children in homes without fathers are more likely to commit a crime, drop out of school, become violent, become teen parents, use illegal drugs, become mired in poverty, or have emotional or behavioral problems. We support the courageous efforts of single-parent families to provide a stable home for their children. Children are our nation's most precious resource. We also salute and support the efforts of foster and adoptive families.

Other than stating the obvious ... that children are better off with *both* parents (unless one of the parents is a reprobate of some kind) ... we really haven't proffered any type of solution in this section. It's really just an attempt to garner *"touchy-feely"* points with the electorate. Along that line, we also don't like *abusive* or *offensive* individuals ... but we *do* like puppies, kittens and bunnies.

Republicans have been at the forefront of protecting traditional marriage laws, both in the states and in Congress. A Republican Congress enacted the Defense of Marriage Act, affirming the right of states not to recognize same-sex "marriages" licensed in other states. Unbelievably, the Democratic Party has now pledged to repeal the Defense of Marriage Act, which would subject every state to the redefinition of marriage by a judge without ever allowing the people to vote on the matter. We also urge Congress to use its Article III, Section 2 power to prevent activist federal judges from imposing upon the rest of the nation the judicial activism in Massachusetts and California. We also encourage states to review their marriage and divorce laws in order to strengthen marriage.

We not only support the Defense of Marriage Act that affirms *"the right of states not to recognize same-sex 'marriages' licensed in other states,"* we would take it one step further. We would support a *Bad Sex* Marriage Act, which would affirm the right of States

not to recognize *"bad sex"* marriages licensed in other States. Most of us have been there, and we think that the *Bad Sex Marriage Act* would stimulate interstate travel and eliminate the cost and emotional pain associated with our present, disjointed system of divorce and dissolution. *"Bad sex"* marriages would simply dissolve when one or more of the parties crossed a State line and declared their relationship to have been fraught with *"bad sex."* Unlike Congressmen, who have Interns, Pages, and Staffers, who benightedly idolize them, most of these poor souls don't have *alternatives* when it comes to gaining a temporary respite from their *"bad sex"* marriages.

As the family is our basic unit of society, we oppose initiatives to erode parental rights.

 **To be more definitive, we would support a No Erosion of Parental Rights Act. We hope that is specific enough for you.**

SAFEGUARDING RELIGIOUS LIBERTIES

Our Constitution guarantees the free exercise of religion and forbids any religious test for public office, and it likewise prohibits the establishment of a state-sponsored creed. The balance between those two ideals has been distorted by judicial rulings which attempt to drive faith out of the public arena. The public display of the Ten Commandments does not violate the U.S. Constitution and accurately reflects the Judeo-Christian heritage of our country. We support the right of students to engage in student-initiated, student-led prayer in public schools, athletic events, and graduation ceremonies, when done in conformity with constitutional standards.

 **We'll go even further. We're not only against *"any religious test for public office,"* we're against *any* type of test at *all*. God only knows, most of us couldn't pass any kind of test.**

And we know it's difficult to *"balance (the) two ideals"* of a *"free exercise of religion"* versus the prohibition of the *"establishment of a state-sponsored creed."* But as we begin *each* of our Congressional sessions with a prayer, as we have since 1789, we will pray for *Devine guidance* to help us sort this thing out.

We affirm every citizen's right to apply religious values to public policy and the right of faith-based organizations to participate fully in public programs without renouncing their beliefs, removing religious objects or symbols, or becoming subject to government-imposed hiring practices. Forcing religious groups to abandon their beliefs as applied to their hiring practices is religious discrimination. We support the First Amendment right of freedom of association of the Boy Scouts of America and other service organizations whose values are under assault, and we call upon the Commonwealth of Massachusetts to reverse its policy of blacklisting religious groups which decline to arrange adoptions by same-sex couples. Respectful of our nation's diversity in faith, we urge reasonable accommodation of religious beliefs in the private workplace. We deplore the increasing incidence of attacks against religious symbols, as well as incidents of anti-Semitism on college campuses.

 **Even when we try to be more like the Democrats by incorporating a variety of *"minorities"* (whether *"oppressed"* or not), we tend to fall short of the mark because we're too subtle.**

While courting the homophobic segment of our society, we do it in the most subtle of ways. If these people are as dumb as we fear, they may not get the point that we are supporting their narrowly sacrosanct views.

While courting those of religious persuasions who have felt *"oppressed"* due to *"anti-Semitism,"* we just don't hammer the point home the way our Democratic adversaries would. Oh sure, we may pick up a few Jewish votes the way we do it, but the Democrats would have broadened the issue to one of *"religious persecution"* and named every religion known to mankind, lumping them in a single group as an *"oppressed*

minority" and claiming to be the *only* Party that's concerned about their ill-fated plight. *They* know how to manufacture votes!

PRESERVING AMERICANS' PROPERTY RIGHTS

At the center of a free economy is the right of citizens to be secure in their property. Every person has the right to acquire, own, use, possess, enjoy, and dispose of private property. That right was undermined by the Supreme Court's Kelo decision, allowing local governments to seize a person's home or land, not for vital public use, but for transfer to private developers. That 5-to-4 decision highlights what is at stake in the election of the next president, who may make new appointments to the Court. We call on state legislatures to moot the Kelo decision by appropriate legislation, and we pledge on the federal level to pass legislation to protect against unjust federal takings.

We will enforce the Takings Clause of the Fifth Amendment to ensure just compensation whenever private property is needed to achieve a compelling public use. We urge caution in the designation of National Historic Areas, which can set the stage for widespread governmental control of citizens' lands.

In Kelo v. City of New London, 545 U.S. 469 (2005), the Supreme Court extended the right of eminent domain to take a private residence for the purpose of private development as long as the private development has a *"legitimate ... public purpose"* rather than the traditional limitation of requiring the taking to be for a clear *"public use."* While we like to bring this up, the reality is that the States will probably resolve this issue by enacting their own new legislation. Oh, and by the way, the upscale housing project that was supposed to generate new tax income the Kelo case (and only cost $78 million in taxpayer funds to secure) *never* came to fruition. In that regard, it ended up just like many of our *Federal* projects.

Supporting Native American Communities

The federal government has a special responsibility to the people in Indian country and a unique trust relationship with them, which has been insufficiently honored. The social and economic problems that plague Indian country have grown worse over the last several decades, and we must reverse that trend. Ineffective government programs deprive Indians of the services they need, and long-term failures threaten to undermine tribal sovereignty itself.

Okay. This is our last ditch attempt to match the Democrats for *irrelevant* tributes that do *nothing* to really improve the plights of *high-profile* minorities.

Republicans believe that economic self-sufficiency is the ultimate answer to the challenges in Indian country and that tribal communities, not Washington bureaucracies, are better situated to craft local solutions. Federal – and state – regulations that thwart job creation must be reconsidered so that tribal governments acting on Native Americans' behalf are not disadvantaged. The Democratic Party's repeated undermining of tribal sovereignty to advantage union bosses is especially egregious.

"Republicans believe that economic self-sufficiency is the ultimate answer to the challenges in Indian country." In other words, we'll keep Manhattan Island ... and you can keep the $24 in beads and trinkets we paid for it.

We also have to be really careful here when we say *"Federal – and state – regulations that thwart job creation must be reconsidered so that tribal governments acting on Native Americans' behalf are not disadvantaged"* since it's treading on Affirmative Action, which we superficially don't support. However, we end on a bright note by taking a shot at *"the Democratic Party's repeated undermining of tribal sovereignty to advantage union bosses is especially egregious."* While we really haven't put forth any solutions, we can *at least* be satisfied with positioning the issue in a way that lets us hammer away at the Democrats and their puppet unions.

Republicans reject a one-size-fits-all approach to federal-state-tribal partnerships and will work to expand local autonomy where tribal governments seek it. Better partnerships will help us to expand opportunity, deliver top-flight education to future generations, modernize and improve the Indian Health Service to make it more responsive to local needs, and build essential infrastructure. Native Americans must be empowered to develop the rich natural resources on their lands without undue federal interference.

When we speak of *"better partnerships (that) will help us to expand opportunity, deliver top-flight education to future generations, modernize and improve the Indian Health Service to make it more responsive to local needs, and build essential infrastructure,"* we mean that we expect the *Indians* to come up with the solutions and the *government* to *supervise* the process and *take credit* for any success it may enjoy.

Crime in Indian country, especially against women, is a special problem demanding immediate attention. Inadequate resources and neglect have made Native Americans less safe and allowed safe havens to develop in Indian country for criminal narcotics enterprises. The government must increase funding for tribal officers and investigators, FBI agents, prosecutors, and tribal jails. The legal system must provide stability and protect property rights. Everyone's civil rights must be safeguarded, including the right to due process and freedom of the press, with accountability for all government officials.

Let's face it: with our non-enforcement of immigration laws, the entire United States has become a *"safe haven ... to develop criminal narcotics enterprises."* But by focusing on the Native Americans' plight, we are able to raise a more *specific*

fear among them and push for that which we best understand: *"increase(d) funding for tribal officers and investigators, FBI agents, prosecutors, and tribal jails."* "Law and Order," baby. That's where it's at!

We support efforts to ensure equitable participation in federal programs by Native Americans, including Alaska Natives and Native Hawaiians, and to preserve their culture and languages. We honor the sacrifices of all Native Americans serving in the military today and in years past and will ensure that all veterans receive the care and respect they have earned through their service to America.

**We included *"Alaskan Natives"* in honor of America's sweetheart, Sarah Palin. Then, we threw in *"Native Hawaiians"* because a few of our older members thought they became a State around the same time as Alaska, and we didn't want to offend them.**

Actually, we were a little scared that we might be missing a few others because, during the campaign, Barrack Obama mentioned that he had already visited *"57 States"* and had *"one left to go."* Then, it occurred to us that this may be one of the reasons he's been so hesitant to release his college transcripts. We can only assume his grades in American History and Geography were right up there with his grades in Economics and Finance.

In any event, rather than ending on a particularly compelling *"high note"* with great emotional appeal, we're ending our Platform right here and right now. Just one more demonstration of how political inept we *really* are.

So there you have it! The Democrats entitled their Platform: *Renewing America's Promise.* We entitled ours: *The 2008 Republican Platform* ... and that pretty much sums up our problem.

The first Tuesday in November of every even year, you get to cast your vote to indicate whether you agree with our Platform or the Democrats'. Please give us your thoughtful

consideration. We'd also appreciate your vote ... *even* if it's just out of sympathy.